Making Blood White

Historical Transformations in Early Modern Makassar

WILLIAM CUMMINGS

UNIVERSITY OF HAWAI'I PRESS
HONOLULU

© 2002 University of Hawai'i Press
All rights reserved
Printed in the United States of America
07 06 05 04 03 02   6 5 4 3 2 1

Library of Congress Cataloging-in-Publication Data
Cummings, William.
Making blood white : historical transformations in
early modern Makassar / William Cummings.
p. cm.
Includes bibliographical references and index.
ISBN 0-8248-2513-6 (alk. paper)
1. Makassar (Indonesia)—History. I. Title.
DS646.49.M35 C86 2002
959.8'4—dc21
2001057020

University of Hawai'i Press books are
printed on acid-free paper and meet the
guidelines for permanence and durability
of the Council on Library Resources.

Designed by Josie Herr

Printed by
Maple-Vail Book Manufacturing Group

CONTENTS

Acknowledgments
vii

Abbreviations
ix

A Note on Makassarese Language and Translation
xi

Introduction: Making a History of Early Modern Makassar
1

PART I. HISTORY-MAKING

1 ∞ *Early Modern Makassar and Its Contexts*
17

2 ∞ *Culture and History-Making*
35

3 ∞ *Transformations in Makassarese Perceptions of the Past*
58

PART II. MAKING HISTORY

4 ∞ *Historical Literacy and Social Hierarchicalization*
93

5 ∞ *Historical Literacy and Gowa as the Center of Makassar*
128

6 ∞ *Historical Literacy and Makassarese Culture*
164

Conclusion: The Force of History
195

Appendix: Early Modern Rulers of Gowa and Talloq
207

Notes
211

Glossary
237

Bibliography
239

Index
253

ACKNOWLEDGMENTS

This book was written on tables and desks overflowing with scribbled notes, printed drafts, and coffee cups in three countries. But it stubbornly refused to stay on those tables or in those notes and has occupied my thoughts and demanded attention at unpredictable moments every day for some five years. At the outset, then, I wish to thank Kiersty, whose editing, companionship, and sacrifices during those five years deserve much more than recognition here.

In Makassar I was buoyed by support from Mukhlis Paeni, then director of the Ujung Pandang branch of the Indonesian National Archives; Djohan Selengke, a tutor who gave unflagging support to a student prone to all manner of questions and requests; and the family of Bapak Guntur in Malengkeri, whose open home and warm companionship made my trips to Makassar enjoyable. In Jakarta we were welcomed several times by Damaihati and Rachamat Sudjana.

Closer to home I have benefited from the encouragement, advice, and support of many. These include my parents, Leonard Andaya, Barbara Watson Andaya, Jerry Bentley, Lisa Birnbaum, David Hanlon, Janna Jones, Sirtjo Koolhof, Campbell Macknight, Cornelia Moore, Mark Neumann, and Bob and Eloise Van Niel.

I would like to thank as well the University of Hawai'i at Mānoa, where this book began as a dissertation; the Fulbright-Hays Doctoral Dissertation Research Abroad Program, sponsors of fieldwork in South Sulawesi and the Netherlands; the American-Indonesian Exchange Foundation (AMINEF); and the staffs of the institutions that allowed me access to their collections. These include the Koninklijk Instituut voor Taal-, Land- en Volkenkunde and the Universiteits Bibliotheek in Leiden, the Koninklijk Instituut voor de Tropen in Amsterdam, and the Arsip Nasional Republic Indonesia in Ujung Pandang.

Like other authors, I have learned that writing a book such as this is much more than an intellectual endeavor. I thank you all, and hope you realize the pleasure I take in recording your presence within the pages of *Making Blood White*. Unless otherwise indicated, photographs and maps included in the text are my own.

ABBREVIATIONS

ANRI	Arsip Nasional Republic Indonesia
BKI	*Bijdragen tot de Taal-, Land- en Volkenkunde van Nederlandsch-Indië*
BL	British Library, Department of Oriental Manuscripts
IG	*De Indische Gids*
JAS	*Journal of Asian Studies*
JMBRAS	*Journal of the Malay Branch of the Royal Asiatic Society*
JSEAS	*Journal of Southeast Asian Studies*
KIT	Koninklijk Instituut voor de Tropen
KITLV	Koninklijk Instituut voor Taal-, Land- en Volkenkunde
MS	Matthes Stichting (Yayasan Kebudayaan Sulawesi Selatan)
NBG	Nederlandsch Bijbel Genootschap
SKT	Sinriliq Kappalaq Tallumbatua
SBPK Or.	Staatsbibliotheek Preuszischer Kulturbesitz, Oriental Manuscripts
SSY	*The Story of Syekh Yusuf*
TBG	*Tijdschrift voor Indische Taal-, Land- en Volkenkunde*
TNI	*Tijdschrift voor Nederlandsch-Indië*
UB Cod. Or.	Universiteits Bibliotheek, Rijks Universiteit, Leiden, Codex Orientalis
VOC	Verenigde Oost-Indische Compagnie

A NOTE ON MAKASSARESE LANGUAGE AND TRANSLATION

A translation is a reading that tries to make sense. My experience with translation is inevitably personal, formed out of encounters with languages not my own. These encounters include not only formal study and the struggle to read what seem cryptic and elusive texts, but haphazard experiences ranging from listening uncomprehendingly as an Indonesian instructor recited Javanese poetry in his quivering bass voice to hearing the same Dutch-language pop version of Lou Reed's "Walk on the Wild Side" every morning for weeks in an Indonesian hotel. I know the wonder that comes from learning a foreign language to the point that it enters dreams, that it carries an emotional force all its own, untranslatable.[1] Translation thus stems from both understanding and experiences themselves difficult to translate into words.

I know too that translation is a controversial effort, one steeped in issues of imperialism and incommensurability. As philology, faith in textual fidelity, and the primacy of the author have given way before postmodernism, the belief that texts contain multiple possible readings, and the primacy of the reader, the question before me is how to translate Makassarese texts such as the Gowa Chronicle.[2] Understanding how I tried to capture and pin to paper these ancient texts begins with the social world of Makassar past and present. While recognizing that the translations in this work can only be at best approximations of their Makassarese sense—translations are inevitably "works in progress"—my effort was influenced most by the social context of my own reading and my understanding of the social context of past Makassarese readings of these texts.

Many of my readings of Makassarese texts were done under the guidance of my language teacher, Djohan Daeng Salengke. The son of an adviser to one of the last rulers of Gowa, from his childhood Djohan had firsthand experience reading and listening in the now-lost world of the Gowa palace. His sense of Makassarese powerfully shaped my own. Our work together began with his somewhat paradoxical caution that to read a Makassarese sentence in *lontaraq beru* or *jangang-jangang* script, one first had to know what it said. These scripts, while alphabetic, are incomplete. Glottal stops, nasalized velars, and double consonants are not graphically represented. Readers must simply know that to form the intended Makassarese word these must be added at the correct places. Thus only by knowing the subject of the sentence can it be read. In many ways, written Makassarese is best viewed as a cue or guide to spoken Makassarese. According to some Makassarese, the written script only "becomes" Makassarese when it is spoken aloud. This is obviously a problem for scholars trying to produce transcriptions and translations of texts. There is no standardized, recognized system of transcription or spelling, and published texts and dictionaries do not follow a uniform pattern.[3]

Terse and graphically incomplete, words and sentences can have multiple meanings that must be considered within the context of what is being related before one can divine which words the writer intended. That is, only after reflection and deliberation can one "read" a complex Makassarese statement. Sometimes the choices are stark and a choice can quickly be made. For example, Djohan posed to me the following hypothetical sentence: ᨊᨀᨎᨑᨙᨕᨗ ᨄᨙᨄᨏ ᨅᨒᨉᨈᨚᨀ. This could be transcribed as either *nakanrei pepeq ballaq datoka* or *nakanrei pepeq balanda tokkaq* and thus be read as either "fire consumed the Chinese temple" or "fire consumed the bald Dutchman." At other times simply deciding where words begin and end is difficult, for Makassarese often did not use spaces between words. Coupled with the incompleteness of the script, graphically perplexing sentences such as this— ᨕᨗᨊᨀᨀᨕᨗᨊᨀᨀᨕᨗᨊᨀᨀᨕᨗᨊᨀᨀᨕᨗ (meaning "my older sibling is angry because I yanked out my vegetables")—become possible.

Reading Makassarese is difficult and requires persistence and patience. Often the meaning of a word or phrase becomes clear only later as the context unfolds, demanding that the reader turn back the page and re-read in this new light. Reading Makassarese—scanning, deliberating, choosing, and remaining open to possibilities—involves actively reworking material to achieve a satisfactory, if always tentative, sense. Furthermore, Makassarese composers assumed a whole world of associations and knowledge that future readers would bring to the text.

Defining a word is never a matter of a simple one-to-one unvarying correspondence between languages. Words are read and gain meaning from the web of implications, allusions, and contrasts they have not only with other words in that language, but with the world to which that language refers. Reading the archaic words that have passed out of use in contemporary spoken Makassarese is often a matter of assumption and inference. An inkling of how Makassarese reading is informed not just by other words, but by a world, first came to me when Djohan and I read at the Gowa palace instead of in an office at the Arsip Nasional. Surrounded by its props, the text drew upon these surroundings to become richer and more meaningful in a way that is easier to intimate than define. The way in which I read Makassarese manuscripts today stems most of all from a few such readings at the Gowa palace.

In my translations I have been guided by the desire to reproduce on paper the rhythm of reading Makassarese texts I first encountered in Makassar. To do so I have used commas and semicolons liberally to structure the text. Only rarely do I follow strictly the breaks (∴) the Makassarese composer placed within his text. Instead, I use commas and semicolons to mark out what I believe are read as coherent units of meaning, a process that is, of course, a matter of judgment. In my experience, Makassarese reading lontaraq read one statement at a time, scanning, deciding, and then interpreting each such unit as a whole before moving to the next. Makassarese reading has both a staccato rhythm and what can only be described as a declarative confidence in each statement. Texts are composed of these typically short declarations. I have also occasionally changed word order and made other minor adjustments to enhance readability in translation.

In addition, I have tried to be consistent in transcription and spelling. Generally I follow Cense and Abdurrahim, with a few exceptions that I believe more closely approximate spoken Makassarese. In terms of glottal stops, while some authors prefer to use a conventional mark (') to indicate glottal stops, I use a "q" because it avoids the problem of doubling when marking possessives; thus Tunijalloq's rather than Tunijallo''s. Nasalized velars are written "ng," and in doubled combined consonants, only the first letter is written twice; thus manngalle rather than mangngalle.[4]

Introduction

Making a History of Early Modern Makassar

This work is a study of a transformation in history-making in early modern Makassar, South Sulawesi, Indonesia. Why this interest in such a topic in such a place and time? Even asking this question is a sign of the times. The study of history at the end of the twentieth century takes place within a context in which a debate over whether true knowledge about the past is possible frames what historians write. Roughly portrayed, there is a struggle between a positivism bolstered by increasingly sophisticated methods of apprehending the facts of the past, and a relativism that denies the possibility of historical knowledge. Historians influenced by the methods from disciplines such as sociology, anthropology, economics, psychology, and more find themselves with a rich set of tools, models, and questions with which to probe the multiple facets of human life in the past. Other historians, influenced most by postmodern literary criticism, argue that the representations of the past that historians produce are so mediated by unstable language, situated within discursive formations, and shaped by cultural structures that their productions are fictions rather than "true" accounts of a fundamentally ungraspable past.

This debate over whether historical assertions are possible is fought out in publications, conferences, classrooms, and curriculums by disciples of both positions. Each tries to outflank the other, either by studiously arguing against points made by the other or by studiously ignoring their position as absurd or outdated. Straw men and red herrings abound in this debate. Some see in this an age-old ideological opposition between Left and Right; others see a contest between theory and practice. In this debate, "radical" "postmodern" scholars have seized the epistemological and theoretical high ground. Consider Louis Montrose's position:

> By *the textuality of histories,* I mean to suggest, finally, that we can have no access to a full and authentic past, a lived material existence unmediated by the surviving textual traces of the society in question—traces whose survival we cannot assume to be merely contingent but must rather presume to be at least partially consequent upon complex and subtle social processes of preservation and effacement; and secondly, that those textual traces are themselves subject to subsequent textual mediation when they are construed as the "documents" upon which historians ground their own texts, called "histories."[1]

Closer to the world of Southeast Asia, Hendrick Maier challenges the assumption that Malay historical texts were even intended to refer to the "real" world of past events, to be the sort of histories with which we are familiar. Instead of reading Malay *hikayat*s (narrative accounts of the past), referentially as historical sources that can be used to reconstruct the past, what we should seek is a pleasurable and interesting reading that speaks to us in the present. While we can examine how readers in different positions and periods made sense of a given work, imbuing it with their presumptions, questions, and perceptions, no one reading of a *hikayat* can be considered true or accurate. Nineteenth-century Malays and contemporary Malays, early colonial officials and late colonial officials, not to mention postcolonial scholars, all read *hikayat*s differently. There can be, he argues, no final reading.[2]

According to Maier, then, scholars should abandon the sure-to-fail effort to reconstruct the authentic past. Contrast this with Keith Windschuttle's position against what he sees as the onslaught of "theoretical and literary interlopers who are now so hungrily stalking the corridors." In his provocatively titled *The Killing of History: How a Discipline is Being Murdered by Literary Critics and Social Theorists,* Windschuttle maintains that traditional historical narrative and inductive reasoning remains a reliable, objective way of pursuing truth and knowledge about the world that faces no devastating philosophical obstacles:

> Although they are narratives of unique, unrepeatable events and are not involved in formulating general laws or making predictions, historical explanations share [scientific] characteristics with several other fields of study including evolutionary biology, geology and recent approaches to cosmology. Like these fields, the history of human affairs is defined by its study of

the variance over time of its subject matter. Again, like them, its explanations are grounded in contingency. What happens in history is not random but is contingent upon everything that came before. . . . Historians adhere to a disciplined methodology that involves the construction of explanations from evidence. The evidence they use is not given but is something they must, first, discover and second, analyse for authenticity and significance for the explanation. . . . Although much historical research may be inspired and initiated by historians' values and theories, the kind of documentation and reference citation used within the discipline means that their explanations can be tested, corroborated or challenged by others. Hence the *findings* made by historical explanation are the product of a properly scientific methodology.[3]

On one side, then, is a faith in the essential soundness of historical narrative and analysis, and on the other an equally strong faith that what historians write can never reliably represent the past.

This debate and the search for a decisive conclusion will certainly continue, for at issue is what form the doing of history will take in the future. Stanley Fish has argued that this opposition between two armed camps is misguided. He believes that theorizing the possibility of historical knowledge and giving historical accounts of the past are two separate activities. Once the influence of class, gender, race, and culture are acknowledged, and the inherently and ultimately tentative and partial nature of all knowledge about the world is granted, Fish asks, "Where then does this leave us? Precisely where we have always been, making cases for the significance and shape of historical events with the help of whatever evidence appears to us to be relevant or weighty."[4]

Yet there is a danger here of partitioning intellectual work, allowing "traditional" historians to blissfully go on doing what they have always done, not needing to heed the insights and implications of postmodern questioning, while relieving "new" historians and literary critics of the effort and responsibility of actually saying something about what happened long ago and what this means to us today. This balkanization is the norm within many history departments, where seminars on "historiography" are sequestered from seminars on "history" proper. Students are encouraged to find the proper balance. Some theory is good (but not too much), and it certainly should not interfere unduly with writing a dissertation about what happened in the past.

This work on early modern Makassar is framed by the context of this debate. It cannot resolve the debate to anyone's satisfaction, nor is that its intent. My position will surely be clear in its pages. More importantly, this work asserts that a valuable contribution may be to shift the terms of the debate by focusing on studying *how* the past is apprehended, by studying what Greg Dening calls "history-making" as a practice. Surely it is here in this activity, in questions of what the past means and what people in the present do with the past, that the epistemological status and knowledge of the past converge.

And indeed within history as a discipline and Indonesian studies in particular, the nature and effects of history-making have begun to attract attention. In a fine study John Pemberton describes how the past as ritual has been deployed in New Order Indonesia to promote and fetishize political stability.[5] Part of an oppositional collection of scholars centered at Cornell University who decry the policies of the Suharto era, Pemberton critiques the perverse and political ends to which this conception of Indonesia's past has been put. But here too there is a danger of implying that while all history-making is partial, this particular form of New Order history-making is exceptionally vile and damaging. It is but a short step to a discourse analysis that focuses exclusively on the genealogy of this history, tracing its offending origins back to the Dutch colonial period, and in so doing eliding the many other historical discourses that have made their presence felt in the archipelago. For instance, a growing body of nuanced and cogent studies investigate New Order (and post–New Order) cultural politics and seek out and give space to alternative locations and possibilities. The position they occupy emphasizes borders, margins, exile, alterity, and subalternity as an alternative to the centrist positions and practices of the New Order.[6] In terms of intellectual force within the American academy and within Indonesian studies, tropes of borders, margins, exile, alterity, and subalternity have occupied the center of authority, united by political opposition to the Suharto regime and philosophical opposition to its policies. A worthy and important project, by omission this populist discourse nevertheless valorizes and legitimizes in the name of the "Indonesian people" other unexamined but presumably less destructive and distorting forms of history-making. Nor is it far from here to romanticizing a dichotomy between New Order histories and other "authentic" or noncoercive forms of history-making.

In fact, any form of history-making—any situated use of the past in the present—is inherently a practice with disproportionate social and political effects. I am certain none of the authors just cited would disagree. But there has been very little explicit effort to perform genealogies of the many other forms of history making that have developed within Indonesia, to see both the creative force they have and the social and political effects they nourish. It is at this position, within a context of recent literature on Indonesia and framed by a larger intellectual debate over the doing of history, that *Making Blood White* is situated.

Making the Past Present: History and Its Manifestations

That the past is a resource upon which humans draw continuously each day is all too often overlooked. Yet it is the past that offers the raw material out of which we construct our selves and societies. It is in our histories that we explain who we are. The imagining of our identities, social lives, and perceptions of how the world works always and inevitably involves making histories from the past. Indeed, this activity is, as Greg Dening remarked, "so ordinary and easy an act that we do not have a word to describe it." Elaborating further, he writes,

> What I do here so self-consciously we all do unreflectively every day of our lives. In gossip, in nostalgic memories, in family anecdote, in toasts and speeches, in anniversary ceremonies, in *rites de passage,* in symbolic actions, we are always making History by crafted stories. We live by and in our crafted stories. Our social and cultural life is a theatre in which we display both ourselves and a significant past. And the meaning of our stories is us, in our roles, in our relationship, in the structures of our society, in the systems of our culture.[7]

By virtue of being made in the present, histories inescapably speak to and of the present. Often subtly, but rarely simply, histories contain reflections of the present. The kind of stories found fit to tell about the past cannot but mirror the class, gender, ideological, and historical background of the teller. Yet too often historians acknowledge this inevitability with reluctance and regret, believing that it compromises and devalues an older and nobler search for knowledge. But for those interested in history making, this entanglement of past and present offers a rich field of study. It is the use to which the past could be put that I will focus on.

The past can be drawn upon in a multitude of ways. Most common, perhaps, is seeking in the past shared origins and experiences at the expense of differences and divisions, thereby promoting the feeling, and thus the reality, of social unity. At the other extreme, and common too, is the politically interested selection of particular facts and plots from all the past has to offer in order to bolster and justify the dominance of certain social groups. Social rivalries without rival histories would be rare indeed.

The act of history making, and the social, cultural, and political contexts in which it is always enmeshed, was as much a feature of early modern Makassar as it is today. For Makassarese too the past offered a space in which they could speak to themselves and others about their cultural values, social relations, and political formations. Certainly it would be an error to say that before the spread of literacy Makassarese were without history—that is, without stories they recounted about the significant past.[8]

However, with the spread of literacy, even a literacy restricted to an elite, the nature of the stories Makassarese told about the past changed fundamentally in form and content. Makassarese created new kinds of histories that served new purposes. Chronicles, genealogies, king lists, treaties, diaries, law codes, and advice about how to govern flourished beginning in the sixteenth century. All bridged past and present in novel ways. The wide-ranging social, political, and cultural effects of these new kinds of written histories on Makassar are the subject of this book. But if Makassarese written histories in particular will merit close attention, it would be useful to consider more broadly the mediums in which the past is made present.

The past travels to the present by a number of routes. We live amid the past, surrounded by monuments, names, buildings, objects, habits of thought, patterns of behavior, and turns of phrase that bring the past into the present. These material and immaterial traces of the past are so ubiquitous that we often forget they exist, but as David Lowenthal writes, "The past is everywhere. All around us lie features which, like ourselves and our thoughts, have more or less recognizable antecedents. Relics, histories, memories suffuse human experience. Each particular trace of the past ultimately perishes, but collectively they are immortal. Whether it is celebrated or rejected, attended to or ignored, the past is omnipresent."[9] The past, living and thriving in the present, gives meaning to our lives without which we would quite literally be lost and bereft of identity. This crucial past is brought forward through the years in a variety of mediums, but four seem particularly important: places, practices, objects, and narratives.[10] Of these four, historians are specialists in the last, focusing their attentions on the efforts of people who consciously make histories out of the past. Yet the other three are equally worthy of our attention, and in many societies carry the burden of the past into the present. Consider each of these four in turn.

Historical places allow us the illusion of traveling back in time. Sites as simple as a bend in a river and as complex as the vast, managed monuments of national governments stand for a past that on the one hand is no more, but that on the other hand survives in our memories and attendance at such "historical" sites. They urge that the past not be lost. This attention to identify particular locations as places where the past is recalled is universal. Among the Apache, named places served as spatial anchors in traditional narratives, "summarizing them, as it were, and condensing into compact form their essential moral truths."[11] Among the Ilongot of northern Luzon, Renato Rosaldo discerned a sense of time rooted in movement between places. Ilongot associated places with past events, travel with the passage of time. History was seen as a journey along a path, as a movement through space in which "people walk along a trail and stop at a sequence of named resting places."[12] Like movement itself, Ilongot perceived history as unpredictable and improvised rather than obeying a fixed pattern.

In this predilection to encode the past in a spatial landscape Apache and Ilongot are not alone. In as distant a time and place as revolutionary France, reformers in Caen plotted a revolutionary procession that bypassed old routes, skirting religious and political sites associated with a tainted past, to establish in travel a commemoration of the revolution. "The festival that they invented erased memories" and, in so doing, attempted to define the shape of later historical memory.[13]

Not all places are equal in historical value. Although there are no people without history, there are places without history. Some sites are extraordinarily rich. Sigmund Freud imagined a Rome in which all its myriad historical layers, its "long and copious past," coexisted in the present. "On the Piazza of the Pantheon we should find not only the Pantheon of today as bequeathed to us by Hadrian, but on the same site also Agrippa's original edifice; indeed, the same ground would support the church of Santa Maria sopra Minerva and the old temple over which it was built. And the observer would need merely to shift the focus of his eyes, perhaps, or change his position, in order to call up a view of either the one or the other."[14] The material traces of many eras survive and cluster at this one location, making modern Rome a fascinating mélange of historical events, structures, and people.

Elsewhere, a single event may vest a place with extraordinary and durable significance for later inhabitants and visitors. To its citizens, the assassination of President Kennedy in Dallas haunted the meaning of that city's significance in American history for decades. So ripe with historical meaning are places such as Hiroshima and Agincourt that merely to speak their names is to conjure up entire histories. Naming in fact is a powerful way of charging a place with historical meaning. European explorers during the early modern era consistently (re)named newly encountered areas, symbolically establishing them within a model of the world based on European thought and interests. Not dissimilarly, Chinese travelers inscribed the landscape by physically engraving literary texts onto stone landscapes. "The text altered the scene by shaping the perceptions of later travelers and guiding those who sought to follow in the footsteps of earlier talents. Often, local figures would request or commission such inscriptions by notable visitors to signify the importance of such a place. Certain sites thus became shrines in the literary culture, eliciting further inscriptions through the centuries."[15]

In contrast to sites redolent with past associations, other places seem to have no remembered past. In the Makassarese *Sinriliq Kappalaq Tallumbatua,* its hero journeys from place to place, from community to community, crossing long distances in between that in contrast to these communities have no apparent significance. Such wastelands may of course become inscribed with historical meaning or may already have meaning for others. But never does the past lie evenly upon the land. Any landscape may be viewed as a mosaic of locations with differing histories that are themselves continually debated and changing. This past is encoded in the landscape and read when places are visited, passed, and mentioned. We live in a landscape that cannot but bear witness to the past that preceded us.

As important a medium as places for preserving the past are the practices carried out at them. Practices—and in particular those recognized with the status of "rituals"—are of course politically charged instruments designed to shape social relations in the present, as many have recognized.[16] But actions are also a form of history-making. Rituals such as the revolutionary procession in Caen can be read as affirmations of particular interpretations of past events. Constructing a ritual to be witnessed by a wide public is one effective means of visibly making a history of the past. On Sumba in eastern Indonesia, annual *pasola* jousting has been transformed from a religious rite in which the historical relations between communities was dramatized to a folkloric celebration of "traditional culture" staged for tourists and visiting dignitaries. Both are performances that present the past with very different terms and meanings, making a history as they are enacted.[17] Among the Toraja in central Sulawesi, each year before sowing new rice a rite known as *medatu* was performed in which Toraja went down to pay symbolic tribute to the ruler of Luwuq in exchange for the fertility this sacred center provided. Other communities gave tribute of cloth, slaves, or a buffalo horn filled with gold, but all these ritual exchanges enacted an initial alliance between highland and lowland as well as annually confirming this historical link.[18]

Paul Connerton cogently argues that repetitive, formal actions are effective mnemonic devices, more effective in fact than written texts. "Ritual movements preserve," he writes. "This is the source of their importance and persistence as mnemonic systems. Every group, then, will entrust to bodily automatisms the values and categories which they are most anxious to conserve. They will know how well the past can be kept in mind by a habitual memory sedimented in the body."[19] Shared social or communal memories in particular are best preserved in the public, ritual actions that groups enact together. In practices, like places, the past survives.

The ritual exchanges between Toraja and Luwuq allude as well to the importance of objects as vehicles for bringing the past into the present. One aspect of this importance is the physical presence of objects within the community. Janet Hoskins describes the centrality of such history-laden objects in affirming community identity in the present.

> In a nonliterate society, where "documentary evidence" takes the form of tombstones, heirloom urns, and sea worm swarmings, ritual provides the locus for an imaginative reflection upon the past. The material traces of the ancestors are assembled for collective examination, their names are repeated in prayers and invocations, and their continuing power is "tested" through propitiatory offerings. This ritual experience is, in the end, a form of self-knowledge.[20]

Objects have a unique ability to make the past visible, to give it a tangible form. Being present, they bear direct witness to the past and are thus often the locus or reference point for historical claims. In such societies we might speak like Hoskins of a "great things" tradition of history instead of a "great men," "great women," or we should add "great events" approach to the past.[21] But while such objects themselves are incontrovertible, the historical meanings they carry are always contested and dependent upon who possesses them. For example, the Elgin marbles taken from Athens and currently found in the British Museum can be used to make a variety of histories: of rapacious British imperialism, of modern Greek inadequacies, of a universal cultural heritage belonging to all humankind, of a glorious past that belongs to and in Athens.

Even more than possession of places, possession of objects carries with it the right to incorporate them into histories, to determine how the past will speak to the present. Possession, as it were, is nine-tenths of the past.

Objects also are superbly malleable assests in history-making because, being durable, they survive for generations and are passed on from one person or group to another. Objects can circulate socially in a way that places and practices cannot. This attribute has long attracted attention; among anthropologists discussion of "the gift" as a topic of analysis has a lengthy history.[22] Circulating in this fashion, objects acquire new historical meanings as the traces of previous owners become part of an object's significance. Which objects become the focus of such attention is unpredictable, for any object can be made to carry semantic meanings. The exchange of cloth, for example, is used in many societies to speak about relationships between people, between groups, and with the unseen world.[23] In Makassar, the *Sja'ir Perang Mengkasar* describes how Sultan Hasanuddin sent his ally, the victorious ruler of Talloq, a gold-patterned chintz, then upon his return presented him "a gift of raiment, the choicest cloths from the regions to the West, glittering as though they were made of glass." Other nobles too were given first a headdress, then cloth, a kris, a cutlass, and a ring.[24] More than mere rewards, these items bore with them the power and prestige—the indelible imprint—of their royal giver. This new past gave them new historical meaning. For these reasons and more, objects from the past play a crucial role in later history-making. This role, however, is never simple. As Greg Dening wrote of Europeans in the Marquesas, their "problem was to transmit across the beaches their own particular signs of institutions and roles. How could Cook communicate the idea of property when even he himself could not make explicit all the interconnections of religion, law, government, economy and value that were contained in a simple nail?"[25] Objects from the past are suspended in the webs of culture, structures of society, and discourses of power of the present. The histories that can be made with them are always partial. All of these contexts make and remake objects from the past.

In summary, to places, practices, and objects histories attach. Places, practices, and objects bring into the present the past about and with which histories are made. Tied to each are narratives short or long about the past they incarnate. They anchor the past and make it available to those in the present. Though not often viewed in this light, written histories perform the same function.

Typically, a historian would not feel the need to justify relying on written sources from the past to construct his or her history, but a word about precisely this is important. Makassarese historical texts take center stage in this work not simply because they are the abundant and comfortable material I am accustomed to, but because of their privileged status within Makassarese historical discourse. In most societies written histories carry only a small portion of the past into the present. Naturally this is true of oral societies such as early Makassar. But in Makassar the advent of historical literacy brought about a revolution in history-making. The histories contained in written manuscripts occupied a prestigious and lofty social position. Places, practices, and objects did not diminish in significance, but indeed established the paradigm in which Makassarese viewed historical manuscripts. These manuscripts were ritually venerated sacred objects carefully preserved at guarded locations. The nature, significance, and effects of this expansion of the past in the present are the subject of the chapters that follow.

Early modern Makassarese brought the past into the present using all four of these mediums. From locations as specific as the installation stone of the *tumanurung* in Kale Gowa to places as large as Gowa (the largest and best-known Makassarese polity) itself, Makassarese believed that certain spots were charged with historical potency where the past remained alive in the present. Rituals carried out at such places were also acts of history making. The installation of Gowa's rulers was a per-

Figure 1. Historical reenactment of *kalompoang* cleansing ritual

formance that re-created the founding of Gowa at the *tumanurung's* descent. This was a history made to privilege Gowa, just as annual Idul Fitri celebrations at the Ballaq Lompoa (Gowa's royal palace) commemorated the coming of Islam to Makassar in a history that bolstered Gowa's status. Figure 1 shows part of a 1997 ritual procession drawing water from a well with which to cleanse Gowa's sacred *kalompoang*, or regalia.

Among the most historically potent objects through which the past flowed in Makassar were the named royal crown (Salakowa) and sword (Sudanga) of Gowa. Possessing them made their bearer symbolically (and at times effectively) the rightful descendant of Gowa's founders. Beginning in the sixteenth century, written manuscripts were a medium in which new histories of the past were preserved. The past itself seemed to adhere to and survive within these written vessels. All of these modes of making the past present are examined in the chapters that follow. Particular attention, however, is paid to Makassarese history-making at the conjunction of the historicity of places, practices, and objects: written accounts of the past. The advent of written histories engendered powerful changes in Makassarese society, and these changes will be my particular focus.

The Argument

This study examines the ways in which the past was conceived, interpreted, and used in early modern Makassar. More exactly, it is a study of a shift in historical consciousness, and of the social, cultural, and political effects that shift had, following the advent of literacy in early modern Makassar. History in Makassar was always about more than the past. The past gave the present meaning, and histories were the medium in which those meanings were conveyed, asserted, and debated. Makassarese based political struggles and social rivalries on historical claims. More than this, the forms in which Makassarese wrote about the past were closely tied to particular political and social formations. Historians studying early modern Makassar cannot but be struck by the uncanny correspondence between the social and political order that Makassarese created and the histories they wrote during this period. The kinds of histories Makassarese wrote belonged to this age, and when this age was no more, changes in how Makassarese thought about and wrote about the past were inevitable. An extraordinary example concerns chronicles.

After the final defeat of Gowa in 1669 by the Dutch East India Company and their Bugis allies, Makassarese no longer added to the Gowa and Talloq chronicles. The chronicles, products of and about a golden age of glorious achievements by these twin polities, had lost the social context that gave them meaning. To continue to write chronicles made no sense in Gowa. In his 1759 history of Makassar, Roelof Blok, the Dutch governor at Makassar, wrote that Makassarese told him they had deliberately stopped adding to their chronicles and would not continue until they regained their independence from the Dutch.[26] After 1669 the chronicles would acquire new meanings from changed circumstances, increasingly betokening a distant, proud past that Makassarese hoped would return, but that contrasted strikingly with the meager present. Chronicles would be copied, but not composed.[27] There developed, it seems, a sense in Makassarese minds that the periods before and after the conquest were distinct eras. The past later Makassarese sought to bring into the present was the revered past of the preconquest era, a golden age unsullied by defeat and decline.

The most essential idea argued in this work is that histories are not just records of the past, but themselves forces or agents that affect the course of developments. Though hard to pin down precisely, things variously described as "historical consciousness," "mentality," and "perceptions of the past" do exist. They are not simply structured by the prevailing social, cultural, or ideological contexts in which they are made; they also shape those contexts. More than just mirrors supposedly allowing us access to the "spirit" or "mind" of an age, histories of the past should be the focus of explicit study as historical objects in their own right. Certainly more difficult to study than the economic, political, or social forces for which most historical sources seem best suited, they are nonetheless no less potent engines capable of preserving or transforming the worlds in which humans live. The three parts of this study examine an evolution in historical consciousness among early modern Makassarese and trace the effects this had on the way they constructed their world.

With an eye then toward larger issues, part 1 of this study describes the manuscripts and stories in which Makassarese made their histories in the sixteenth and seventeenth centuries. Chapter 1 provides the reader discussions of three crucial contexts that frame this work: the ongoing scholarly debate over how to evaluate Indonesian historical texts, an overview of the historical trends and events in sixteenth- and seventeenth-century Makassar, and an assessment of the central place of culture in this study of early modern Makassar. Chapter 2 undertakes the laborious but essential work of describing the evolution of written scripts and genres of historical writing in early modern Makassar. Special emphasis is placed on the social and cultural context in which these new forms of history-making developed. Chapter 3 then examines the passage from oral to written histories. Understanding their fundamentally different forms, concerns, and social functions is an essential prerequisite to measuring the impact and significance of written histories in and on Makassarese society.

In part 2 the nature and consequences of this shift in how the past was made present in written histories are examined in three related areas. Chapter 4 explores how written histories were vital in the creation of a new, increasingly hierarchically ranked social formation based on a fundamental distinction between red-blooded and white-blooded descent. Most critically, written histories describing the descent of "nobles" from a white-blooded heavenly being *(tumanurung)* separated and elevated this social elite from red-blooded Makassarese "commoners." Chapter 5 examines the parallel process of political centerization, in which new pasts displaced old and in so doing established Gowa as the center of Makassarese society. Gowa increasingly became both the model by which other Makassarese polities judged themselves and their past and the location of the most significant historical events in Makassar's past. Chapter 6 turns to the influence of written histories in creating the idea that Makassarese possessed something called "a culture" that could be defined and to which they could refer. This process enhanced the ability of white-blooded Makassarese to reinforce their privileged social position, reifying and extending a stratified social hierarchy by making it part of the "core" of Makassarese culture. Though described sequentially, these processes were simultaneous; each depended on and was strengthened by the others.

Finally, the conclusion briefly revisits the main threads of argument made in earlier chapters, but takes as its main task considering the implications this work has for the study of the past in early modern Southeast Asia and beyond. It offers an assessment of the predominant way historians perceive the study of this place and time and suggests an approach to the region that promises to enrich and extend not only our understanding of the past, but of how the past might be better approached in the histories we make. As a beginning toward this end we turn first to the world of history-making in sixteenth-century Makassar.

PART I

History-Making

∞ *1* ∞

Early Modern Makassar and Its Contexts

This work examines changing ways of making histories in early modern Makassar, South Sulawesi, Indonesia. "Makassar" refers simultaneously to a language, those who speak it, and the region where they live. In contemporary terms, Makassar is a regional language, with approximately 1.5 million speakers, in the southern and western portions of the Republic of Indonesia's South Sulawesi province. It is important to distinguish between all of Makassar and Gowa, the Makassarese polity that most dominated its neighbors and is now seen as the heartland of Makassarese culture and the main site of Makassarese historical developments. This study is centered on a particular time: the early modern era or, for Makassar, the sixteenth and seventeenth centuries.[1] This is the period during which Gowa rose, flourished, and eventually fell in the late 1660s. Nevertheless, topics such as the influence of literacy and historical consciousness are not so neatly confined to time periods, and from these two centuries I will look both backward to the fifteenth and forward to the eighteenth centuries and perhaps beyond. This work is not, it will soon become apparent, a descriptive account of the events and trends of the past. It is not a narrative of that past, but a study of how Makassarese perceived and made use of their past in the histories they made. To make a crucial distinction, the past is comprised of events that have taken place, history-making is the action of interpreting that past in the present, and histories are the tangible products of this interpretive activity.

First, some preliminaries. In addition to the wider contest over the nature of history-making, this work is situated within two more specific contexts. First, this research is based on readings of local historical manuscripts, an endeavor with a long and contested history within Indonesian studies. Therefore I will consider how other scholars have approached Indonesian historical texts and how Makassarese histories might be examined in light of these efforts. Second, although this work is not a narrative reconstruction of early modern Makassarese history, the historical context of "what happened" is a helpful aid in following the arguments of later chapters. The remainder of this introductory chapter examines these contexts—one historical and one historiographical—and relates them to the larger aims and scope of this work.

READING TEXTS IN INDONESIAN STUDIES

Is there a history in this text? This question has been the focus of several generations of vigorous debate among Indonesianists. Beginning in the 1930s a duel of sorts began when C. C. Berg undertook his critique of the work of N. J. Krom. Krom believed that there was a layer of facts within Javanese historical texts that the careful reader could discover and put to use. Berg argued that these texts were not works of history, but political charters and myths written for purposes of legitimation or even magical instruments. At first glance historical, Javanese texts claiming to recount the past were in fact only useful as sources for the political and cultural milieu of the era in which they were composed.[2] This debate, framed anew by each subsequent historian working with Indonesian historical manuscripts, has dominated the handling and interpreting of local-language source materials and the construction of a fuller picture of the society and history of the archipelago. Most typically, historians have attempted to fish for historical facts that can be verified or that at least are not contradicted by "sounder" European sources. This effort to place European and Indonesian sources side by side, however, has affected what kind of Indonesian texts have been seen as useful. In Adrian Vickers' words, "The answer has usually been to seek those forms of traditional writing which seemed to resemble Western forms of history and incorporate them into narratives about specific regions." Setting the pattern for many later studies, Husein Djajadiningrat's method in his *Critische Beschouwing van de Sadjarah Banten* was to "select a text which was closest in form to a [Western] 'chronicle,' and examine it for historical data."[3] But as the comments of Maier cited in the Introduction suggest, many within the field of Indonesian studies are no longer satisfied with an approach that salvages "facts" from Indonesian texts to construct modern, linear narratives modeled after the experience of history in the West. Yet such doubts have not characterized the study of South Sulawesi texts.

The smaller circle of scholars studying South Sulawesi has been a comparatively quiescent oasis within this maelstrom of debate. Indeed, debate has been rare, and scholarly consensus the norm. Scholars have consistently praised Bugis and Makassarese historical texts for their sober, matter-of-fact, unadorned, and thus to Western historians familiar and reliable accounting of the past. To cite one representative example, in contrast to the otherness of Javanese chronicles Noorduyn wrote that in South Sulawesi, "the writers have confined themselves to recording facts" and that chronicles "were regarded as the historical writings par excellence."[4] South Sulawesi chroniclers have been seen as engaging in well-known and recognizable tasks, not something culturally alien. The record of Western scholarly praise for the restrained, unembellished, and dependable chronicles of the Bugis and Makassarese is long and ongoing. There is a comforting myth—itself nourished by contemporary Indonesian historians working within the discourse of Indonesian national history—that all historians of the archipelago—past and present, Indonesian and Western—have been engaged in the same empirical enterprise of recording and reconstructing the area's past on essentially the same historiographical model and with virtually the same assumptions about what it means to make histories of the past.

The nearly pervasive view in the field of South Sulawesi studies is that historical texts provide the factual building blocks with which a clearer picture of the Bugis and Makassarese past can be gained. More than most, scholars of South Sulawesi have stuck to their texts. In this, the work of South Sulawesi scholars is increasingly at odds with how other Indonesianists are approaching and making use of texts. To be sure, there is no approach in Javanese, Balinese, or Malay textual studies that has risen to dominance or been widely hailed as breaking the deadlock of opinion about the nature of historical texts in the Indonesian archipelago. The debate of Krom and Berg remains a jumping-off point for discussion. Differences in scholars' approach derives in part, and perhaps in large, from choices about their respective objects of study. For the philologist, the text alone commands attention, removed from its historical context. For the historian, texts are mined for information to help build a narrative of the past comprehensible to Western readers. For the anthropologist, the thought encoded in historical narratives is paramount. The approach taken depends on whether historical texts are treated primarily as objects of study in their own right, as potential historical sources, or as a means of entry into ways of thinking. The link between what exactly one chooses to study and the way in which sources are read toward that end is intimate, even determinative.

There have been important contributions to debate over the historicity of texts in the field of Balinese studies, and it is useful to briefly consider these developments. The historical parallels between Bali and South Sulawesi are numerous. The premodern political landscape of both regions was marked by competition between polities struggling for preeminence and accompanying fluctuations in the presence of centralized authority. Each has been characterized by patterns of autonomous historical development despite being geographically poised on the eastern edge of the Java Sea. The two evidence strong links between historical production and political rivalry as well as traditions of treating written texts—especially historical texts—as sacred objects. Methodologically, scholars of preseventeenth century South Sulawesi and pre-nineteenth-century Bali have little European archival material to work with, guaranteeing the centrality of local historical materials in both fields. There are, in other words, numerous areas of correspondence between both the regions and the nature of the scholarship they inspire. These correspondences are especially relevant for a study of the connections between history-making and social, political, and cultural change. Immediately useful in this context are recent analyses of Balinese traditions of written composition, historical genres, and the social, political, and historical contexts in which histories of the past were produced. Both Helen Creese and Raechelle Rubinstein, for example, have analyzed the Balinese *kakawin* (poetic historical accounts written in Sanskrit meter or meters derived from Sanskrit metrical principles) tradition as a historical practice rooted in and generative of social conditions, political struggles, and cultural values.[5] There is, in short, good reason for scholars of South Sulawesi to look at Bali and elsewhere for resonances, parallels, and contrasts that can help counter the tendency toward myopia characteristic of Indonesian studies.

In this book I read Makassarese historical texts at different times as objects of study, as historical sources, as means of entry into another mentality. I do so, however, in unequal measures. The smallest portion is reserved for presenting critical editions of previously unpublished Makassarese texts; only in a few cases are different manuscript versions compared and judgments made about what is the most likely original reading. Consulting Makassarese historical texts for facts with which to construct a narrative history of early modern Makassar also occupies my attention only peripherally; in any case the outline of such a narrative is presented below. By far the predominant focus of my attention will be the historical consciousness Makassarese expressed in their histories. But I do not confine my analysis to a few texts, nor do I believe that texts alone constitute the world of study that should command our attention. This study concentrates on the visible historical effects of a transformation in how Makassarese perceived the past in the early modern era. Histories not only mean, they do; they not only offer us insights (of whatever sort) into the past, they also have demonstrable and decisive effects on the social world in which they are produced and in which they continue to reside. The details and implications of this approach to Makassarese histories will be unfolded beginning in the next chapter. First, however, I consider the historical context of Makassar in the sixteenth and seventeenth centuries.

THE RISE OF GOWA: A BRIEF ACCOUNT

Defining the place and time this work considers might help to situate it. It is important to note that this is neither a chronological narrative nor a comprehensive thematic treatment of the events, trends, and changes in sixteenth- and seventeenth-century Makassar. Neither a political, economic, nor social history of that place and time, it does not present an overview organizing and summarizing Makassar's past. For this reason, readers might well appreciate a précis outlining just such a history as an orientation and framework in which to place the people and places mentioned in the chapters that follow.

Histories of early modern Makassar have typically been formed in one of two molds. Perhaps because of the important place Makassar occupied in archipelagic trading networks, the concomitant Western tradition of seeing Makassar primarily as a port, the greater accessibility of European sources concerned with the visible world of trading and economic fortunes, and a Dutch colonial tradition of locating significant cultural, social, and political achievements almost exclusively in Java, most histories have framed Makassarese history as the product of economic developments. In these histories trade is the dominant force, and economic transformation the substructure undergirding the events and changes of that period. The most sophisticated and recent such treatment is Anthony Reid's *The Age of Commerce,* in which Makassar plays a key role as one of the polities most able to capitalize on rising international commerce in the fifteenth century and most subject to its decline in the seventeenth century.⁶ Not wrong, but rather one-sided, this work exemplifies how Western scholars in particular have understood and described Makassarese history.

Indonesian historians have cast this past into a different form. The key date in the Indonesian historiography of sixteenth- and seventeenth-century Makassar is, in fact, 6 November 1973. On that date, by Presidential Decision No. 87, Sultan Hasanuddin (r. 1653 to 1669) was formally enshrined in the pantheon of Indonesian national heroes. Those making history in independent Indonesia celebrated Hasanuddin for his valiant but unsuccessful resistance to Dutch invasion. In this presentation of the past, Hasanuddin takes his place alongside other revolutionary Indonesians participating in the nonpareil heroic story of modern Indonesia: the anticolonial struggle for freedom. Makassar's past is made on a stage on which Indonesians waged an archipelagic-wide fight for independence, a past culminating in the 1945–1949 Indonesian national revolution ending Dutch colonialism.⁷

Both these molds, Western and Indonesian, present Makassar's past in terms of a remarkably similar plot.⁸ In brief, the unifying and dominant development during the sixteenth and seventeenth centuries was the rise and fall of the kingdom of Gowa. Like bookmarks, the rise and fall of Gowa mark out a defined historical period. Beginning around 1500, Gowa grew in size and influence, increasingly drawing other Makassarese communities into its orbit. This golden age ended catastrophically in 1669 with the final defeat and conquest of Gowa by the Dutch East India Company (VOC) and its Bugis allies. Here, briefly recounted and with the aim of providing the background for the themes discussed in this work, is that tale.⁹

Much of early Makassarese history remains unknown. Archaeological findings and to a lesser extent historical linguistics have yielded some generally accepted statements about Makassar before the advent of historical chronicles in the sixteenth century. The Makassarese language belongs to the Western Malayo-Polynesian branch of the Austronesian language family. Taiwan is the most likely homeland of the Proto-Austronesian ancestor of Makassarese, and speakers of Proto-Austronesian began moving southward through the Philippines archipelago about thirty-five hundred years ago. By perhaps three thousand years ago groups of these seafaring explorers began settling in South Sulawesi.¹⁰ As part of this larger Austronesian family, culturally, socially, and linguistically Makassarese have widespread parallels with other Austronesian speakers from the western Indonesian archipelago to Polynesia. Based on linguistic data, Roger Mills suggests that among South Sulawesi languages Makassarese broke off earliest from Proto–South Sulawesi, its speakers moving southward along the west coast (and perhaps the east coast as well, to be later displaced and forced southward by Bugis migrations) from the northern portion of the peninsula into the regions where Makassarese is spoken today (map 1).[11]

Archaeologists have unearthed clues to early Makassarese society in sites within South Sulawesi. Most notably, there is significant archaeological and toponymic confirmation of Makassarese trade with Javanese and Malays. In the area of Bantaeng on the south coast of the peninsula, archaeologists have unearthed evidence of ancient and widespread trafficking in ceramics, statuary, bronze and iron artifacts, and other goods. The fourteenth-century Javanese poem *Nagarakertagama* mentions Bantaeng, Makassar, and the island of Selayar as "countries" known to Javanese traders.[12] That Makassarese were long involved in commerce with groups from the western archipelago is clear, though beyond that it existed we know little of this trade. Another early center of commerce appears to have been the Siang area north of present-day Makassar. Before the rise of Gowa, Siang was the port foreign traders most frequented on the west coast of South Sulawesi and may have been a regional power with considerable influence in the fifteenth and earlier centuries.[13] Archaeological finds thus suggest that the Gowa area was a comparatively isolated backwater, with traders and goods flowing into Makassar from Bantaeng to the south and Siang to the north. Similarly, the best-known and richest sites of pre-Austronesian habitation, referred to as Toalian, come from limestone caves in Maros, north of Gowa as well.

What conclusions can we draw from this scattered evidence? Given their voyaging Austronesian heritage and what we know of Makassarese by the arrival of Europeans in the archipelago, there is no reason to doubt that seafaring has been an important and continuous feature of Makassarese society. Makassarese took part in the trade networks that criss-crossed the archipelago and that by the early modern period carried them as far as the north coast of Australia.[14]

While our knowledge is perforce circumstantial, early written sources and oral traditions also provide some glimpse of political and social organization at the beginning of the early modern era. The Makassarese political landscape appears to have been characterized by the formation and disintegration of federations of small communities. Never

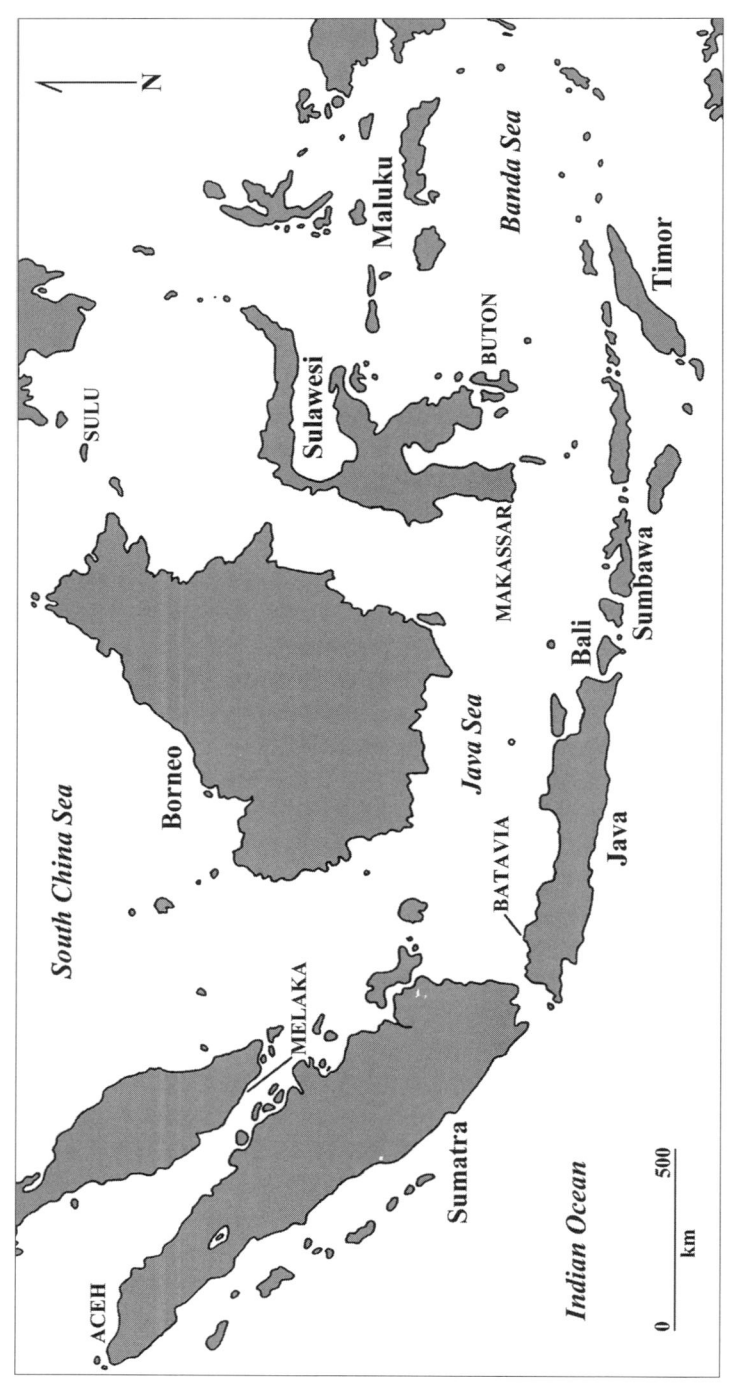

Map 1. Indonesia

centralized, these bonds were affirmed in rituals and marriages rather than permanent institutional arrangements. Kinship, and specifically siblingship, provided the idiom and ideals for those constructing relationships that extended beyond the family and community. How long these arrangements could endure is impossible to state. The most famous such federation was composed of nine small polities that became the core of emergent Gowa. Their leaders were collectively known as the Bate Salapang (The Nine Banners)—sometimes called the Kasiang Salapang. The *Gowa Chronicle* describes the extraordinary foundation of Gowa as taking place when a stranger-lord named Karaeng Bayo (Lord of the Sea) married a heavenly being *(tumanurung)* that descended bearing powerful regalia at a spot that became the sacred center of Gowa. The nine nobles of the Bate Salapang promised them allegiance and service in exchange for certain rights, and this royal pair's offspring became the first ruler or *karaeng* of Gowa. Gowa itself, as David Bulbeck's archaeological survey indicates, was essentially an inland but near-coastal agrarian polity that moved seaward by "capturing" small coastal trading polities such as Polombangkeng and Sanrabone.[15] The most important of these coastal communities was Talloq, an offshoot of Gowa and destined to be Gowa's closest partner.

For present-day historians reviewing Makassar's past, Makassarese step from shadows into light in the early sixteenth century. The unparalleled source that makes this movement possible is the *Gowa Chronicle*. With it begin accounts of the deeds and accomplishments, marriages and offspring of the reigning rulers of Gowa. Paired with the *Talloq Chronicle,* a vast if not unproblematic new source of information about Makassar becomes available. Less recognized are the substantial lacunae in these chronicles. Most significantly, they discuss and center historical developments on Gowa and its environs, discussing other areas of Makassar—including Siang and Bantaeng, which archaeological findings indicate were of considerable importance—only as they interacted with Gowa and Talloq. With no comparable sources from other Makassarese areas, historians have been quick to equate Gowa's history with Makassar's history as a whole. Thus by dint not only of its considerable accomplishments in the early modern period but because of the uneven landscape of sources, the rise and fall of Gowa frames and guides all the historical narratives describing early modern Makassarese history.

Karaeng Tumapaqrisiq Kallonna is the first Gowa ruler whose reign the *Gowa Chronicle* describes at length.[16] While his accomplishments are perhaps all the more impressive because of the paucity of information about his predecessors, there is no doubt that decisive changes during his reign transformed Gowa. Ruling from late 1510 or early 1511 to late 1546, Tumapaqrisiq Kallonna laid the foundation for Gowa's later domination of Makassar. Among his accomplishments the *Gowa Chronicle* mentions the first written records, laws, and declarations of war. With Gowa's long list of conquests of other Makassarese communities during his reign, the dramatic rise of Gowa's influence throughout Makassar began. Many of those "conquered" were defeated in battle and forced to acknowledge Gowa's sovereignty, but this did not mean permanent submission or immediate incorporation into Gowa's growing empire. Ties of marriage, exchanges of sacred regalia, commercial access to overseas valuables brought to Gowa, population resettlement, and other factors had to do their slower work before early relations based on defeat in war could give way to more stable links tying and subordinating outlying Makassarese communities to Gowa. At the same time, Gowa employed its growing and formidable military might as far afield as Bugis Boné and Sidenreng, while signing a treaty with Luwuq. Gowa's horizons moved quickly from the small stage of local politics to wars, treaties, and trade with polities across the peninsula and beyond. During his reign too Makassarese traded at Melaka and welcomed Portuguese merchants to Gowa (map 2).

The expansion of Gowa's influence—militarily, economically, politically—begun under Tumapaqrisiq Kallonna continued throughout the early modern era. Gowa's sixteenth-century rulers descended from Tumapaqrisiq Kallonna. He was succeeded by his sons Tunipalangga (r. late 1546 to early 1565) and Tunibatta (ruled for forty days in 1565), Tunibatta's son Tunijalloq (r. 1565 to late 1590), and Tunijalloq's son Tunipasuluq (r. late 1590 to early 1593). The *Gowa Chronicle* records impressive accomplishments during these reigns as well, and historians have followed the chronicle in recounting them. Under Tunipalangga a range of specialized craftsmen began to work for the ruler: ironsmiths, goldsmiths, builders, shipwrights, blowpipe makers, weaponsmiths, ropemakers, and more. Bricks were fired, gold smelted, and gunpowder mixed. Weapons and agricultural implements were improved. Earthen forts began to be buttressed with brick walls. Communities as far away as Mandar in central Sulawesi now acknowledged Gowa's suzerainty. Tunibatta died fighting the Bugis, but Gowa's rise continued during the reign of his son Tunijalloq. He worked hard to further the efforts of his predecessors. He strengthened defensive forts along the coast with powerful cannons, improved Makassarese ships and weapons, and patronized court scribes. Trade flourished, and Tunijalloq sent envoys abroad and made alliances outside of Sulawesi with the rulers of Mataram, Banjarmasin, and Johor, and with rulers in Maluku and Timor. Tunijalloq built a mosque for the burgeoning Malay community, who themselves may have begun proselytizing among Makassarese. After some time Tunijalloq felt that Gowa was strong enough to challenge the Bugis again, and in 1582 the Bugis states of Boné, Soppeng, and Wajo were forced to band together in a triple alliance against Gowa. By the end of Tunijalloq's reign Gowa was without doubt the preeminent power and commercial center in South Sulawesi. The *Gowa Chronicle* remembers Tunijalloq's son and successor Tunipasuluq as a despot known for arbitrary behavior. Only fifteen years of age when he came to power, Tunipasuluq exiled or seized the property of many nobles, presumably removing resistance to his efforts to centralize and reorganize Makassarese social relations and manpower obligations. Many Malay traders and

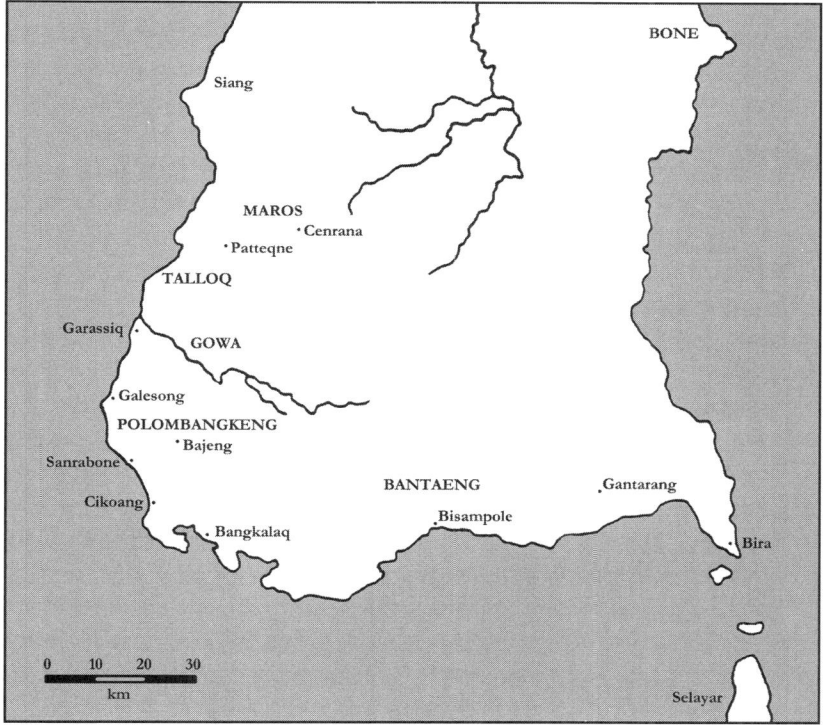

Map 2. Makassar and Its Environs

Makassarese fled during his brief reign, opposing his demands for subservience or fearful that his gaze would next fall upon them. Finally, the nobles of Gowa and Talloq collectively deposed Tunipasuluq; he died in exile on the distant island of Buton twenty-four years later.

This story of Gowa's sixteenth-century rulers and accomplishments seems to call out for words such as "flourish," "rise," "expand," and "progress." From one small polity among many dotting the Makassarese landscape to the dominant power in the peninsula, Gowa's rulers turned an unpromising beginning into a tale of impressive proportions. Anthony Reid summarized it as "one of the most rapid and spectacular success stories which Indonesian history affords."[17] Of most of the Makassarese communities that gradually were pulled into Gowa's orbit we hear little, except for those few such as Talloq, which became an intimate partner in this project, and others such as Maros and Polombangkeng, previously powerful communities situated near Gowa. Within this narrative of increasing growth and success the Gowa and Talloq chronicles record several turning points. The deposing of Tunipasuluq was clearly one, but two others ultimately were of greater significance.

The first of these two sixteenth-century turning points was a war fought between Gowa and its allies against the combined forces of Talloq, Maros, and Polombangkeng in the 1530s. Gowa was victorious and simultaneously gained access to the manpower and rich agricultural lands of Maros and Polombangkeng and the maritime trade of coastal Talloq. This access must have been decisive in fueling Gowa's rise. Significant too was the beginning afterward, as yet tentative, of a close partnership with Talloq that would flourish in the seventeenth century. The second major turning point came in perhaps 1561, when a group of Malays approached Tunipalangga and asked for a place to dwell. This was certainly not the first time that Malays and Makassarese encountered each other. Malays had been trading at Makassarese ports for decades, and some groups settled in Makassarese coastal communities after being forced from Melaka by the Portuguese conquest in 1511. Makassarese too may well have been known in Melaka: the Portuguese merchant Tomé Pires mentioned traders from the "Macaçar islands," while the *Gowa Chronicle* noted that Karaeng Tumapaqrisiq Kallonna came to power in the same year that Melaka was conquered.[18] But now a pattern of intermittent or seasonal interaction with Malay merchants gave way to the regular, everyday contact that only a permanent community could facilitate, and Malay mercantile acumen and commercial contacts throughout the archipelago accelerated the pace and profitability of trade at Gowa. The war of the 1530s and the close contact between Makassarese and Malays that began three decades later were of profound importance for Gowa's later history.

Reading the chronicles carefully also reveals significant trends shaping Gowa and Makassar during the course of the sixteenth century. Most evident, Gowa's rulers began to create a hierarchy of positions and titles that would endure beyond the lifespan of personal and kinship links between individuals. The two most important were probably those of harbormaster *(sabannaraq)* and an adviser to the ruler known as "the speaker of the land" *(tumabicarabutta)*. Other officials included a trio of ministers *(tumailalang)* that acted as intermediaries within Gowa. Individual nobles now occupied these permanent positions, each of which had defined duties, privileges, and ritual roles. Some communities were transformed into appanages for the noble who held the title—the *karaeng*-ship—of that area. In addition, a bewildering variety of local titles were arranged over time into a coherent hierarchy. The most powerful rulers of important communities were titled *karaeng;* the lords of the Bate Salapang and other local lords were titled *gallarrang;* leaders of smaller communities were called *kare, datuq, loqmoq,* or one of several other titles. The ruler of Gowa alone was addressed as *somba*. More important than these individual designations was the recognition that they represented particular ranks or positions within a Makassarese society whose pinnacle was in Gowa. Not rigid or unchanging, this evolving hierarchy of positions and titles nevertheless marked out a comparatively coherent system of relative statuses and clear political and social relationships within an integrated whole.

Accompanying and making possible this growing hierarchy was the increasing power of the ruler of Gowa. From being an adjudicator of disputes and first among equals, the Karaeng Gowa became an august ruler with considerable power. The guarantees of noninterference by the ruler of Gowa that the Bate Salapang had been promised when they raised the *tumanurung* and Karaeng Bayo to be their rulers eroded. Originally the source of Gowa's strength, the Bate Salapang were of decreasing significance; more and more prestige, resources, and influence lay with the titled positions and *karaeng*-ships established over the course of the sixteenth century. The Gowa court *lontaraq bilang,* for example, consistently record information about the important *karaengs* of the land, but hardly ever mention the Bate Salapang. The ruler of Gowa and a handful of *karaengs* dominated Gowa's affairs, making decisions and reaping the economic and political benefits that stemmed from their privileged positions. Yet this power was not unlimited. Tunipasuluq's arbitrary actions established the boundaries beyond which rulers could not go, and the belief that rulers must be lawful rather than rapacious remained a potent ideal among commoners.

During the seventeenth century these trends and the general pattern of Gowa's expansion and rising power continued at an even swifter pace. Following the deposition of Tunipasuluq, Karaeng Matoaya, the influential statesman and ruler of Talloq, installed on the throne of Gowa Tunipasuluq's brother (and his own nephew), who would come to be known as Sultan Ala'uddin (r. 1593 to 1639). The new ruler of Gowa was a young boy at the time, and it was Karaeng Matoaya who supervised the rebuilding of a Gowa empire that Tunipasuluq's actions had threatened to destroy. Sultan Ala'uddin remained under Karaeng Matoaya's tutelage for most of his long reign until Karaeng Matoaya's death in 1636. Sultan Ala'uddin considered his uncle his closest adviser, and he followed Karaeng Matoaya's lead in all things. Historians too have noted their close ties and shared accomplishments.

Most commentators have seen seventeenth-century Makassar as dominated by the talents and personalities of its rulers. Two pairs stand out: first, Sultan Ala'uddin and Karaeng Matoaya, then their sons Sultan Malikussaid (r. 1639 to 1653) and Karaeng Pattingalloang, who became ruler of Talloq in 1641. From 1593 to 1654, when Karaeng Pattingalloang died, Gowa flourished. By all accounts a gifted, industrious, and wise man, Matoaya presided over Gowa's rise from a local power within South Sulawesi to a key power within the Indonesian archipelago. Pattingalloang shared the outstanding character and abilities of his father. Crucial to this success were the close bonds the rulers of Gowa and Talloq forged beginning with Matoaya and Ala'uddin. During this period outsiders often assumed the two kingdoms were one, living up to the famous and long-remembered Makassarese pronouncement that Gowa and Talloq had "only one people but two rulers" *(seqreji ata narua karaeng)*. Among the accomplishments of the seventeenth century were the minting of gold coins, construction of new and more advanced ships, manufacture of cannons and gunpowder, and a tremendous expansion in the brick fortifications protecting Gowa (figure 2), particularly along the coast as the VOC threat became apparent.

The city later called Makassar became a substantial city during the seventeenth century. Its population probably reached a hundred thousand. In addition to Makassarese there were sizable Malay and Portuguese settlements, as well as permanent communities of Bandanese and other Indonesian groups. Dutch, English, Danish, and other Europeans established trading posts, and the city bustled with Arab, Chinese, and Indian traders, Spanish envoys, and many others, all drawn to Makassar by the ability of its rulers to create an entrepôt where a vast range of goods and services was available. The list of goods traded at Makassar was long indeed: sandalwood tribute from the Lesser Sunda islands, rice from Maros, diamonds from Banjarmasin, slaves from Buton, cloves from Maluku, cloth from India, porcelain from China, and much more. Setting the tone for this thriving, cosmopolitan atmosphere were the rulers of Talloq in particular. Matoaya and Pattingalloang were known for their intellectual curiosity in matters ranging from theology to science, from Catholic doctrine to astronomy. Pattingalloang spoke Malay, Portuguese, and Spanish in addition to Makassarese and collected a library of books, manuscripts, globes, and maps that impressed visitors enormously.

However, accompanying this permissive, welcoming attitude toward foreign traders and goods was a powerful military constantly engaged in expanding Gowa's influence. Expeditions of up to a thousand ships were launched to northern and central Sulawesi, Buton, and the Lesser Sundas. Within South Sulawesi one observer reported that

Figure 2. Walls of Makassarese fortification at Somba Opu

the rulers of Gowa could muster a force of thirty-six thousand men with ease; another reported a hundred thousand. Bugis rebellions against Gowa's overlordship were put down ruthlessly. Makassarese who violated the prerogatives the rulers granted themselves were punished, often executed, swiftly and dramatically. Neither "liberal" nor "tyrannical," the rulers of Gowa and Talloq by the middle of the seventeenth century commanded impressive military power and oversaw a bountiful commercial haven.

Punctuating this continuing narrative of rulers overseeing the expansion of Gowa during the seventeenth century were two important watersheds. The first was conversion to Islam in 1605, the second an emphatic declaration of resistance to VOC pressure that set the stage for their final confrontation in the 1660s. Muslim Malays had been visiting and residing in Makassar for a century or more before the rulers of Gowa and Talloq converted to Islam. Quite probably, individual Makassarese converted before 1605, but on September 22 of that year Karaeng Matoaya formally and publicly embraced Islam; he was followed soon thereafter by Sultan Ala'uddin (the Islamic title by which this first Muslim ruler of Gowa is known). In a society where rulers were the focus of social life and its norms, other Makassarese quickly followed these rulers. Some Makassarese resisted formally accepting Islam, and "conversion" itself is best understood as an ongoing process rather than a single transformative event. For example, lowland Makassarese populations participated in Islamic practices and identified themselves as Muslims long before highland Makassarese, who often equated entering Islam with political submission to Gowa. Nevertheless, Karaeng Matoaya and Sultan Ala'uddin fundamentally changed South Sulawesi. Matoaya and Ala'uddin launched campaigns known as "wars of Islamization" throughout and beyond the peninsula. Between 1608 and 1611 all the major polities of South Sulawesi south of the highland Toraja were forcibly converted to Islam. Overseas areas conquered or under the influence of Gowa, such as Bima on the island of Sumbawa, were similarly compelled to convert to the new faith. This explicitly Islamic Makassarese identity did not cause major social changes in the seventeenth century, but it did become an important idiom in which Makassarese political relations were expressed, and it did establish Gowa as an Islamic polity on a par with Aceh, Banten, and the other major Islamic courts dominating the archipelago.

The second major event that punctuated and transformed Gowa also took place during the reign of Sultan Ala'uddin. VOC efforts in the eastern archipelago in the early seventeenth century focused on capturing and enforcing a hoped-for monopoly on valuable Maluku spices. Gowa was an important node in spice-trading networks, and its open trading practices and activities within Maluku constituted the most damaging obstacles to VOC aims. Responding to Dutch requests to refrain from the profitable spice trade, Ala'uddin purportedly declared, "My land is open to all nations" and "God has made the earth and the sea and has divided the earth among men and given the sea in common to all. It has never been heard that anyone should be forbidden to sail the seas." This outright refusal to accede to VOC wishes, and Gowa's continued activities in the Maluku area that the Dutch now considered their personal sphere of influence, placed Gowa and the VOC on a collision course. A pattern of violent incidents followed by halting efforts at reconciliation culminated in a 1660 war in which the VOC seized and kept Gowa's coastal fort at Panakkukang. Dissatisfaction with the unfinished state of affairs festered, and in 1666 the final war began. The Dutch, aided by Bugis led by Arung Palakka, utterly defeated Gowa in 1669; its population was scattered, its defenses were demolished, and faith in its prowess was vanquished. In the decades after the conquest, Gowa itself nearly ceased to exist. In a letter written to the Dutch governor-general shortly

Figure 3. Tombs of the rulers of Gowa

after the conquest of Gowa in 1669, one ruler of Gowa asked for pardon. Likening Gowa's Makassarese vassals to children in a family ripped asunder, the sultan wrote that because of sickness and death throughout the land it had not been possible even to find out the names of all the ruler's children.[19] The last independent ruler of Gowa, and the one who oversaw the debacle, was Malikussaid's son Sultan Hasanuddin (r. 1653 to 1669). Following the conquest he abdicated, and died soon after. With his death the *Gowa Chronicle* ends too, a poignant recognition that a glorious era had come to a close.

These are the main story lines and episodes in the accepted narrative account of early modern Makassar. In general the rise and fall of Gowa is told with an emphasis on how economic success in trade fueled Gowa's political expansion. Commerce provided the wealth, resources, and opportunities that were the raw materials of political and military prowess. The most successful works tracing this parabola are those of Anthony Reid. In several articles, then in his two-volume study *Southeast Asia in the Age of Commerce 1460–1680*, Reid, using Makassar as a major and indeed paradigmatic case study, argued his thesis that an upswing in commerce fueled political centralization. In this interpretation Makassar stands as an extraordinary example of what ambitious and talented men could accomplish given the vistas that an explosion of trade opened up beginning in the late fifteenth century. Ironically, it was precisely this commercial success and military might that attracted the ire of the VOC. Gowa became the VOC's chief rival in the eastern archipelago. A half century of misunderstandings, violent incidents, reconciliations, blockades, and other armed conflicts culminated in the 1666–1669 wars in which the VOC and their Bugis allies conquered Gowa. Never able to regain its autonomy, and fundamentally transformed by the VOC presence, Gowa fell, and its early modern golden age came to an abrupt end. With this narrative of Gowa's history recalled in outline, we can now turn to the cultural world of early modern Makassar.

∞ *2* ∞

Culture and History-Making

This chapter examines the relationship between culture and history-making, an examination that goes to the heart of ethnographic history. In particular, I consider the role culture plays in contemporary history-making about early modern Southeast Asia, then the aspects of Makassarese culture that shaped the practice of history-making during that period. I argue that awareness of Makassarese perceptions of language and the social position of written texts as sacred objects are central to understanding the progression from orality to literacy discussed in chapter 3.

Writing Makassarese History

Debate over the significance of culture in the past and in the histories made of it has a long pedigree in the Western historical tradition. Conflicting visions of what forces are of greatest importance in driving change and shaping events are at the heart of this ongoing debate. Among historians of Southeast Asia, a dominant way of framing and understanding the early modern period is now emerging. The force held most responsible for establishing the temporal boundaries of the period, the common social features of its societies, and the historical trends that affected the development of the region as a whole is commerce. The historian at the forefront of this effort to frame the characteristics that defined and the trends that shaped early modern Southeast Asia is Anthony Reid. It is in his work that the coherence of the period is most cogently argued for and its lineaments most ambitiously described. It is his work too that is most often cited by both specialists and scholars outside the field seeking to understand this period in Southeast Asia's past.

There are two reasons that economic arguments appear to be the most effective in explaining the events of the early modern era. The first is the long-standing, even primary value accorded to economic forces in shaping the world in which we live. The second stems from the nature of the sources commonly available to historians of the period.

The records, travelogues, reports, and books written by European visitors to the region provide the most abundant source of firsthand accounts of what was taking place in the early modern period. The observations of traders, missionaries, government agents, and explorers are often perceptive, but they reflect European politics, values, and activities as much as they do Southeast Asian ones. So too Europeans came with specific purposes and projects. Whether their mission was to convert the heathen, chart unknown lands and bring back information about exotic peoples, or pursue commercial ventures that would enrich themselves and their investors, Europeans were not just spectators, but spectators with specific interests. Certain features of Southeast Asian life, and certain activities, were worthy of note. Strange cultural practices formed one significant body of observations, while political, economic, and military dispositions formed another. Often the same source blended titillating exotica with precise information about trading activities. Most important, it was the public, observable world of Southeast Asian activities that European visitors viewed and described. What exactly, we should ask, was visible to observation? The answer is what Southeast Asians did and what they had: the public practices and the material face of early modern Southeast Asian life.[1] In no other sphere of human life is economic activity as evident.

It should come as no surprise, then, that Reid views the early modern age as "the age of commerce." But during what period did commerce not influence this maritime region of voyaging and crossroads? The key issue is not whether commerce had important effects on early modern Southeast Asia—it certainly did—but whether this was an age *defined* by commerce. Is it in fact correct to posit commerce as the primary historical force defining the period and transforming the region?

We might ask whether in his keen effort to establish the importance of trade Reid is not asking too much of commerce. Of the links between the profits and products of trade on the one hand and certain political and social changes on the other hand there is little doubt. Ambitious leaders able to monopolize or dominate commercial transactions gained important foreign allies, access to firearms, cloth, and other trade staples, and a hard-to-quantify elevated social status because of this special relationship. Many rulers along the littorals of Southeast Asia quite clearly took advantage of such possibilities to gather to themselves a larger and better-armed entourage, a wider network of allies, and the ability to more effectively control manpower reserves than hitherto had been possible. In the early modern equivalent of arms races, rivals without such access were increasingly eclipsed by fortunate and formidable rulers. There is no reason to doubt this development, well documented for many areas of maritime Southeast Asia. But can all the major developments of the early modern period be traced to this economic wellspring of change, even in such places as obviously dependent on trade as Makassar? Could there not be more at work, albeit less visibly at first glance than economic changes?

This study begins from the desire to expand the kind of explanations we might make and the kind of understandings we might gain from a wider range of historiographical perspectives. I argue that cultural, social, religious, and intellectual formations are historical forces in their own right. The relevance of economic forces cannot be denied with the wave of a hand, but neither can the fundamental significance of cultural values be elided without reducing the complexities of human social life to misleading simplifications. Examining local perceptions of language is a first step in conveying the rich potential that Makassarese historical culture had to shape the Makassarese social world.

Perceptions of Language in Early Modern Makassar

As a window into Makassarese perceptions of language, one of the shortest extant Makassarese texts is also the most revealing. A short lontar palm roll in the Koninklijk Instituut voor de Tropen in Amsterdam has the following text.

Following the words [undecipherable][2] *makes very great the prosperity of all the communities above the winds and below the winds. He makes ruling decisions with the justness of Allah ta'ala. Whoever reads or hears and then acts on them, the words of this document will be advantageous to him. He is called a wise person.*

This text was a talisman in two senses. First, it contained a sacred Arabic statement that the writer may not have been able to read in Arabic, and may not have known the meaning of, but that he recognized and was able to speak aloud. He clearly believed that voicing these sacred words could have powerful effects: the *words* are a talisman. Second, as an *object* the physical lontar palm roll was a talisman. Portable, the roll itself was valuable and potent even when simply carried and not "activated" by being read. It was a sacred object that like a kris or a bezoar stone conferred its magical power on its bearer.[3]

The unintelligibility of Arabic for most Makassarese only reinforced the sense that speaking Arabic was a potentially powerful way of affecting the human world. As Benedict Anderson wrote of Arabic in Java, "Arabic was maintained as the language of 'initiation' precisely because Arabic was *not* understood; the whole point of a spiritual ritual in an uncomprehended language is that it manifests power, and implies a deliberately nonrationalist mode of cognition."[4] Except for those few early modern Makassarese who through long study knew Arabic well, the language of Islam consisted of memorized mantras whose original semantic meaning did not cross or only imperfectly crossed cultural boundaries. Among the Minangkabau, Arabic seals "contained" words of this sacred language that made the seals themselves evidential signs of Allah.[5] Elsewhere in Sumatra, Barbara Andaya writes, even among illiterates, "the king's seal was resonant with sacred powers" and in some cases the wax seals of letters were eaten because they contained the power of the signatories.[6] The unknown Arabic phrase on this small lontar palm roll is what Vicente Rafael called an "opaque signifier": sounds to which Makassarese attached meanings and significances probably quite distant from their semantic meaning in Arabic.[7]

Moreover, this text is far from the only evidence that Makassarese saw language in general and written texts in particular as capable of affecting the world around them. Numerous oral traditions evince the power of spoken and written language in early modern Makassar. One of the most dramatic oral histories conveying this sense describes the coming of Islam to Makassar. It tells of the arrival of Datoq of Bandang, who was destined to convert the Makassarese to Islam. After stepping ashore, Datoq of Bandang surprised and confused the people by continually praying aloud and expressing his wish to meet with the ruler. Hearing of this, Karaeng Matoaya left his palace to go see the stranger. At the gate as he left, Matoaya met an old man who asked where he was going. The old man then wrote something on Matoaya's thumbnail and sent his greeting to the stranger with the ruler. When Matoaya and the stranger met at the beach, the stranger saw that written on Karaeng Matoaya's thumbnail was the sura Al-Fatihah and said that the old man must have been an incarnation of the prophet Muhammad himself.

Karaeng Matoaya immediately converted by uttering the confession of faith and began to spread Islam among the Makassarese.[8]

Another version of the coming of Islam omits the meeting with the old man, instead telling that Karaeng Matoaya greeted the stranger at the palace gate after the latter stepped ashore. Here, without being taught, Karaeng Matoaya welcomed the stranger by speaking the customary Islamic greeting, *Assalam Alaikum Wahrahmatullahi Wabarakatuh.* To some Makassarese this proves that Islam was already present in South Sulawesi before the arrival of missionaries. In particular, they believe it indicates that the prophet Muhammad must have appeared in Gowa earlier. The spot where this meeting took place at the palace gate is seen as a sacred locus of spiritual power even today.[9] This version is interesting not only as an effort to claim that Islam was indigenous to South Sulawesi, but again because of the prominence of speaking Arabic. Makassarese, it seems, saw Islam as remarkable because of its stress on spiritually powerful spoken incantations. Indeed, for both Arabs and Makassarese Islamic language was compelling. The Islamic command is "Recite!" and at the very heart of conversion was the spoken profession of faith.

Links between manuscripts and sacredness are well attested to in much of the archipelago. Balinese regard *kakawin* texts, for example, as supernaturally powerful objects dangerous to the uninitiated. Written letters themselves have a divine origin and can be manipulated to influence events. In such a cultural context, writing becomes a religious act comparable to yoga.[10] For Makassarese, Islam was easily intelligible as a path to spiritual power and took its place alongside existing traditions emphasizing the power of spoken language.

Anthropologists have been quick to recognize the significance accorded spoken words in general and ritual speech in particular in Indonesian societies.[11] Writing was a practice infused with mystery and power across the archipelago.[12] As C. C. Berg wrote of verbal magic among the ancient Javanese, "Observing that words sometimes make human beings behave in accordance with the sense they convey, many people believe words to possess an inherent power which may affect situations and dead objects as well, and priests to possess the gift of handling such powerful words."[13] Inscribing such words on objects is another way of making them efficacious. The Makassarese word for writing *(ukiriq)* in fact means "to carve or inscribe." Inscriptions in the old Makassarese script found on bricks used in Makassarese fortifications suggest the magical potency these characters originally may have had. Nor did this sense that written symbols are powerful talismans disappear with the advent of literacy. VOC officials were confused by the fact that Bugis and Makassarese considered written treaties to be physical tokens standing for entire social relationships rather than simple contractual agreements spelled out in articles.[14] Writing, like ritual speech, is a cultural act laden with meanings that stretch far beyond the need to communicate or record information.

Among early modern Makassarese, the best-known activity centering on ritual speech involved oaths. Before battle and at the installation ceremony of high-ranking nobles, their warrior followers swore oaths known as *aru*. Each warrior chanted an oath of loyalty while dancing aggressively and wielding his kris. The bellicose tone of the *aru* and its ritual presentation conveyed martial ferocity. Makassarese believed that such an oath not only stoked men's warlike fires, but bound them to their chanted words. To break their word invited the gravest consequences: exile or death in life and everlasting ignominy in people's memory. Here are three verses of an *aru* Makassarese remembered as being spoken by warriors of Gowa before their *karaeng*.

> Note, *karaeng!*
> May I be greatly pardoned, my lord,
> in front of your magnificence,
> in the presence of your loftiness,
> beside your splendor.
>
> My words are eternal, *karaeng.*
> You are the wind, *karaeng,*
> and we are the leaves.
> You are the water, *karaeng,*
> and we are floating pieces.
> You are the needle, *karaeng,*
> and we are the sewed thread.
>
> If later it is not as
> it is in my *aru* before you,
> plant a forked stick on my grave,
> on my footsteps.
> Change my name,
> curse my descendants.

> Tell to children,
> tell to those not yet born,
> [this is what happens to]
> a person who speaks so
> and then does not fulfill his words.[15]

It was against this cultural backdrop that literate history-making developed: Makassarese perceptions of written language derived from their perceptions of spoken language. The beliefs that surrounded and explained the powerful effects of spoken sacred or magical language established the framework within which written language would be understood, a framework and way of seeing the past that decisively influenced how, why, and to what effect Makassarese wrote histories.

Makassarese Writing History

The most important feature of the Makassarese historical manuscripts I will be concerned with in this book is their presence as vessels containing the once-spoken words of Makassarese ancestors. Writing recorded speech so that it could be respoken at a later time. Reading, to make an obvious point, was performed aloud, not silently. It remained speech, and here it is useful to recall the incomplete nature of Makassarese scripts. Not all sounds are graphically represented, and the reader must know how to convert this written shorthand into correct speech. Meaning is not conveyed until written words, having been spoken once, are spoken again. This characteristic was the source of much of writing's mystique and power for Makassarese; to hear again the very words of a long-dead but much-revered ruler inspired awe. To disregard or violate that ruler's words invited disaster. As Lorraine Gesick argues in the case of southern Thailand, the voice of Thai kings was the source of the sacredness of southern Thai historical manuscripts.[16] Writing was a sacred talisman or physical token that contained words from the past. Writing allowed the past to exist in the present. It was this ancient status that gave written Makassarese its aura and guaranteed its power.

In the early modern period Makassarese produced historical manuscripts of several sorts. The best-known are chronicles *(patturioloang)*. Alongside these texts were treaties, customs, declarations of war, genealogies, datebooks, and more. Dating specific genres and analyzing their historical and conceptual relationships is a difficult and controversial task. Briefly, it seems that during the sixteenth century Makassarese moved from first writing information about the past to composing the lengthy and elaborate *patturioloang*. Thus, the *Gowa Chronicle* reports that during the reign of Tumapaqrisiq Kallonna (r. c. 1510 to 1546), the harbormaster and *tumailalang* I Daeng Pamatteq first "made Makassarese *lontaraq*" *(ampareki lontaraq Mangkasaraka)*.[17] The chronicle also recalls that Tumapaqrisiq Kallonna "made written treaties with the person from Maros named Karaeng Loe of Pakere, the ruler of the people of Polombangkeng called Karaeng Loe of Bajeng, the ruler of the people of Boné called Boteka; together they made treaties." Finally, the chronicle notes that "this ruler was the first to make written laws [and] written declarations of war" *(iapa anne karaeng uru mappareq rapang bicara timutimu ri bunduka)*.[18] Makassarese *patturioloang* are not mentioned by name.

At about the same time during the reign in Talloq of Tunipasuruq (r. c. 1500s to 1540 or 1543), the *Talloq Chronicle* reports that "writing first became good" *(nauru mabajiq ukirika)*.[19] The chronicle does not report what was written. From the corpus of surviving Makassarese manuscripts, it seems certain that when Makassarese began to write in earnest in the sixteenth century they wrote about the past. It is equally clear what they did not write: trade or harbor records, literary compositions, religious tracts. This may seem surprising. B. F. Matthes first noted the dearth of Makassarese literary and religious compositions not adapted from Malay and Arabic, particularly in comparison with the Bugis.[20] Indeed, one of the most conspicuous differences between Bugis and Makassarese is that the enormous Bugis epic known as the *I La Galigo*, by some reckonings the world's longest epic composition, is unknown among the Makassarese. Later commentators have reached similar conclusions. G. K. Niemann concurred with Matthes, writing, "Makassarese literature consists mostly of translation."[21] The best-known form of Makassarese "literature" is texts recording versions of epic oral compositions called *sinriliq*, a tradition that began to be recorded on paper comparatively recently. Modern Indonesian evaluations of "Makassarese literature" are devoted almost entirely to this oral tradition.[22] Makassarese oral literature is rich in poems, epics, riddles, stories, and other forms of composition.[23] Yet given the importance of trade and the complexity of transactions during the sixteenth and seventeenth centuries at Gowa's busy port, the absence of a corpus of Makassarese manuscripts concerning commerce is puzzling. Possibly such records were kept in Malay at the harbors and destroyed during the wars of the 1660s, but certainly we would expect some to have survived. Unfortunately this riddle cannot be solved here. The fact remains that when Makassarese began to make manuscripts in the sixteenth century, the texts they made were overwhelmingly concerned with the past.²⁴

The question of the origins of the Makassarese scripts has received much attention but resulted in little agreement. The ultimate origins of both the *jangang-jangang* (old Makassarese) script and the *lontaraq beru* (new Makassarese) script may never be known (see figure 4, in which

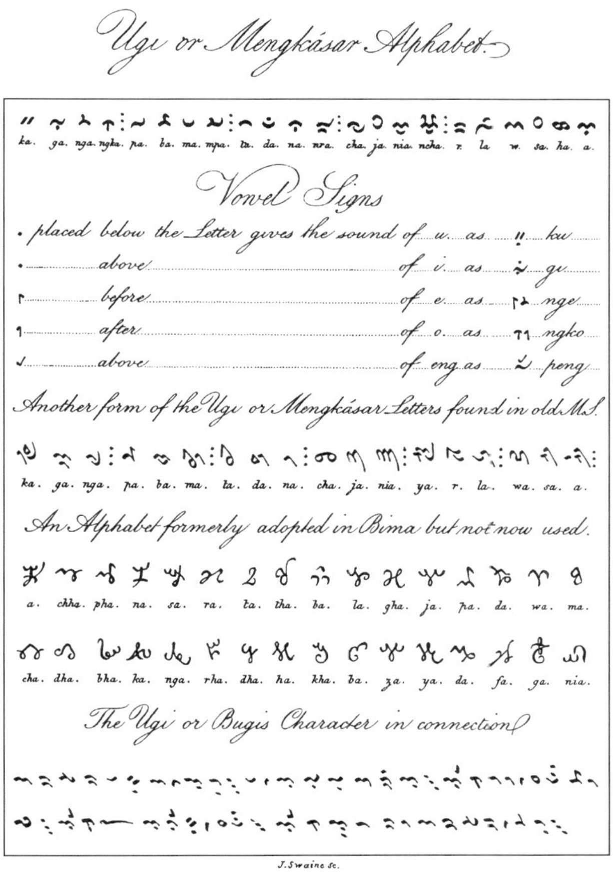

Figure 4. Raffles' "Ugi or Mengkásar Alphabet" (Reprinted from Thomas Raffles, *The History of Java*, volume 2, Oxford University Press, 1965 [1817])

the top line depicts the *lontaraq beru* script and the *jangang-jangang* script is described as "another form of the Ugi or Mengkásar letters found in old manuscripts"). In conception at least they were based on Indian models of alphabetic scripts.²⁵ Both predate the 1605 conversion to Islam, after which a character "ha" (∞), which graphically mimics the same letter in Arabic, was added to the *lontaraq beru* script to enable Makassarese to transcribe this common Arabic sound.

The *jangang-jangang* script never had this additional phoneme; it was also less standardized graphically, making it more difficult to read. But this older script did not die out. It was used for such important manuscripts as the 1667 Treaty of Bungaya, as well as the two oldest extant Makassarese *patturioloang* (BL 12351 and KIT 668/216). I think that this older script was culturally viewed as more arcane, rarified, and hence more spiritually powerful than the *lontaraq beru* script, which came to be used widely by Bugis as well as Makassarese. The perception of this script brings to mind attitudes toward Sanskrit in Bali and Java, where different scripts and materials were seen as appropriate to particular genres or types of writing.²⁶

Possibly, too, Makassarese used *jangang-jangang* in certain texts to distinguish themselves and their past from Bugis, who also wrote in the *lontaraq beru* script. These factors would account for the continued use of *jangang-jangang* in certain manuscripts. Whatever their ultimate Indian origins, the Makassarese language they transcribed contained few words derived from Sanskrit; most of those that did probably entered the language through Malay.²⁷ Makassarese believed their scripts to be their own; they carried no memories of nonnative origins, though during the seventeenth century after adopting Islam some Makassarese began to write using a slightly modified Arabic script known as *serang* (figure 5).

Why did Makassarese begin writing histories at this time instead of another, and in the forms they did instead of others? We cannot be certain. The most obvious answer is to give credit to the Malay presence in Makassar beginning in the sixteenth century. Malays certainly carried written historical traditions with them, as they did Islam and other cultural practices that influenced South Sulawesi. Yet this path of influence is unlikely, or unlikely to have been direct. The *Gowa Chronicle* bears little resemblance to Malay *hikayat* such as the *Sejarah Melayu* or the *Sja'ir Perang Mengkasar,* a fact that I will return to in later discussions. Nor did Makassarese write *patturioloang* using the Arabic script, a method of transcription far more complete than *lontaraq beru* or *jangang-jangang* scripts. In addition, to my knowledge no Makassarese history refers to

Malay histories of any sort. J. Noorduyn too was skeptical of arguments that Makassarese historical writing developed or derived from Malay or other foreign historical traditions. As he put it, "There are several essential and striking differences from other Indonesian historical writing such as Javanese historiography. This seems to exclude any strong influence from outside as a simple explanation of its origins." Rather, he describes

Figure 5. *Serang* script

South Sulawesi histories as a type of historical writing that "developed independently along its own lines."[28]

Historical chronicles *(patturioloang)*, treaties *(ulukana)*, oaths (variously known as *tunra, sapatta,* or *sumpa*), customs *(rapang* or *rapang bicara)*, social regulations *(parakara)*, declarations of war *(timu-timu bunduq)*, datebooks *(lontaraq bilang)*, and genealogies all shared the ability to conserve words and deeds from the past. In written manuscripts the past was preserved unchanged. For example, the most famous pronouncement in Makassarese history is an oath that bound together Gowa and Talloq. In the seventeenth-century golden age of Gowa and Talloq's partnership, Karaeng Matoaya of Talloq recalled that his father Tumamenang ri Makkoayang was the first ruler of Talloq to proclaim that Gowa and Talloq were "only one people but two rulers."[29] A rare manuscript written in the old Makassarese script briefly recounts the moment in which the pronouncement was first declared.[30] The text records the formulaic oath spoken by the rulers of Gowa and Talloq, Tunijalloq (r. 1565 to 1590) and Tumamenang ri Makkoayang (r. early 1540s to late 1570s). The language is elaborate and visually powerful, calling upon common images of sailing and navigation to evoke the sense of cooperation and unity of purpose necessary to sail a ship or to establish a close political alliance.[31]

Take out the words of Tunijalloq and Tumamenang of Makkoayang spoken to their father and uncle [Tunipalangga]. "We are the rudder; we bail [water from the boat]; we handle the sails until we arrive. If it sinks, we sink; we only hope. One people but two rulers. Someone, even if they only dream of setting us in Gowa and Talloq against each other, that person is cursed by Rewata."

The oath this manuscript records probably dates from 1565. In that year Tunijalloq unexpectedly ascended the throne after his brother Tunibatta was killed after ruling Gowa for only forty days. At the same time Tunijalloq became ruler, Tumamenang ri Makkoayang was appointed to be the first *tumabicarabutta*, the highest-ranking official charged with carrying out the commands of the ruler of Gowa. According to the *Talloq Chronicle*, "With the death of Tunibatta, he [Tumamenang ri Makkoayang] was installed in Gowa as the speaker of the land by the people of Gowa alongside Tunijalloq."[32] As rulers of Gowa and Talloq, Tunijalloq and Tumamenang ri Makkoayang worked closely together, forming the foundation for the remarkable seventeenth-century partnership between these two polities. As important as the oath itself is the existence of a manuscript, written in the archaic Makassarese *jangang-jangang* script, that preserved this historical moment and testified to its truth.

Similarly, *rapang* texts explicitly recorded the spoken guidelines or advice of renowned and revered ancestors, particularly the rulers of Gowa and Talloq. Like treaties and declarations of war, *rapang* were short and collected into compendiums. One Makassarese manuscript (ANRI 62/1), for example, contains more than three hundred such articles or entries. *Rapang* manuscripts are common in Makassar and often copied. Makassarese regularly copied a core set of *rapang* from the rulers of Gowa and Talloq, then added *rapang* from local rulers and respected religious officials. Unlike some other genres of writing, *rapang* followed no single pattern of either composition or compilation. Instead the Makassarese mixed and arranged *rapang* entries with great freedom. One of the most commonly encountered *rapang* reads as follows.

These are the messages of Karaeng Matoaya, named Sultan Abdullah, to Karaeng Tumamenang of Bontobiraeng. He said, "The things I will present you, these words are of five kinds. If you know them, this is the foundation for ruling well. First, if you do something watch for its consequences. Second, do not be angry if you are corrected. Third, respect honest people. Fourth, do not listen to hearsay; later you will hear the true news. Fifth, you will quarrel if you become angry." [33]

This example displays the characteristics found in most *rapang*: attention to the sacred ancestor whose words are being remembered, emphasis on the preservation of his exact words, and belief that the past is the proper measure for behavior in the present.

Datebooks or *lontaraq bilang*, sometimes misleadingly referred to as "diaries," probably developed last among all the genres of Makassarese historical writing and on the surface most resemble the efforts of Western historians to record the past.[34] As an illustration of the concerns and style of *lontaraq bilang*, the following are the entries for the year 1648.

2 February (Sunday)	Karaeng Paqbundukarg died.
20 March (Wednesday)	The female *karaeng* of Popoq died.
5 April (Saturday)	Karaengta of Tamasongoq gave birth to a son by Tumamenang of Jungtana named Manginara Majuddin, Daengta Daeng Mattiro.

12 May (Monday)	The mother of the ruler named Karaengta of Bontoa died.
14 June (Saturday)	Daengta Daeng Naratang had a daughter named Habibah.
3 August (Monday)	Karaeng Jipang died when still young.
11 October (Wednesday)	I Maqminasa Daengta Daeng Sannging died.
30 September (Friday)	Friday prayer services were begun in Bontoalaq.
30 November (Monday)	The son of Karaeng Salaparang (on Lombok) named Ammasa Pamayan became ruler of Sumbawa.
8 December (Wednesday)	A house was built for a large bell.
9 December (Thursday)	I Assing died.[35]

As this excerpt conveys, noble births and deaths were the most frequently preserved events in *lontaraq bilang*. Other notable happenings, such as construction projects, the installation of nobles in important positions, divorces, natural disasters such as fires and earthquakes, the arrival of foreign ships and delegations, unusual events such as eclipses and comets, the departures and arrivals of rulers, and more all find places in *lontaraq bilang*. Makassarese did not preserve these events because of an inquisitive wish to explain how the present came to be (there are no causal links in *lontaraq bilang*) or because of a penchant for recording events so the past could be objectively known, but out of a desire to convey the past to the present.

Makassarese viewed *patturioloang* and other historical texts, both the physical objects and the texts they contained, as sacred heirlooms from the ancestors. Words could not be altered at will, for fear of incurring an ancestor's wrath and because of the strong desire to preserve the prestigious heritage the words represent. Scribal error, of course, did occur, sometimes with significant results. For instance, in one manuscript the copyist incorrectly added a vowel mark, transforming "those not conquered by Gowa" (ᨈᨊ ᨊᨕᨔᨑᨙᨕ ᨁᨚᨓ) into "the people conquered by Gowa" (ᨈᨕᨛ ᨊᨕᨔᨑᨙᨕ ᨁᨚᨓ). This significantly if unintentionally altered the meaning of the passage.[36] For the most part, however, it is noteworthy that the dozens of extant Gowa and Talloq *patturioloang* are all copies or versions of the same work. Never, it seems possible to conclude, did a Makassarese chronicler set out to rewrite the past or reinterpret what had been set down in previous *patturioloang*.[37]

Striking evidence of this is provided in the case of the *Gowa Chronicle*. Four descriptions of the text over a period of more than two centuries are nearly identical. Speelman's description of a *Gowa Chronicle* he saw shortly after the 1669 conquest of Gowa matches almost exactly the *Gowa Chronicle* that Roelof Blok described in 1759, another *Gowa Chronicle* manuscript copied in 1795, and the text B. F. Matthes collected and published almost a full two centuries later.[38]

Numerous manuscripts, in fact, attest to the importance of preserving exactly the words and customs of the ancestors. One common *rapang* article stated that forgetting treaties was once a frequent cause for warfare. Another declared that if people in a conquered land did not remember the laws of their ancestors they would never return to freedom. A third cautioned people never to forget their origins.[39] Makassarese wrote histories in a cultural context that prized the source and exact transmission of words spoken earlier. Many *rapang* begin with phrases such as "Spoke Gallarrang I Kare Mangaliki, these are the words of our Karaeng Tumamenang ri Ujung Tana."[40] Oaths too praised and demanded that words be remembered. One oath began, "May I be like a candle melted by the heat of its flame, like salt dissolved in water, if I forget."[41] Manuscripts were more than mere histories. They were the very past made present when the words they recorded were respoken, and such a function inspired awe and presumed great spiritual power. As objects, manuscripts offered a connection to a moment of origins in which were unleashed generative powers whose traces still had effects in the world.

Makassarese attitudes toward manuscripts containing words of the ancestors have parallels throughout Southeast Asia. Raechelle Rubinstein describes Balinese belief in the potency written characters inherently possess and the concomitant need for accuracy in recopying to preserve their "life-force."[42] To this day many Balinese believe that the goddess Saraswati dwells in the letters of the Balinese script. Among the Gayo of northern Sumatra, chanted spells often included tales of origins as an essential step in unleashing the power of the utterance. So too in southern Thailand the act of copying a manuscript was itself seen as a means of extending the power of the ancestors whose utterances they recorded.[43]

The survival of the past in written texts is worth dwelling on at least briefly, for it indicates the ways in which early modern Makassarese perceived the past differently from modern historians. There are no simple comparisons here. Above all, writing ethnographic history is an experience in alterity, an effort conceptually to jump and find one's footing in a new cultural milieu. We come to understand this new terrain by comparing it with our own. The most important difference between Makassarese conceptions of the past and my own lies in how the past was envisioned in relationship to the present.

In contrast to modernity's sense of the past as fleeting and separate from the present, Makassarese saw the past as a vibrant and vital part of their lives. But while not shunted aside and dismissed, neither was the past envisioned as a totality of all that had gone before. Certainly Makassarese did not conceptualize the past as we do, spatially imagining it as a single, vast panorama stretching behind us to the beginning of time. One kind of history of the past may have had little to do with another kind of history of the past. There were different histories for different purposes. *Patturioloang* have much in common with genealogies, for example, but little in common with *lontaraq bilang*. The two senses of the past these genres seem to imply did not conflict, but neither did they take their places as part of some larger History. There was, it seems, no single History because there was no single past.

Moreover, there was no similarity to the modern historian's voraciously devouring sources to produce as complete and detailed an account of the past as possible. Much of this difference derives from the modern, Western assumption that all accounts of the past are representations. That is, contemporary historians see history-making as an effort to produce an account mimicking the past as closely and comprehensively as possible. Historians are ultimately in the business of making narratives. To make our histories, we search out every possible fragment of information we can about the past, treating these fragments as sources with which we construct our representations. The belief that a larger whole can be known by examining its component parts, and more particularly by establishing the causal links between these parts or moments, is another fundamental principle of modern, Western history-making. Though these methods may seem natural, even inevitable, they are in fact cultural practices and not universal perceptions.

Makassarese, by contrast, seem to have viewed their histories not as representations of the past, not as imitations of something separate and irretrievable, but as preservations of the past still alive, relevant, and immediate to the present. To construct an account of the reign of a particular ruler, for example, Makassarese chroniclers did not seek out every available source for information, then weave these facts together into a history. They did not see themselves as removed from the past, as reconstructing the past lest it be gone forever. From the Makassarese cultural context, then, referring to something as "historical" means that it comes from and incarnates the past, not that it is about the past. A historical manuscript does not describe the past from a distance, but embodies the past in the present. The Makassarese sense that past and present are not severed from one another is anecdotally but usefully illustrated by comparing English and Makassarese language. In English the concept "in front" may mean either physically situated before one or temporally in the future, while "in back" means behind one or in the past. By contrast, in Makassarese *"riolo"* means physically in front or earlier in time, while *"riboko"* means physically behind or later in time.[44] If speakers of English orient themselves toward time by facing the future, speakers of Makassarese orient themselves toward time by facing the past. In contrast perhaps to a Westerner's sense of separation from the past is the strong sense of continuity and attachment between past and present that Makassarese felt.

Any account of history-making in early modern Makassar, or in any other place and time, must confront the difficult questions of the culturally ordered ways in which people apprehended the past. Like all products of human endeavor, histories are culturally grounded.[45] Because they are so deeply ingrained in a person's worldview, it is difficult to see that one's own perceptions of the past could be different. One goal of ethnographic history is to emphasize this sense of contingency, to realize that even something as fundamental as how time seems to work is not universal. To gain a measure of distance from one's own fundamentals is the first step toward being able to see those of another place and time. Universal assumptions will not do; neither will dichotomies of East and West or Modern and Primitive. The explicit contrast between Makassarese senses of history and the kind of history and historical consciousness my work represents is an important context for this work. So too Makassarese histories were made and possessed in a social world concerned with spiritually powerful objects, a context that would dramatically influence Makassarese history-making and its effects.

THE SOCIAL FORCE OF THE WRITTEN PAST

The crucial question for any ethnographic historian is where and how to begin writing about the culture of the area he or she studies. In the past this question had a straightforward answer. Colonial ethnographies of Makassar followed a standardized format in which categories such as character *(eigenschappen)*, religion *(godsdienst)*, and customs and practices *(gewoonten en gebruiken)* had discrete, prepared slots. The task of the ethnographer across the archipelago was to fill in the data under these uniform headings. Such summaries are perforce short and cannot but simplify, reduce, and homogenize complex, even contradictory, systems of thought and ways of behaving. Yet culture cannot be abstracted from its own webs of significance: the social and political contexts in which it is enmeshed. Nor can it be reduced to rules and structures without transforming something subtle, rich, elusive, and supple into a reified totem that belongs to the world of ethnology and its dusty shelves. To read the pages that follow, one should have some preliminary grasp of important aspects of Makassarese culture, but the challenge is to provide this beginning without engaging in the simplifications of colonial ethnographies. To begin this exploration of Makassarese culture, consider the dilemma I faced when I began to study Makassarese histories.

The greatest difficulty I faced as an outside scholar trying to learn about Makassar's past was not mastering unusual scripts or dealing with archaic language, but merely gaining access to manuscripts. Makassarese regard manuscripts as sacred, powerful objects capable of affecting those who possess, recite, and hear them. As the *Story of Syekh Yusuf* declares, "Whoever reads or hears reads [this], that person has entered into the radiance of Tusalamaka (Syekh Yusuf)."[46] In my research, the aid of a Makassarese assistant was crucial. Family and social ties allowed Djohan to borrow or copy manuscripts that would never be shown to an outsider. In some cases, even Djohan was not allowed to see the original manuscript, though he was able after several visits to persuade a secretive owner to make a copy of the text. For example, the owner of one text from Sanrabone was at first suspicious of surrendering his heirloom manuscript to Makassarese from another community. Yet after realizing that Djohan was working on my behalf—on behalf of not only a non-Makassarese scholar, but in fact an American who intended to write about Makassarese history—he decided that publicizing Sanrabone's illustrious past could help compensate for the almost exclusive attention historians have paid Gowa to the neglect of other Makassarese polities. Viewing the situation from this angle, he made a copy of the manuscript for Djohan to deliver to me. However, at other times nothing would persuade the owner of a manuscript to surrender its secrets.

Occasionally the existence of hidden manuscripts was known, and even their contents, but reading the manuscripts was not possible. For example, tales were told of a manuscript from the reign of Sultan Hasanuddin that purportedly described events during his reign not recounted in either the *Gowa Chronicle* or the Gowa court *lontaraq bilang*. Exactly what these events are (if the claim even is true) is unsure, but the owner of the text swore that he would never allow Djohan to see the manuscript; perhaps Djohan would be allowed to see it after the owner dies, when the decisions regarding its preservation and access fall to the next generation. Similarly, I was never able to read a manuscript telling about a particular incident in the history of Gowa and Sanrabone. This text purportedly records a story about how a ruler of Gowa was afraid of death and consulted his counterpart and vassal in Sanrabone, who had mystical knowledge about the afterworld. The ruler of Sanrabone promised that he would accompany the ruler of Gowa when the latter died so that Gowa's ruler would not have to face the afterworld alone. And indeed, though still healthy, Sanrabone's ruler knew when the ruler of Gowa's death was approaching and summoned his own relatives to prepare them for his imminent departure. When the ruler of Gowa died, the ruler of Sanrabone died too, fulfilling his promise. Thus the general outlines of the text in this hidden manuscript are apparently known, though the story's accuracy obviously cannot be checked. Djohan reports that the Dutch scholar J. Noorduyn asked Djohan's father to acquire this manuscript, but he could not, for the same reasons it remains unavailable to me today. First, there is the power latent in ancient manuscripts that makes their unveiling dangerous and their possession an asset to be closely guarded. Second, the mystical knowledge of the ruler of Sanrabone is discussed in the text, and Makassarese strongly believe that information about the inner beliefs and practices of mystical Islam can be revealed only to fellow Muslims, not to Christian scholars.

This cloak of secrecy and potential danger is not a simple barrier between Makassarese and non-Makassarese. Makassarese scholars moving outside their own networks of kinship and social relations face the same cultural beliefs about manuscripts. Many Makassarese who have inherited manuscripts preserve them unopened in chests or cases. When questioned, they may no longer know what the manuscripts are about, only that they are sacred. It may be that particular ritual strictures about how *lontaraq* are stored, like practices noted in one Balinese case by Raechelle Rubinstein, also govern accessibility.[47]

In other cases Makassarese may preserve and guard manuscripts they know are sacred, but whose script they cannot even read. Tales abound of people who opened manuscripts without making the proper offerings to the ancestors whose words they contain, or to a vague spirit of the manuscripts. Some tell of these transgressors being bitten by poisonous black snakes inside the manuscript case or of being struck by lightning and killed. There are others who when approached by local scholars who want to examine or borrow a manuscript to make a microfilm copy insist that proper rituals be observed and that the manuscript travel under a yellow umbrella that in the past was the preserve of Makassarese nobles. In one case, the carefully handled manuscript of a family who no longer dared open the case but who generations ago had been instructed to preserve its contents turned out to be only a receipt for the sale of a horse. And more than once I eagerly awaited a manuscript whose contents had been vaguely described as being about the history of a particular community only to discover that the Makassarese text was a copy of part of the *Makassaarsche Chrestomathie*, a Dutch publication from the last century. I realized that this printed book had, ironically, become a source of hallowed writings about Makassar's past that some Makassarese used to create their own sacred manuscripts.

Inscribing and uttering written words were performed as rituals among Makassarese. This duty is most evident with Islamic materials, where writing and reciting intersected with older Makassarese traditions holding that blood *(ceraq)* was a sacred and potent essence capable of bestowing power on what it consecrated. Objects such as royal regalia, the Qur'an, and the banners of communities were smeared with blood *(aqceraq)* to magically strengthen them, especially before battle.[48] In lessons teaching children to recite the Qur'an, the text was smeared with blood as a sign of honor and perhaps also to "activate" the power lying latent in its words. Similarly, those who performed the sacred duty of copying the Qur'an were given gifts such as chickens, white cloth, and gold. Before beginning such work, copyists smeared blank paper with the blood of a rooster and a hen sacrificed for the occasion, a recognition that inscribing the words could unleash potent forces.[49] In the Makassarese *Story of Syekh Yusuf*, the writer declared, "Whoever from the *ummat* of Nabi Muhammad who after me can listen to the stories of Tusalamaka [Syekh Yusuf] whether they read it, store it in their house, or firmly believe it in their heart, clearly all their sins will be forgiven."[50] In the seventeenth century, the Frenchman Nicholas Gervaise reported that Makassarese believed sickness to be caused by evil spirits that had to be exorcised. For such exorcisms, Islamic "priests" wrote the names Allah and Muhammad on slips of paper pinned around the bed on which the afflicted person lay, creating a barrier of sacred written words capable of driving away spirits.⁵¹ All these examples suggest that, like ritual speech, in the hands of a capable and confident user written language was a tool that could be wielded to influence the physical and the spiritual world. But as objects, written manuscripts made language and the past available in new ways.

The sacredness of Makassarese manuscripts derives in part from the social role they play in society. As spiritually potent objects, manuscripts belong to the larger cultural category of *kalompoang*. Commonly translated as "regalia," the meaning of *"kalompoang"* embraces greatness, magnificence, or anything that displays such qualities, in addition to referring specifically to physical heirlooms such as swords, banners, and manuscripts. Makassarese considered *kalompoang* to be objects whose potency derived from their ancient and otherworldly origins. Oral histories typically relate how these sacred objects from the Upperworld mysteriously appeared of their own volition in this world. Possessed of an otherworldly spirit, *kalompoang* were capable of influencing for good or ill the lives and fortunes of humans. Because of this power, Makassarese considered (and many still consider) *kalompoang* the locus of social life within the *paqrasangang* or community.

The role of *kalompoang* in Makassarese society has been the focus of much scholarly attention. The historian Leonard Andaya argued that *kalompoang* in general and *gaukang*—sacred stones at the physical center of a *paqrasangang*—in particular were the revered centerpieces of early modern Bugis and Makassarese kingdoms.⁵² In some cases the *kalompoang* were considered the true rulers of the community. Indeed, it appears that Makassarese did not consider human rulers and *kalompoang* entirely separate categories, but rather ones that blurred together; *kalompoang* could be considered rulers and rulers *kalompoang*. The most famous example of this concerns *tumanurung*, mythical beings who descend from the Upperworld and whose marriage to an earthly lord produces children who become the rulers of a new kingdom. All the major polities of South Sulawesi tell origin stories about their *tumanurung* ancestors that emphasize their special status as living *kalompoang*. Collectively the heirs to *tumanurung*, human rulers and *kalompoang* comprised the religious, social, and political focal point of Makassarese community life.

In a similar vein, the Dutch ethnologist Chabot described at length how *kalompoang* and *saukang*—sacrificial altars or miniature houses situated at the consecrated center of a community—were the ritual focus of annual harvest ceremonies. To participate in these ceremonies was to affirm one's membership in the *paqrasangang*. So significant were these practices that the bounds of *paqrasangang* identity itself corresponded to neither residence nor kinship, but was defined by shared reverence for the regalia, sacred stones, or spirit altars of the community.[53] Membership was something that was felt, a shared emotional link to a particular place.[54] Makassarese use the term *pacce* to refer to this sense of empathy and unity within the community; without it there is no *paqrasangang*. One text described "being of one great *pacce*" *(lompo pacceki)* as an ideal within the family.[55] So strong are these feelings that it does not require that all members are related, and those who migrate elsewhere often feel that their true home remains that community.

Appreciating the significance and function of *kalompoang* is essential to understanding the cultural world of early modern Makassar. It is also essential to understanding how Makassarese perceived *patturioloang:* the historical chronicles Makassarese began to write in the sixteenth century. Like *"kalompoang,"* the word *"patturioloang"* has a range of related meanings. Typically translated as "chronicle," *"patturioloang"* literally means "that which is of the ancestors." It referred, then, both to the physical manuscript inherited from the past and the words of the ancestors the manuscript preserved. More difficult to convey is the depth of the sense that *patturioloang* were intimately related to ancestors. Metaphorically at least, ancestors and *patturioloang* were equated and interchangeable in the same way that rulers and *kalompoang* were linked.

Kalompoang, gaukang, and *saukang* and the feelings of *pacce* they created provided an impetus toward social cohesion and a focus for communal identity in early modern Makassar. But this centrifugal movement toward solidarity was matched by a contrasting centripetal tendency in Makassarese society toward divisiveness and fragmentation. Scholars are in universal agreement that Makassarese social relationships have been and continue to be guided by an acute sensitivity to relative status and overt rivalry between near equals. To outsiders, the placid face of harmonious communal life appears dramatically shattered when these status rivalries erupt in confrontation or violence. Keenly aware of their own social position within the community, Makassarese capture the sense of honor and pride they feel, as well as the deep sense of shame when this sense of honor and proper social relationships is violated, with the term *"siriq."* It is the apparent contradiction between practices that create social solidarity and the ever-present potential for rivalry and disruption that has made Makassar so fascinating to outsiders. Both these tendencies and the contrary directions Makassarese felt themselves pulled will surface many times in the chapters that follow.

Scholars examining Makassar's history through manuscripts cannot lose sight of the social place these manuscripts occupy and the cultural beliefs that surround them. Questions about who possessed the past, incarnate in manuscripts, are important in a society that viewed written texts as powerful objects that must be treated with ceremony and reverence lest they unleash destructive forces upon the land. With the advent of literacy, the past, objectified in these manuscripts, became something tangible that could be owned, guarded, and used in the present. The recorded past became an object of tremendous value, an asset enveloped in secrecy and privilege. To possess the past in sacred manuscripts gave one tangible resources to deploy in political and social rivalries. To not possess such a past put one at a tremendous disadvantage in a society in which claims were verified and legitimated by links to the past. Part 2 deals with the social uses to which Makassarese put written histories beginning in the late sixteenth century and the social, political, and cultural effects of these new forms of history-making.

∞ 3 ∞

Transformations in Makassarese Perceptions of the Past

This chapter examines the changes in Makassarese historical consciousness occasioned by the sixteenth-century advent of literacy. This addition of literate to oral history-making had dramatic effects, effects that are examined in detail in part 2. In essence, written composition and preservation of the past in a new form made the past available for use in novel ways. Before turning to these novel uses of the past, however, I explore how writing transformed Makassarese perceptions of the past.

Scholars no longer argue that societies without writing are without history. Instead, it is widely recognized that spoken narratives about the past are a ubiquitous feature of oral societies. Sixteenth-century Makassar was no exception; nor, indeed, is twentieth-century Makassar. In the last several decades numerous Indonesian government projects have collected and published oral traditions about the origins and history of local communities in South Sulawesi. Such collecting began with Dutch missionaries and colonial officials in the nineteenth century. As a stepping-stone to conversion to Christianity, to gain better knowledge of local customs and traditions to abet colonial governance, and in pursuit of a modern scholarly commitment to catalogue knowledge about the world, missionaries, scholars, and officials published Makassarese oral histories. In addition they commissioned, requested, or inspired by example from their Makassarese informants and assistants written accounts of local folklore and traditions.[1]

This urge to document and collect was indeed new. It produced a substantial body of transcribed oral histories to which Indonesian projects continue to add. Some of the Makassarese oral histories used in this work come from published collections of oral traditions. Collected, edited, and set to paper, they are several steps removed from the world in which they were spoken. This distance calls for comment because of the methodological problems it raises: most crucially, can these entexted narratives reliably offer us any insight into the oral traditions of history-making in Makassar, or have they irrevocably crossed a divide that literacy establishes?

At one extreme, a reading of this material would conclude that these stories can only be read as evidence of the discursive fabrication of Indonesian national culture. Such purists might see the context of their production as invalidating the use of stories so mediated by local and national political purposes, concluding that they have nothing reliable to tell us about the local societies from which they originated and the local histories of which they once spoke meaningfully.[2] At another extreme, some would conclude that conceptions of the past are not so easily elided and that such texts merely transcribe without distorting oral traditions.

There is no single or simple way to proceed from this crossroads. I believe that two factors must weigh heavily on scholars searching for answers about oral history-making in printed books and manuscripts. The first is the kind of reading one wishes to make, for each form of textual analysis has different assumptions and demands. The second is the social place of the past, for each society relates to and finds significance in its past in different ways. My choice has been to use published oral traditions, but to do so carefully and well aware of the epistemological dilemmas involved.

Unlike written texts, orally narrated histories are actively present only in the moment of their telling. Written texts lying before us can be skimmed, perused, pondered, reread. All but the most open-ended appear to possess a structure and coherence that invite detailed narrative analysis. To perform such a narrative analysis of a transcribed oral tradition is extremely problematic, for it endows the text with a unity, permanence, and consistency that corresponds poorly to the context of its telling. Once fixed on paper, oral histories can more easily escape the bounds of shared public remembrance, the links to particular places and objects. Manuscripts can be possessed by individuals and can travel in the form of published or collected texts to places far beyond the community in which they originated. Severed from their performance and their reception—which are crucial to the process of making meaning in oral traditions[3]—transcribed oral histories become loosened from their social moorings and the functions they served within the community.

They become artifacts. To overemphasize their narrative coherence or to apply the tools of narratology to the detailed unfolding of the text may reveal more about the process of textualization than about history-making in the oral community it derived from. Textualizing and fixing what was fleeting and textless is a transformation inescapably inherent in the act of writing about those who did or could not. "For us literates, a study of oral tradition cannot but be an exercise in writing. We must begin with the assumptions of the literate and move laboriously toward an understanding of orality through the barriers of our literacy."[4] As Sweeney notes, we tend to see oral traditions as "unwritten writing." It is not so, but this disjunction between oral and written does not automatically invalidate what we literates read in the speech we textualize. Such actions call for caution, not resignation and abdication in the face of these difficulties.

Deliberate transformations in content are as significant as transformations in form. It is easy, for example, to imagine editors willing to shift emphases, alter, or embroider transcribed texts. To my surprise, I sensed no deliberate intervention by Indonesian fieldworkers or publishers, who seem focused on producing books as tangible testament to the success of government-sponsored projects and their own diligence. Editing the content of oral traditions they elicited from informants for books that are not read but stacked in boxes and on library shelves apparently was not worth the effort. Nevertheless, caution is appropriate, and what I read for in these entexted oral histories was both specific and limited to certain kinds of readings. In particular, I focused on the following: recurring themes and motifs; references to people, places, and objects; evidence of what was considered significant about the past and what was not worth recalling. I do not read complex mental perceptions in the play of language, perform symbolic analysis of mythical elements, or claim to see a reliable historical framework in the structure of the narrative itself. Indeed, my primary concern has been understanding the social significance of stories about the past in Makassarese oral history-making.

In *Islands and Beaches* Greg Dening describes contemporary Marquesan society as one with few links to the past. The nineteenth-century ravages of depopulation, cultural destruction wrought by intolerant missionaries, and suicidal violence among Marquesans severed past from present. The Marquesas are perhaps one of the most dramatic examples of the ways in which wrenching social change can create a chasm isolating past from present. A reader of Marquesan oral histories would be hard-pressed to find local oral traditions from before this period of massive trauma. Fortunately the history of Makassar is not so tragic. There the past remains vibrant and alive. The effects of colonial intrusion, modernization, and other historical transformations were by no means insignificant, but they do not approach the thoroughness with which Marquesans became dispossessed of their past. The past survives, and the histories Makassarese narrate convey the continued meaningfulness of their past. One center of history-making and -telling that powerfully attests to the continued force the past holds on imaginations of present-day Makassarese is the tomb of Syekh Yusuf, depicted in figure 6.

In this context where past and present remain linked, I have concluded that publication has not irredeemably transformed these oral histories beyond use or recognition. Nor has the sheer weight of time irredeemably transformed these oral histories. Largely this is so because of the significance and social function of origin stories about the distant past. Here too we must be cautious. I do not claim that Makassarese oral histories in general have been passed down orally unchanged, but that origin stories recounting the foundations of many Makassarese *paqrasangang* have survived with little change because of the importance Makassarese accord beginnings. Even if contained now in government-

Figure 6. Syekh Yusuf's tomb, guardians, and offerings

sponsored collections, the tales themselves are often ancient. This is a crucial point. As accounts of the origins of local communities, the cultural importance of these stories must be recognized. The origins of a community, the history of its settlement and founding ancestor, provided the lodestone for a community's identity.[5] The past gave the community its sense of unity and explained how its people came to live as they did in that particular place. Because of this crucial function, then, these stories represented the most significant past and were remembered. The cultural importance of one's origins, and the often sacred nature of what was related in these accounts, dictated that they be passed down from generation to generation largely unchanged.

In addition to the general aura of sacredness surrounding origin stories, specific social mechanisms ensured their preservation across generations. First, these histories belonged to the community as a whole, not to individuals. They acted as vehicles to carry the heritage that bound that community together. Fundamentally altering a communal memory and the meanings it has requires either tremendous effort or social changes significant enough to transform what those in the present seek in the past. We should not assume that oral memories of the past will naturally and inevitably change over time. Second, their preservation did not depend on human memory and the practice of storytelling alone. Origin histories did not "float freely"; they were tied to specific places and practices that aided preservation and continuity. Paul Connerton's remark that a society's most important memories are conserved in public social practices is important to recall here.[6] The origin story of a community was closely associated with the specific place where the community was founded and to specific objects present at that founding. Together, these stories, objects, and places carried the past into the present. Makassarese origin stories often mentioned and centered on these objects and places. They were recalled in commemorative rituals, most often annually; each year actors endeavored to reproduce the past through its performance. The narrative a community told about its past and the meanings people attached to it could not easily be detached from the sacred places and objects to which the past was tied. Fundamental changes in the content and character of oral histories require changing the historical landscape and surrounding monuments or relics of the past as well, a task that is not easy. Memories, as many studies have shown, can be surprisingly durable.[7] This social context for the recall and remembrance of the past therefore reinforced the sacred and inviolable character of oral histories to ensure that they would be passed from generation to generation with little change.

The presence of what may be perceived as an "authoritative" written version of the past also has significant implications within a community accustomed to making history orally. Such texts have a social currency and power that transform the dynamics of how the past is made present. But these caveats do not mean that transcribed texts of previously oral histories must be disregarded or handled so carefully and with so much qualification that they become of little use. Because of the essentially conservative character of the transmission of Makassarese origin histories, these oral-histories-become-texts do faithfully relate stories and suggest themes, practices, places, and events of significance to the oral community in which they were originally told. Read in this manner, they can be used responsibly in their new form to shed light on conceptions of the past in Makassar before the advent of written histories. A history from Pattalassang illustrates the character and characteristics of Makassarese oral histories.[8]

A HISTORY OF PATTALASSANG

This tells of the rulers of Pattalassang. He who [ruled] before [there was a] karaeng [of] Pattalassang was called dampang *of Pattalassang, before the people of Gowa entered Islam. This* dampang *was the first in Pattalassang. Not well known are his origins or appearance. The last dampang of Pattalassang was named Daeng Maqloteng. He died and was buried in Pattalassang. The last* dampang *of Pattalassang had two children. Both of these children were girls. The oldest was named Dale Tauwa and the youngest was named Belobabaya. The Dampang Pattalassang died, and all agreed that Dale Tauwa would replace her father. [She] was called Kare Pattalassang. After ruling Pattalassang for a while, one day there appeared unexpectedly up in the sky a kite of a material called* cinde.[9] *It was called the Cinde.*

This tells of how the Cinde was taken to be the kalompoang *of the people of Pattalassang. That Cinde was seen one day by the people up in a tamarind tree in the center of a kampung named Saile, north of Pattalassang. Then all the people went to look at that Cinde. At that time there were those who wanted to have it. There were also those who only wanted to see it. The tamarind was of extraordinary size. No one could climb up it. Also, the Cinde was like a flag tied to the top of the tamarind tree, waving like a flag being blown in the wind. Many people prayed that perhaps it would be struck by a strong wind and come free, blown down by the wind, then all would hurry to get it. For a few days people waited below that tamarind tree, but the wind never blew. The Cinde kept fluttering as if it was being blown by the wind, but there was no wind. Because the people considered it sacred, they pounded drums and [played]* pui-pui.[10] *Gongs were struck too. The clamor was loud. After a few more days the Cinde unexpectedly disappeared. All the people scattered, each seeking the Cinde. Not long after all went seeking it, someone saw it at the top of a large campaga*[11] *tree in a kampung named Mamampang, also close to the kampung Saile. Then all the people came again and gathered there. There* pui-pui *were played; there were also people striking gongs and drums. There again the Cinde stayed, waving in the wind as if it was being shaken at the top of the campaga. It was flapping very strongly though there was no wind blowing. After a few more days of that [the Cinde] disappeared there too, moving to a large taeng tree*[12] *close to a great well. This well was called the Great Well by the people of Pattalassang. Amid the clamor of the gongs, the drums, and the* pui-pui, *suddenly the Cinde came down. The Cinde was received by all and brought together slowly to the house of Dale Tauwa. There it was feasted day and night, honored by the people, and made the* kalompoang *of the people of Pattalassang.*

This tells of the summoning of Kare Pattalassang by the somba *of Gowa. One day the story of Kare Pattalassang, that is, Dale Tauwa, was heard by the* somba. *Then she was invited to journey to the* somba's *palace in Gowa, because the* somba *of Gowa also wanted to know Dale Tauwa well. There was a mistake at the time of the invitation by the* somba *of Gowa because it was forgotten by the* somba *to fix the time of her trip. Then one day by chance both the* somba *went to bathe for pleasure at Barombong while also Kare Pattalassang came to the palace of the* somba *of Gowa. Then seen from afar at the* somba's *palace, people clamored all wanting to see the beauty of this Dale Tauwa. Then a wall collapsed in front of the* somba's *palace because all these people wanted to see Kare Pattalassang, because of her great beauty of which tales had been told. Then went Karaeng Baine also to look out from her window. Suddenly, the thought arose in Karaeng Baine's heart that [Dale Tauwa] would replace her later if she were seen by the* karaeng. *Then the door guard was ordered [by Karaeng Baine] to command [Dale Tauwa] to return to her house in Pattalassang. When Kare Pattalassang found out that she had been so insulted Kare Pattalassang cried; then she went back to Pattalassang, returning to her kampung. When she was in the palanquin returning to Pattalassang [Kare Pattalassang] cursed the* somba's *wife so that her face would become hideous. This cursing of the* somba's *wife was to continue through her descendants. Because she was so humiliated by the wife of the* somba, *she wanted to forget this event and asked to abdicate as* kare. *Then after just a few days I Belobabaya was selected to become Kare Pattalassang until [the time she] returned to the mercy of Allah. This* somba *died in war with Boné and is called Somba Tunibatta.*

To mention again the time that Belobabaya governed Pattalassang, they returned and established a friendship with the somba *of Gowa. [Pattalassang] was made one of the Bate Salapang of Gowa. [The ruler] was now called Karaeng Pattalassang. Somba also knew that the Cinde was the* kalompoang *of Pattalassang. Then [the* somba *of Gowa] asked Karaeng Pattalassang for that* kalompoang, *and it was immediately given to the* somba *of Gowa. Also as a sign of his happiness the* somba *of Gowa gave Karaeng Pattalassang a* kalompoang *named Alakaya. This Alakaya was a flag* kalompoang. *Thus it was until the death [of Belobabaya]. The grave of Belobabaya is also called the Great Grave.*

This history consists of four short narratives. Linked in chronological order, the four vignettes tell of the first rulers of Pattalassang, the coming of the *kalompoang* to Pattalassang, the story of Gowa and Pattalassang's first relations, and the story of the establishment of Pattalassang's friendship with and political allegiance to Gowa. All four segments, then, focus on beginnings. In fact, orally composed Makassarese histories typically devote themselves almost exclusively to origins. The prominence of origin stories in Makassarese historical horizons stems from the social significance these beginnings have for later communities.

At its most fundamental, the basis of a *paqrasangang* identity is the collective memory of a shared origin in the distant past. This sense of belonging is historical: the community is an entity that has persisted for a long time. The popular—that is, oral—history of a community in the present is always the story of its origins, of the past that literally gave birth to the present. Historical memories, then, are clustered at these moments of beginnings.

In Makassar, the importance of origin stories coupled with naturally better recall of recent events gave (and gives) oral histories a shape like a barbell: a great deal of attention and memory is devoted to the most distant past, followed by decades or centuries in which the community persisted but details are forgotten or quickly glossed over, followed by another bulge of detail about the generations immediately preceding the present. In the case of Pattalassang, stories from local inhabitants provided the colonial official M. J. Friedericy a wealth of detail about the founding and early rulers of Pattalassang and a fair amount of information about the most recent generations but little more than a list of rulers' names connecting the two periods. The era in between was neither of great cultural significance nor easily recalled. Of three intermediate rulers it was remembered only that one was a drunk and ruled for a short time.[13] Inasmuch as only eight rulers were mentioned during a span of three centuries, it is clear that the inhabitants of Pattalassang forgot a number of rulers, and in some cases the reigns of two or more rulers may have been compressed into one.

Unlike the history of Pattalassang that Friedericy collected, the account above does not continue up to the present, omitting entirely any mention of later rulers.[14] It is, in fact, more of a teardrop than a barbell. This is worth noting, for if the purpose of history is to link the present with the distant past, in Pattalassang people apparently did not base this linkage on continuity, on the ability to trace an unbroken line of descent. A narrative does not have to link past and present in the way we conventionally imagine. The early rulers of Pattalassang are certainly important in the account, but they themselves are not the focus of these narratives. As the history explained of the first ruler, "Not well known are his origins or appearance." In this oral society, the past was not tied to the present through king lists, royal genealogies, or *patturioloang* that privilege a ruling group or line. Put another way, rulers did not monopolize or control access to the past. The reckoning or tracing backward of genealogical lines did not structure oral history-making in Pattalassang. Rather, the recall or perpetuation of particular moments in the past, their survival in memory, structured history-making.

The centrality of the Cinde in the second vignette and the contrasting relatively meager memory of Pattalassang's first rulers in the first vignette underscore the commemorative nature of history-making in Pattalassang. Nothing loomed larger in the historical horizon of the people of Pattalassang than the Cinde, the sacred object from the past still preserved and guarded in the present. The Cinde—a physical token of their history—anchored the past in oral Pattalassang historical consciousness in two ways: as the comforting proof that their histories were true and as the focal point for commemorative ritual activity.

Sensitive to their lack of a written history and cognizant of the frailty of memory, rural Makassarese today frequently point to their *kalompoang* as proof that the stories they tell are true. Aware that they cannot meet other canons of proof, to be able to point to an irrefutably present token of the past verifies the stories that concern these objects. The veracity of a story about an ancestor who had supernatural abilities, for example, is demonstrated by pointing to the mountain he lived on or the well from which he swam out to the ocean. The trees, settlements, and well that infuse the second Pattalassang vignette evidence how a sense of memorable places structured the past. The truth of the history of a *paqrasangang* and the pride contemporary inhabitants derive from its ancient origins are demonstrated by reference to the *kalompoang* whose origins their stories recount and to the places where founding actions took place. Memories of the past attaching to objects and places is a theme I will return to throughout this work. The Makassarese cultural perception of historical objects recalls Annette Weiner's comments on inalienable objects in general, comments worth quoting at length.

> The primary value of inalienability, however, is expressed through the power these objects have to define who one is in an historical sense. The object acts as a vehicle for bringing past time into the present, so that the histories of ancestors, titles, or mythological events become an intimate part of a person's present identity. To lose this claim to the past is to lose part of who one is in the present. In its inalienability, the object must be seen as more than an economic resource and more than an affirmation of social relations.
>
> Inalienable wealth takes on important priorities in societies where ranking occurs. Persons and groups need to demonstrate continually who they are in relation to others, and their identities must be attached to those ancestral connections that figure significantly in their statuses, ranks, or titles. To be able to keep certain objects that document these connections attests to one's power to hold oneself or one's group intact. For to give up these objects is to lose one's claim to the past as a working part of one's identity in the present.[15]

The crucial point to underline for our purposes is that certain objects and places not only figured prominently in the content of Makassarese oral histories, but guided history-making as a practice. The Cinde not only played a central role in what was remembered about the past in Pattalassang but was at the center of historical activity. To view the Cinde, to use it in annual rituals, or to speak of it evoked tales of the past. History-making was rooted in this object. Stories attached to the Cinde. A clear indication of how strongly *kalompoang* structured and gave meaning to oral histories comes from texts describing how communities lost their *kalompoang*.

The *Gowa Chronicle* provides several examples of a common event in Makassarese history: when Gowa conquered another community it often seized the community's *kalompoang* and took them back to Gowa. For example, when Karaeng Tunipalangga (r. 1546 to 1565) conquered Lamuru, he took its *kalompoang,* a sword named I Lapasasri.[16] Similarly, a recorded oral history from Bontonompo strongly asserted that it had had *kalompoang* in the distant past but that Gowa took these sacred objects away when it conquered Bontonompo.[17] The trauma this loss of the lodestone of a community's history and identity created is illustrated by a manuscript recording events that took place before and during the Makassar war of 1666–1669. It tells of the community of Paceqlang and its *kalompoang.* The text recounts that Paceqlang originally had several sacred items that came from Luwuq. When the founder of the community disappeared, he took all but one, a sword named I Tamalamba, back to Luwuq. When Gowa conquered the area in the sixteenth century, it seized this sword. The text describes the disasters that the community, bereft of *kalompoang,* suffered. Crop failure, famine, banditry, natural disasters, and more all awaited a community that had lost its *kalompoang.* Later, to the community's good fortune, the ruler of Paceqlang acquired a new *kalompoang,* a kind of talisman the ruler tied around his waist. The sense in which this object became the center of Paceqlang's identity is captured in the declaration that "if it goes to the west, you people of Paceqlang go west too."[18] Stronger still, the allies of the ruler of Paceqlang swore an oath not to covet this new *kalompoang:* "May my life deteriorate and come to misery, may I be without descendants, may it be hard to find food, may I live life like a chicken, may I scrounge for food in muddy waste water if I hold the *kalompoang* and am not truly a person from Paceqlang."[19]

This tale, forty-two pages in all, was purportedly written by the brother of the first *gallarrang* of Paceqlang after the conquest of Makassar in 1669. The history it tells, however, is not framed by the momentous events of that war. They are mentioned in the text, but the plot of the text is the loss and recovery of sacred *kalompoang* in Paceqlang. The story of these objects, rather than the story of Paceqlang's rulers or the war between Gowa and its enemies, provides the framework that gave this history meaning. As in Pattalassang, *kalompoang* dominated historical memory in Paceqlang. Helen Creese notes a similar concern in a chronicle recounting Majapahit's conquest of Bali. "Rather than the initial conquest, it is the power of the regalia and *pusaka* weapons brought from Majapahit, and the dispersal of the noble ancestors to all parts of Bali that are pivotal in the Babad Dalem prose account."[20] The sense of continuity between past and present was preserved by remembering the stories that surrounded the Cinde, an object that transcended the ephemeral coming and going of individual rulers.

This brings us to the third part the history of Pattalassang recalls: the story of its first relations with Gowa. Oral memories of the past were not distributed evenly chronologically or socially. Rather, oral histories clustered around certain topics. One of the most important topics in Makassarese oral histories is the origins of their first relations with Gowa. History did not begin with Gowa, but the forging of ties to Gowa did mark an important watershed in the historical consciousness of many Makassarese.

The only datable reference in the Pattalassang stories is to Tunibatta, who ruled Gowa for only forty days in 1565. There is no other mention of dates, years, or time periods. The past was not remembered as we moderns remember it—that is, as a chronicle of events placed against the omnipresent backdrop of advancing time. Instead, time passes in vague, conventional passages of "after a while" and "not long after." Breaking up this what seems to our minds frustratingly unsystematic vision of the past are only a few meaningful watersheds. The Pattalassang stories, for example, were written down after conversion to Islam and take pains to explain that these histories are from a period "before the people of Gowa entered Islam," even though at one point the death of Kare Pattalassang is described as the time she "returned to the mercy of Allah."[21]

Significant watersheds in the history of Pattalassang were marked by the acquisition of the Cinde and incorporation into Gowa. The first divided what can aptly be called "history" from "prehistory," for before the Cinde there was no community to speak of and hence no socially meaningful past. The second separated the period of origins from the later past, conceptualized within the context of Gowa's period of preeminence. The history of nearly all Makassarese communities can be divided into two periods: pre-Gowa and post-Gowa. This disjunction is not surprising given the extraordinary influence Gowa exercised over so much of Makassarese society during the sixteenth and seventeenth centuries. However, in addition to shaping the general context of the past, and in so doing pressing itself onto the historical memory of Makassarese, Gowa is specifically remembered for the moment when it was first able to conquer or incorporate local communities. As in the history of Pattalassang, this event often was recalled in terms of sexual possession.

Stories of sexual jealousy and vengeance were common mediums in which Makassarese expressed their desire for political autonomy. The third story from Pattalassang is a rare female-centered account of how efforts to create links between communities through intermarriage were riven with tension and hostility. Many oral and written treaties between communities contain oaths preventing the theft, seizure, or seduction of women by outsiders. The effort of Makassarese men to protect "their women" from the predatory advances of men from other communities is one of the most persistent themes in Makassarese society.[22] For example, oral traditions recalled that when Sudiang became part of Gowa's governing council (Bate Salapang) in the sixteenth century, the ruler of Gowa agreed to the declaration by the *gallarrang* of Sudiang that "you will not filch eggs from my egg-basket, you will not arrogantly take my women."[23] A century later, Makassarese nobles deliberately insulted Arung Palakka and mocked his manhood by stealing "his women" several times in the 1670s.[24] The tension and violence that surround such abductions remain a factor in Makassar today. As Chabot observed, the insult the woman's male relatives feel *(siriq)* compels them to avenge the family's sense of honor by killing the man who ran off with their daughter, sister, niece, or cousin.[25]

As it is told in this story, Pattalassang's female ruler not only got the best of the queen of Gowa, but retained Pattalassang's autonomy. To have become of wife of the ruler of Gowa would have meant, as the *Maros Chronicle* explained in a similar situation, becoming inferior because a woman would have been surrendered to another community.[26] This vignette, I believe, recalls to the people of Pattalassang both their ancient independence and their admirable resistance to Gowa. In fact, as the final part of the oral history emphasizes, the people from Pattalassang remember their past relations with Gowa in terms of equality rather than submission.

The last of the four oral accounts from Pattalassang tells of the friendship and alliance the rulers of Gowa and Pattalassang established. Here too *kalompoang* played a prominent role. In Makassarese eyes, nothing could more closely bind two communities than exchanging *kalompoang*. In so doing each became a part of the other. Never again could the history of Pattalassang be imagined without the inclusion of Gowa. Pattalassang would forever imagine its identity in commemorative rituals and stories that tied that identity to Gowa. This mingling of pasts with Gowa is found in other Makassarese oral histories as well. Oral histories were tied to local objects or places and focused unevenly on topics of local significance, but by also describing a community's links with Gowa, the histories recalled the most important historical event since a community's founding.

Like sacred objects, sacred places functioned as anchors of history. Stories about the past adhered to both, and in the presence of both the past was communally commemorated. Chabot collected a story telling of the origins of the sacred spot of the community of Bontoramba and how the spirit of the land came to dwell there. Despite its brevity compared to the histories from Pattalassang, readers will immediately note many of the same features: the emphasis on explaining beginnings, the importance of objects in the account, and the lack of any effort or need to continue unbroken the story into the present.

The story of "the lord of the land" called Besenga. Once upon a time there was a courageous man who lived in Bontoramba. This man lived along the main road. Now at that road, whenever there were people who passed by with their sarong over their heads or with a parasol, these people immediately died of supernatural causes. Because of this, after some time this man was called a man of violent deeds. Finally, the man issued this statement: "If in the future I am no longer here (I will have disappeared) and if you want to give me something, there is a stone there in the middle of the land; there you must give it to me. But this stone will later move to the south of the country, to the mango tree. When the stone has arrived there, erect a house for me so that I will be able to live there." When he had delivered this, he disappeared.[27]

At this point it is useful to recapitulate the most salient features of Makassarese oral histories as represented by the histories from Pattalassang. Their most notable feature was a focus on the origins of their community, its sacred *kalompoang,* and their links with Gowa. Remembering and telling these histories provided the basis for a community's identity. The social weight placed on origins, coupled with the frailty of memory, gave oral histories a teardrop or barbell shape. Makassarese oral histories were not conceived of as a continuous account or chain linking the past and the present, but as stories that commemorated or restaged foundational events. Typically, these stories attached to the *kalompoang* that served as the locus of ritual activity for a *paqrasangang* or to the sacred spot where the community was said to have originated. The oral history of a Makassarese community placed comparatively little attention on genealogy and rulers, but it did acknowledge the watershed effects the expansion of Gowa had throughout Makassar. Stressing some periods rather than others, and some topics rather than others, these oral histories were certainly not comprehensive or systematic, but they represented what Makassarese saw as socially significant in their past.[28]

While students of other societies in and beyond Indonesia may recognize aspects of Makassarese oral history-making, it is important to remember that these are not universal characteristics of an oral culture. History-making is a social practice, deriving much of its purpose and character from social features and practices that vary substantially among oral societies. By way of contrast, James Fox's study of oral histories on another eastern Indonesian island, Roti, reveal a different sense of the past. Unlike Makassar, Rotinese have traditionally had specialist reciters who preserved and chanted extended genealogies of clans and lineages.[29] Unlike Makassarese oral histories that almost exclusively recalled founding events, Rotinese histories traced backward an unbroken chain from the present to the past. Continuity was a key feature of Rotinese oral genealogies, a feature absent in Makassar. The roots of this difference probably lay in differences in social structure and, thus, in differences in what the past was expected to do in the present. Roti possessed strong corporate descent groups—segmentary lineages with clans —that provided an overall framework for a history-making that emphasized genealogy and continuity. Makassarese possessed no such corporate kin groups and, not deriving their identity from such groups, had little reason to preserve the past in a way that explained and supported these groups.

Many other Makassarese oral histories that follow similar patterns could be cited. The history from Pattalassang and the shorter history from Bontoramba are typical of the perceptions and accounts of the past found in local communities in both twentieth- and sixteenth-century Makassar. But as the previous chapter discussed, in the sixteenth century Makassarese began to write histories, and when they did so they wrote about their past in ways different from the oral histories they had remembered and told. It is to the shape and nature of written histories that we now turn.

Tunipasuluq's Reign in the *Gowa Chronicle*

Tunipasuluq, the ninth *karaeng* of Gowa, ruled from late 1590 to early 1593. Virtually everything historians know about him derives from one section in the *Gowa Chronicle*. Like each ruler the chronicle discusses, Tunipasuluq's reign forms a self-contained, coherent narrative unit within the larger chronicle. The bulk of the *Gowa Chronicle* is composed of these accounts of *karaengs*' reigns, eight in all. Here is the section about Tunipasuluq.[30]

Karaeng Tunijalloq had a child Karaeng Tunipasuluq. Karaeng Tunijalloq died and Karaeng Tunipasuluq inherited the throne. His personal name, may I not be cursed, was I Tepu Karaeng. His royal name was I Daeng Parabung. Before he became ruler he was called Karaeng Bontolangkasaq. After he began ruling, he expelled I Daeng ri Tamacina as tumailalang, taking his servants and assigning them to one of his personal followers. He installed as tumailalang Karaeng ri Patteqne, named I Tamanggoa. His royal name was I Daeng Arenne. [Karaeng Tunipasuluq] was fifteen years old when he became ruler and ruled for two years before being deposed. He was the first karaeng to meet in battle the people of Boné at Meru and triumph over Daeng Marewa in Kaluku. He conquered Buluq Loe. After he was deposed, he entered Luwuq and in Luwuq entered Islam. Twenty-four years after being deposed he died over on Buton. He had three children by a female slave, one girl and two boys. After he was deposed in Islamic year 1026, during the month of Rajab, Christian year 1617 on July fifth, Karaeng Tunipasuluq died eastward on Buton. It was this karaeng who organized the karaeng's subjects, forming the people into nine banners and establishing the "half-banners."[31] *He also was the karaeng who first took a liking to small firearms, iron vests, swords, and long-bladed kris. Only three nights after Tunijalloq died, he was installed by Karaeng Matoaya with what belonged to him [as ruler]. He also did not allow subjects to pay homage to his two older siblings. This Karaeng Tunipasuluq, even if they committed no wrong, would on a whim have them killed. The Javanese left,*[32] *and all the anaq karaeng fled. The ones who did not flee were: Karaeng Matoaya, Karaeng ri Barombong, Karaeng ri Dataq the child of Karaeng Macaqdia, Karaeng ri Baroqbosoq, Karaeng ri Alluq, the child of Karaeng Matoaya, Karaeng ri Maros, Karaeng ri Patteqne. There were many other actions of his known as bad. Said people who knew [firsthand of his misdeeds], we should not know, it is not good for us to speak of them. This karaeng was karaeng of Gowa and karaeng of Talloq. After the karaengs of the people of Maros died out, he was also the first [from Gowa] taken as karaeng by the people of Maros.*

As scholars working with South Sulawesi *patturioloang* have noted, each reign follows a standard formula.[33] The rulers' names and titles, conquests and accomplishments, wives and children are listed in roughly that order. It is this propensity to record information familiar to Western historians that has led many to pronounce (with palpable relief)

South Sulawesi *patturioloang* "sober" and "factual" records amenable to historical study, in contrast to the "mythical" and "unreliable" chronicles of Java.[34] For many too, this would seem to be one effect of the shift from orality to literacy: a movement from unreliable to reliable, from mythical to historical. However, such a view of what is "going on" in the account of Tunipasuluq's reign is quite limited. A text is not simply material in which to dig for facts that can be appended onto the historian's narrative; a history such as this is more than a source.

To begin, in the *Gowa Chronicle* account of Tunipasuluq's reign, all action is linked to and initiated by the ruler; there are no events that take place independent of his actions and no events that originate elsewhere and affect the ruler. Other people and places enter the chronicle only by virtue of their connections with the ruler. Each reign in the *Gowa Chronicle* repeats this effect, producing a vision of history radiating out from a chain of active rulers affecting and shaping the lives of others.

Marshall Sahlins referred to the perception that the world is dominated by or revolves around towering figures as "heroic history." Because of the cultural or cosmological weight given to rulers, the implications of their acts are far greater and the effects more far-reaching than those of others. "This really *is* a history of kings and battles, but only because it is a cultural order that, multiplying the action of the king by the system of society, gives him a disproportionate historical effect."[35] In Makassarese *patturioloang,* time and historical significance are not simply related to the lives and activities of rulers in the way that U.S. presidents can be said to have a disproportionate historical effect. Time and historical significance flow from and only exist in terms of rulers. In the *Gowa Chronicle* the age of some rulers when they ascended the throne is given, and for some the length of their reign is recorded as well. But these dates are not encompassed by a calendar or timeline outside of the rulers' lives until the arrival of Portuguese and Malays bringing Christian and Muslim calendars in the early seventeenth century.[36] The lives of rulers structured the past.

In these written histories individual rulers replace sacred *kalompoang* and places as the conceptual anchors for understanding and recalling the past. In the histories of Pattalassang, if there is a central focus of historical attention it is the Cinde, not the rulers of Pattalassang. This progression from regalia to rulers as the centerposts of Makassarese history will be examined in detail in chapter 4, but it is useful to note here.

Another noteworthy feature of the written history of Karaeng Tunipasuluq's reign is its genealogical content. It might be expected that genealogies would be the preserve of oral history; we commonly associate family knowledge with memory rather than with the formal accounts of written history. While this might be the case in Roti and elsewhere, however, it is not true of Makassar. Scholars have commented on the shallowness of genealogical memory in Makassar. Chabot described how Makassarese used broad categories that were easy to assimilate people into, rather than finely graded kinship categories. In the generation above one's self, for example, everyone except one's parents are known as *toa,* while everyone without exception two generations above one's self are known as *puri.* In the generation below one's self everyone except one's children are known as *kamanakang,* while everyone without exception two generations below one's self are known as *cucu.* Makassarese rarely retained genealogical information further back than three generations.[37] As suggested in the discussion of Roti above and in the previous chapter, this information was neglected not because illiterate Makassarese were incapable of such an act of memory, but because it had little use in their social world. Shelley Errington's assertion that Bugis nobles actively forbade Bugis commoners from possessing written genealogies cannot be confirmed for Makassarese but could well be accurate.[38]

The recording of detailed genealogies belonged to the period after the adoption of literacy. The social circumstances and effects of this new genre are discussed more fully in chapter 4. For the moment it is enough to give an example of how abundant and complex written genealogical accounts often were. The selection below comes from the reign of Karaeng Matoaya (r. 1593 to 1623) in the *Talloq Chronicle* and comprises merely one part of the genealogical information included in his reign's account.[39] Divided here for convenience, the first section mentions one of Karaeng Matoaya's wives and his eight daughters and one son by her, the second section details the children by that one son of Karaeng Matoaya, and the third section returns to list his eight daughters by that wife.

Another of his wives was a person from Binamuq. Her mother was from Baroqbosoq, her father was a friend of I Lolopujiang. She was named I Bungasaq. They had eight daughters and one son.

His Arabic name was Abdulkadir, his Makassarese name was I Mallawakkang, his royal name was I Daeng Sisila, his karaeng-*title was Karaeng Popoq. He was in charge of the* tumakkajannang. *Now when Karaeng ri Popoq first mar-*

ried [it was to] a child of Tumamenang ri Gaukanna. He who was called Karaeng Popoq did not yet have children before he was widowed. After he was widowed, Karaeng Popoq married a child of a gallarrang from central Gowa. Her personal name was I Bayang, her royal name was I Kare Pate. They had six children: five boys and one girl. These are the names of the boys: I Madaeng, his Arabic name was Mahmud, his royal name was Daeng Maqbali, his karaeng-title was Karaeng Bontomanompoq, he was in charge of the tumakkajannang. Another son, his personal name was I Mamma, his royal name was I Daeng Mamaro. Another son, he was named I Yumaraq, his royal name I Daeng Mabella. Another son was named I Borahing; he was still small when he died. Another son was named I Tulolo; he was still small when he died. His daughter was named I Mina, her royal name was I Daeng Majannang. Another wife was Karaeng ri Pattong. Her personal name was I Sinungku, her royal name was Daeng Yannu. They had two children: one son and one daughter. The son was named I Manngemba, his royal name was Daeng Mattayang, his karaeng-title was Karaeng Bontopanno, his Arabic name was Abdul Gafur. He was raised to become tumailalang by Tumamenang ri Lakiung, replacing Karaeng ri Bisuli as tumailalang. Their daughter was named I Maluq, her royal name was I Daeng Talebang. Another wife had one son who died when small. Another wife also had one son who died when small. These were the children of Karaeng ri Popoq.

Another was a daughter whose name is unknown. She was taken to be the milk-sibling[40] of Tumamenang ri Bontobiraeng, but died when still small. Another daughter was named I Bissu-tatumagisiq, her royal name was I Kare Tonji, she was called Daengta ri Manngeppeq. Another daughter was named I Patimaq, her royal name was I Daeng Rinangke. Another was named I Yadaneng. Another daughter was named I Kare Manassa, she was also Daengta ri Pattingalloang. Another named I Yani died when still small.

This selection of detailed, nested genealogical information illustrates well the central place kinship relationships had in Makassarese *patturioloang* and in seventeenth-century Makassarese social life. The ability to track complex kinship links and the social need to do so both stem from the period after the advent of literacy in Makassar. Makassarese nobles proved adept at manipulating marriage possibilities and kinship relations. Marriage was a useful tool with which to build political support and mobilize followers, and nobles did not hesitate to parlay genealogical knowledge and ties into formidable blocks of support. Affines were especially valuable from this perspective. Shelly Errington described how Bugis nobles carefully guarded their genealogies and at the same time strategically married "centrifugally" outward. Well-designed matches "reeled in" distant cousins on the fringes of the family, reanimating kinship bonds that generations of marriages had eroded.[41]

Before moving on, it is again helpful to summarize the most notable features of Makassarese written composition as illustrated by the *Gowa Chronicle*. The *Gowa Chronicle* has several introductory sections, which will be presented below, but the bulk of the chronicle consists of eight sections recounting the eight reigns of successive rulers of Gowa. Viewed as a complete work, the *Gowa Chronicle* has a shape as distinctive as that of the history of Pattalassang. In this history, the teardrops and barbells of oral memory are replaced by linked narrative blocks, chronologically contiguous and standardized in format. Unlike oral histories, there seems to have been a clear conception of what a "chronicle" was as a work, what it should contain and how it should be written. In addition to this standardized, even shape, the *Gowa Chronicle* is remarkable for the cosmological centrality it gave rulers. Defining and structuring the past, rulers played the same role as anchors for written history-making as did *kalompoang* for oral traditions. Finally, the volume of detailed genealogical information present in written chronicles contrasts sharply with Makassarese oral traditions' lack of interest in kinship history.

From the perspective of narrative structure and content, Makassarese oral and written histories are fundamentally different. It would be easy at this point simply to conclude that a "transition" from orality to literacy radically transformed Makassarese conceptions of the past. In some ways this is true. The break, however, is not as straightforward as the texts above may suggest. The relationship between orality and literacy was more complex than a simple transition. The facets of this relationship, and in particular the symbiosis between oral and written histories, are the focus of the next section.

Orality, Literacy, and Makassarese *Patturioloang*

In an important article two decades ago, Christian Pelras first spoke of the interchange between oral and written material in South Sulawesi. Pelras argued that the distinction between oral and written literature was of secondary importance in studying Bugis literature, which should be considered a unified body of oral and written traditions. The two traditions are indivisibly tied to each other: most tales have both oral and written versions, and each medium borrows elements from the other.[42]

Although oral and written histories were more socially distinct in early modern Makassar, the two forms of history-making were linked. This section examines the interdependence of oral and written Makassarese histories from two perspectives: the influence of oral forms of composition on written composition, including the inclusion of oral histories within the framework of written histories, and the symbiotic relationship between oral and written knowledge of the past.[43]

The influence of existing patterns of oral composition on written histories immediately strikes the reader of the first pages of the *Gowa Chronicle*. Many of the hallmarks of oral composition that scholars have identified as being characteristic of oral composition in general or the Indonesian archipelago in particular can be found in the *Gowa Chronicle*.[44] Foremost among these are parallelism and the use of formulaic or stock phrases.

The passage that opens the *Gowa Chronicle* derives from ritual speech. Though difficult to translate, and having phrases whose meanings are elusive, the chronicle's beginning might be read as follows.

This is the story of ancestors of the people of Gowa. May I not be cursed, may I not be destroyed, naming, recounting the ancient karaengs. *Those who recline on royal couches, those who rest on royal couches, those who are of the purest gold, the chain of kings. This is recited so that nothing is forgotten by our children, by our grandchildren, by our descendants. Because if it is not known, there are two dangers: either we will feel ourselves to be* karaengs *too, or outsiders will call us common people.*[45]

The strong oral residue in this written text is immediately evident. The formulaic phrases comprise a ritual speech no longer uttered but rather set down in writing. The text displays an oral narrative organization of paired phrases in which the second phrase emphasizes and slightly restates the first phrase—"Those who recline on royal beds, those who rest on royal beds, those who are of the purest gold, the chain of kings." Even reading the passage silently one can sense the way in which aural rhythms predominated. These ritual speech patterns can still be heard in Makassar today. Reading the passage aloud in Makassarese in particular, it is difficult not to fall back on the stylized rhythms of chanted speech.

Throughout the Gowa and Talloq *patturioloang* there are stock phrases borrowed from oral composition. The use of these conventional phrases makes *patturioloang* the genre of Makassarese written histories easiest to read. The most common of these phrases were (1) "This was the first ruler to . . ." or "This was the ruler who . . ."; (2) "Another wife of . . ." or "Another child of . . ."; (3) "He had a child . . ."; (4) "This ruler was not praised as . . ." or "He was only praised as . . ."; (5) "This ruler conquered . . ." Originally used in oral composition to aid recall, the stock phrases used in Makassarese *patturioloang* underline the topics that were at the center of written accounts of the past: the deeds of the ruler, his wives, and descendants; his conquests; how he was remembered. Writing in early modern Makassar was not the interiorized expression of an "author" in the modern sense, and hence the effort to distinguish stylistically one's writing as a literary composition that we associate with writing was an alien concept.[46] Employing recognizable formulas, rather than creative and varied manners of expression, was a practice inherited from oral composition that became the norm in written *patturioloang*.

Oral histories influenced written histories in more than style of composition. Chroniclers incorporated many oral traditions within written histories. In particular, Makassarese recalled the distant past of polities such as Gowa in often mythical tales of their origins. Later, when written *patturioloang* were composed, these tales became the first section of *patturioloang*. Ian Caldwell has detected a similar pattern of oral stories being incorporated into written chronicles among Bugis.[47] Both the Gowa and Talloq *patturioloang* can without too much difficulty be separated into orally composed and literately composed halves. In terms of content and narrative style the two halves are distinctive.

The *Gowa Chronicle*'s opening ritual speech is followed by an oral history of the founding of Gowa. In particular, it relates how a being who mysteriously appeared from the Upperworld—a *tumanurung*—married a powerful earthly man of unknown origins and founded the ruling line of Gowa.

Tumanurung *married Karaeng Bayo, the father of Tumassalangga Barayang.*[48] *She was called by the people of old* tumanurung *because unknown were her origins and her manner of death. It only was said she disappeared. She was married by Karaeng Bayo; as for Karaeng Bayo, unknown too were his community. It was only said that purportedly he was brothers with Lakipadada, who it was said bore Sudanga. Karaeng Bayo wed* tumanurung *and had a child Tumassalangga Barayang. For three years he was in the womb. When he was born, he came out and could immediately run, immediately knew how to talk. His mother was troubled by the people who said he was a misshapen person. The reason he was called Tumassalangga Barayang was because of his shoulders: one side went up, the other side went down; and his ears: one was gnarled, the other was overlarge; the soles of his feet were the same length to his heel as to the front of his feet; his navel was large. From the moment that he became* karaeng, *for those reasons the people said he was a misshapen man. But his mother said, "Why do you say that my son is a misshapen man? For his shoulders are Barayang shoulders, his ears are flanking [?] mountains. A hair snapping in Java he hears. A dead white buffalo in Silayar he smells. The white spot of a leech [?] in Bantaeng he discerns. His feet are like scales. His navel is a great well. His hands are hollowed-out extremities. When they scoop they have taels of gold. When they scoop they fold* karoaq-*cloth. When they scoop they let his men walk in multitudes." After her child grew up, she split her necklace in two. Half was given to her child. She entered her chamber, then was no longer inside. That necklace, half of which was given to her child, was called I Tanisamaang.*[49]

At this point in the chronicle the presence of the narrating writer is first felt. Having recorded the story above, he wrote, "[As for] Tumassalangga Barayang, nothing is spoken of his wife or his death. It was only said by the people of old that he disappeared. He purportedly said to the people, 'Sit, you.' Then he went out into the mountains north of Jonggoa. There was thunder, then rain while it was sunny, then he could no longer be seen." With this the chronicler had reached the limits of oral knowledge about the past. As with the oral histories from Pattalassang above, the people of Gowa remembered tales about foundational events, but they did not preserve an unbroken narrative from those origins to their present. Without this knowledge, and without written sources to rely on, the chronicler continues, "Until Tunatangkaqlopi from Tumassalangga Barayang, their wives are not known. Not known too are their children except those who inherited the rulership. Not known also are their wars. Not known further is how long they ruled because there were not yet lontaraq."[50] The next section of the chronicle, a genre that unlike oral histories did value the ability to trace an unbroken chain from the present into the past, is a list of successive rulers of Gowa with only short fragments of oral knowledge remembered about each ruler. The *Gowa Chronicle* lists six rulers in this section, but it is impossible to know if there were others who were subsequently forgotten. This transitional period, in which there is neither abundant oral tradition for the chronicler to rely upon nor written sources, marks the shift from oral to literate composition in the *Gowa Chronicle*. The remainder of the chronicle comprises eight accounts of the rulers of Gowa from Tumapaqrisiq Kallonna in the early sixteenth century to Sultan Hasanuddin, whose rule ended in 1669.

Sometimes Makassarese today ask questions about the past to which no written or oral histories provide answers. For example, while Sudanga, the sword of Lakipadada, became one of the most powerful *kalompoang* in Gowa, many Makassarese today wonder what happened to Tanruq Ballanga, the sword of his brother Karaeng Bayo. Why is nothing known about the fate of this potentially powerful *kalompoang*?

While this mystery remains, what chroniclers did not set down on paper was often remembered and passed down orally. A prominent example of orally preserved accounts of events too dangerous or controversial to record in written manuscripts concerns the death of Tunijalloq in 1590. The *Gowa Chronicle* only reports, "His demise was a death of being cut down aboard ship, north of Agangnionoq and seaward of Lipukasiq, during the harvest season in Maros. On the third night of the month of Muharram he was cut down by his milk-sibling; a man from Majannang named I Lolo spoke not and cut him down."[57] The most fascinating question is why a man so close to Tunijalloq—culturally a sibling and intimate follower—killed him as he sailed away to war. Why was this tantalizing fact omitted from the chronicle? It appears, however, that the reason did survive in oral memories. Nearly a century later, Makassarese nobles in exile told Nicholas Gervaise about how an earlier ruler was killed aboard ship by another Makassarese noble.[58]

Recounted by Gervaise as a scandalous and shocking tale from the exotic Orient, the story describes how a ruler of Gowa, not satisfied with the great number of concubines he had, became infatuated with and took for his own a wife of one of the most powerful lords at court. This lord was grieved but had to hide his resentment at losing her until the chance for revenge appeared. While the ruler was aboard one of his magnificent royal barges, the jealous husband slipped aboard among the rowers. He entered the cabin, stabbed the ruler of Gowa to death, then threw himself into the sea and was never heard from again. As punishment, his nearest relations and dearest friends were seized and thrown into cauldrons of boiling water until dead.[59] Gervaise reports that this was a story about Sultan Malikussaid, the father of Sultan Hasanuddin, but this is incorrect. The *Gowa Chronicle* says nothing noteworthy about Malikussaid's death, only that it occurred.[60] The story Gervaise heard could only be about Tunijalloq, whose posthumous name in fact remembers him precisely as "the one who was cut down."

Why was nothing of this story, even if embellished in Gervaise's account, included in the *Gowa Chronicle*? Certainly many present must have known why I Lolo went out of control and killed his ruler. This portion of the *Gowa Chronicle,* after all, was certainly composed within living memory of the event. Was it unseemly to preserve the reason behind this flagrant assault on royal prerogative and power? Could it have been considered dangerous to do so? Did later rulers of Gowa prefer that the arbitrary behavior of Tunijalloq that led to his death not be recalled? Did they fear the remembering of such an act of regicide? These are all possible reasons, but memories of sexual rivalry and possession were probably the most dangerous memories of all in Makassar, and their recall could at a later time too easily fuel anger and violence. Whether a dangerous or simply uncomfortable memory, the unmentioned history behind this episode is not the only place in the *Gowa Chronicle* where chroniclers elided potentially flammable histories.

The greatest silences in the written *patturioloang* of Gowa and Talloq concern the tension and violence that marked their early relations. All available written and oral sources describe Talloq as an offshoot of Gowa (map 3). The sixth ruler of Gowa, Tunatangkaqlopi, had two sons, Batara Gowa and Karaeng Loe ri Sero. As the beginning of the *Talloq Chronicle* cited above explained, at Tunatangkaqlopi's death the two brothers quarreled, and Karaeng Loe ri Sero eventually left Gowa to found Talloq with the support of a portion of the Gowa nobility. Despite the detail in the account, little is actually spoken about the quarrel between the two brothers. In particular, we can only guess how the quarrel arose and what they quarreled over. However, an oral history first written down in the nineteenth century explains that the two brothers quarreled over who would possess the *kalompoang* and thus succeed their father. Indeed, this history claims that Karaeng Loe was the elder brother and Batara Gowa usurped his proper position.[61] The truth of the account is impossible to verify, but the explanation is precisely the kind of oral history that often survived alongside more cautious written histories. Moreover, as Ian Caldwell notes, stories of disaffected brothers founding new settlements are a pan-Austronesian phenomenon and well known in South Sulawesi.[62]

Another episode of violence between Gowa and Talloq took place around 1540, when Gowa defeated an alliance of Talloq, Maros, and Polombangkeng in war. The *Gowa Chronicle* describes the war in detail but again does not explain the circumstances that caused the war, saying, "There were no words put in the *lontaraq* about the war; it was just recorded that they fought."[63] But here too there are other sources that

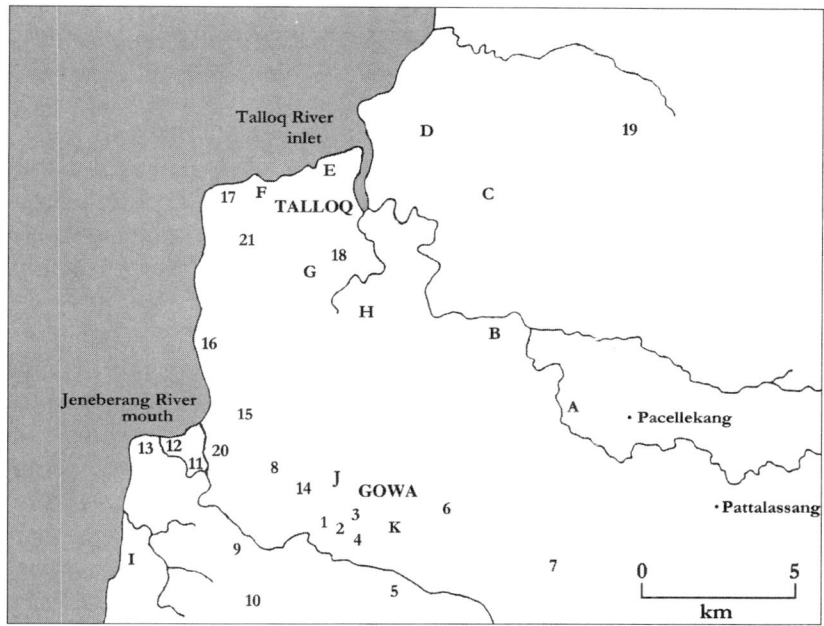

Map 3. Gowa-Talloq Heartland

Toponyms Associated with Gowa

1. Dataq, Lakiung
2. Bisei
3. Tomboloq
4. Old Gowa Fort
5. Mangalle
6. Saumata
7. East Bontomanaiq
8. West Bontomanaiq
9. Gantarang
10. Kanjilo
11. Lekoqbodong, Somba Opu
12. Garassiq
13. Panakkukang
14. Mangasa
15. Jongaya
16. Mariso
17. Ujung Tana
18. Camba
19. Sudiang
20. Bontotangga
21. Bontoalaq

Toponyms Associated with Talloq

A. Bangkalaq
B. Moncong Loe
C. Leang
D. Parang Loe
E. Campagaya
F. Pattingalloang
G. Karuwisi
H. Panaikang
I. Barombong
J. Karunrung
K. Paqbineang

supply answers. An oral tradition recorded later describes the background to this war. Before the ruler of Gowa Tumapaqrisiq Kallonna was succeeded by his son Tunipalangga, Tunipalangga ran off with Balu Maqlonjoka, a daughter of Karaeng Tunipasuruq, the ruler of Talloq. Insulted by this affront, the ruler of Talloq refused offers of compensation and other efforts by Gowa to make amends, sent word of this offense to his allies in Maros and Polombangkeng, and marched on Gowa in war.[64] In fact, at a later point the *Gowa Chronicle* mentions this episode but fails to connect it to the description of the war with Talloq. "Before he became ruler he ran off with Balu Maqlonjoka, and after running off with Balu Maqlonjoka angered Karaeng Tunipasuruq. He set the people of Gowa and the people of Talloq against each other."[65] The rift caused by Tunipalangga's running away with Balu Maqlonjoka was not completely forgotten. But such a story, liable like the one behind the death of Tunijalloq to open old wounds, was dangerous and better left unwritten. Orally the story was preserved for some three centuries before being written down in the nineteenth century.[66]

In these stories, oral accounts preserved what had remained unwritten. But this is not the only way that oral histories complemented written histories. Frequently, written manuscripts refer to people, places, events, and objects about which oral memories contained fuller accounts. Oral histories elaborated upon terse and skeletal written histories. These accounts were revived in the act of reading, "triggered" by the written text, and so brought into play with written histories.

As both the tangible remains of the past and as the focus for history-making, objects and places were the triggers of historical memories. When viewed or spoken of, Makassarese recalled the histories of which these objects and places were a focal part. Histories attached to these objects and places, dominating and structuring Makassarese historical mentality. The relationship between oral and written histories worked in a similar manner. Oral histories attached to written histories, complementing what was not written down. Reading manuscripts with a Makassarese is like tacking back and forth while sailing into the wind; eager to help explain their past, Makassarese will constantly be reminded of other stories, other histories that flesh out sparse written accounts of the past. Oral memories clustered around written texts. Rather than a simple passage from one to the other, then, oral and written histories existed in a complex, symbiotic relationship in which each informed the other, functioning more as complements than as opposites.

Conclusions: Transformations in Makassarese Historical Mentality

This chapter began by presenting and contrasting representative examples of oral and written Makassarese historical accounts. The differences between the two are striking. Oral histories focused on origins, particularly the origins of a community, its *kalompoang,* and its links with Gowa. Commemorating these beginnings provided the locus of a *paqrasangang*'s identity. This emphasis on remembering origins gave oral histories a teardrop or barbell shape. In these conceptions of the past there was little effort to maintain an unbroken chain linking past and present, whether composed of rulers or of other genealogical ties. Written histories focused on the lives and reigns of rulers, the dominant figures who gave the past its shape and history-making its focal point. Obeying a standardized model of what a written chronicle of the past should contain, these histories resembled narrative blocks. Chronologically linked and full of detailed genealogical information, these histories emphasized continuity between past and present.

The most socially significant differences between oral and written histories concerns what they emphasize as the anchors of the past. Makassarese did not conceive of the past as a vast space regulated by a homogenous linear time and filled with discrete facts and events. To know the past did not mean striving to comprehensively retell it in the present. Early modern Makassarese histories centered on particular times and topics that were socially meaningful. Oral histories were attached to and about places and objects, while written histories were attached to and about powerful rulers. This change in how the past was viewed and how histories of it were made hints at the transformative possibilities ushered in by the presence of written histories in early modern Makassar.

It would be a mistake, however, to focus primarily on the cognitive dimension of the advent of historical literacy. History-making, whether oral or written, was a practice situated in the immediate social world. Indeed, one cannot write abstractly and generally about the transition from orality to literacy because there was and will be no such universal transition. History-making, both oral and written, is a social practice embedded in local worlds, even local worlds open to influence from the outside such as Makassar. The dynamic between oral and written may well be different in each society. This point bears emphasizing because much of the scholarly literature about literacy and orality concerns Europe. In Makassar, the most evident result of the advent of literacy was not a change in the capacity to remember and the attending information revolution that many have identified as the paramount effect of literacy in Europe. What must be underscored here is that historical literacy in Makassar ushered in new ways of recalling the past. It made the past available and manipulable in new ways. What changed in sixteenth-century Makassar, in effect, was the social position of the past and its ability to be used in the present. The Makassarese world was profoundly transformed by the new uses to which the past was put. We need, then, to explore more fully the social, political, and cultural changes that the advent of historical literacy brought about. Part 2 has this exploration as its task.

PART II

Making History

∞ *4* ∞

Historical Literacy and Social Hierarchicalization

Part 2 of this work examines how the changing conceptions of history that literacy effected led to tangible and remarkable social, political, and cultural changes in sixteenth- and seventeenth-century Makassar. Literacy, of course, was not the only force at work, and all historical change cannot be traced to it alone. But new ways of conceiving the past played often pivotal roles in shaping or giving form to the changes afoot in Makassar. This chapter examines the effects of the new ways of imagining the past that literacy sparked in creating a more hierarchical, ranked social order. The idea of a ranked social order based on historical claims, which many have seen as a "classical" feature of Makassarese society, took root and blossomed in this period.

The idea of rank itself, of course, was not new to Makassar during this period. Social differentiation by rank is one of the most evident hallmarks of all Austronesian societies, from Bali to Hawai'i and more. As the historical linguist Robert Blust has noted, the concept of being cursed or "swelling"—*bassung* in Makassarese—as a result of offending or violating the status of a higher-ranked individual was ancient and widespread among Western Malayo-Polynesian societies.[1] Early Makassarese society was certainly no exception. To argue that literacy created the idea of social division by rank in formerly egalitarian oral cultures is mistaken. Rather, the argument here is that literacy increased and augmented an existing cultural trait, that literacy was a catalyst spurring to unprecedented heights the widespread Austronesian tendency to divide people by rank.

As the effects of historical literacy were complex, so too the ways in which the past made itself felt in the present, thereby increasing social differentiation in Makassar, can be approached from several perspectives. This chapter maps out three facets of this process of social hierarchicalization and, concomitantly, three ways that writing about the past made its presence felt in early modern Makassar. First, the establishment of a legitimizing standard of historical descent based on white blood is discussed as the critical move separating nobles from commoners. Second, the effects of making and possessing written genealogies is explored. Third, I examine the increasing sense fostered by writing histories that the past can be possessed and the social consequences of this new attitude toward the past.

Making Blood White

The *Gowa Chronicle* includes a telling explanation of why the work was composed. As cited in the previous chapter, the chronicler writes, "This is recited so that nothing is forgotten by our children, by our grandchildren, by our descendants. Because if it is not known, there are two dangers: either we will feel ourselves to be *karaengs* too, or outsiders will call us common people." The double purpose of this statement—to differentiate oneself from those of lower rank while not transgressing the prerogatives of those of higher rank—is an exemplary case of a widespread Makassarese emphasis on knowing one's proper social position. Ethnographers have repeatedly cited the pervasiveness of status rivalry in modern Makassarese society and its influence in every realm of social life from weddings to political machinations.[2] The urge to improve one's own status, and the keen sense of competition with others of similar status, seemingly knew (and knows) no bounds in Makassarese life.

It is difficult to grasp the extent to which visible signs of hierarchy and status came to pervade early modern Makassarese life. Although Makassarese read these signs with a fluency we cannot capture, it is possible to gain a sense of how displaying and measuring status were constant Makassarese preoccupations. The marking of status was most visible on ceremonial occasions in which Makassarese carefully and deliberately presented interpretations of social relations.

Indeed, marking status began quite literally at birth. Nineteenth-century ethnographies note that the placenta was preserved in an earthen pot and either buried or hanged in a tree seven days after birth among commoners, and either nine, fourteen, or eighteen days among nobles, depending on their rank.[3] Festivities continued to mark the elevated rank of noble children. A year or two after birth the infant's hair was ceremonially cut for the first time, a modest and unremarkable occasion for commoners but accompanied by great feasting and celebrations among nobles.⁴ Again among noble families, at about age six a feast was held marking the first occasion when the child's feet were allowed to touch the ground *(nipaonjoki butta)*. Eerdmans commented that in the past this ceremony had taken place at age two or three. Writing in the 1680s, Gervaise said that this ceremony was held among commoners four or five months after birth but that high-ranking children were carried and not allowed to touch the ground until age eight or nine. Moreover, Islam gave this event further sacred connotations and embellishments. Noble parents brought their child to the mosque for purification and to present him to Allah. Five or six *ulama* said prayers over the child's head, each in turn cut part of the child's hair, a boy's feet were set down on the blade of a sword to make him fearless in battle, and finally the *ulama* gave him the name of an Islamic saint. Then parents took the child home to feasting, dancing, and celebration.⁵

During the course of the seventeenth century, Makassarese incorporated Islamic rites into the fabric of social life as further occasions to mark social position. Gervaise described circumcision ceremonies as grand and solemn. When the child was approximately eight or nine, Islamic *ulama* were consulted to choose an auspicious day for the event.⁶ A buffalo was sacrificed to Allah the day before and its head removed. The day of the ritual the youth bathed in a copper kettle for an hour. Then the priest brought the buffalo head, set it down on a carpet or mat, covered it with a cloth, and placed the boy between the two horns. After saying a prayer, he performed the circumcision; then three days of celebration, dancing, and games commenced. Meanwhile, the boy was kept in bed for forty days. If the boy came from a noble family, the ceremony was markedly more solemn and expensive, with up to a hundred buffalo sacrificed. That same day all the suitably aged boys of the father's vassals and neighbors were circumcised as well, an act deliberately intended to reproduce in the next generation an existing hierarchy of social relations.⁷

In addition to the ritual performances themselves, the social gatherings and celebrations afterward were public demonstrations of status. The amount of food served, the number and rank of guests, the number of servants mobilized, the quality of the entertainment, and the length of the festivities all indexed social status. Even what food helpers prepared reflected the jostling of status rivalry: those of higher status prepared vegetable dishes or made expensive desserts in the kitchen, while those of lower status did the messier work of cutting meat, squeezing coconut pulp, and plucking chickens in the yard.[8] Punctuating social life at births, hair cuttings, circumcisions, teeth filings, marriages, funerals, and other events, each gathering presented a social map of the relative status of a given family. The most detailed exploration of the way in which questions of status permeated every aspect of social gatherings in South Sulawesi in Susan Millar's work *Bugis Weddings*. Indeed, there is no shortage of evidence to suggest that marriage ceremonies function as social mirrors across Indonesia. From the Balinese epic *Parthayana*, which is structured around Arjuna's relationships to women, to the Bugis epic *La Galigo*, which uses marriage rituals to exemplify the nature of the social order, to John Pemberton's analysis of Surakarta royal weddings, Indonesians have always recognized marriage ceremonies as carefully constructed claims to power.[9]

The best-documented historical description of a ritual process as a social mapping is found in Gervaise's discussion of Makassarese funerals. He described seventeenth-century Makassarese funerals as magnificent and pompous.[10] Funerals were so important as registers of status that even the poor saved money so they would not be embarrassed. Among the nobility the corpse was prepared with great care. The body was washed in the house five times: with clean water, water with earth steeped in it, water mixed with powder of perfumed wood, juice of citrons, and sweet waters and essences, their expense determined by the wealth and rank of the family. The body was clothed in a long white robe and a white turban, wrapped in a sheet, and placed in the largest room of the house, itself draped in white. Perfumed pots were set up to give off pleasant odors while mourners came to express their sympathy and to affirm links with the family of the departed.

The funeral procession was an even more conspicuous display of tokens of rank. The body was brought to the mosque in a palanquin covered with white cloth and carried by slaves. The chief *ulama* sat beside the body if the deceased was of high rank; if of lower rank, the body was carried by relatives or hirelings and the chief *ulama*, if he attended, followed on foot. Several people with perfuming pots walked ahead of the palanquin, while others followed behind scattering pieces of gold, silver, or copper to the poor, again according to the wealth and rank of the deceased. Another European observed that in funerals, "the Moors of Macasar usually have four Boys very well clad at the four corners of the Bier, which is very large. Every one of them carries a Fan and fans the dead Body which goes in the middle, which is to cool the Soul, because of the great heat it endures in the other world. This myself I have seen."[11] After prayers in the mosque a second procession led to the burial site. For high-ranking deceased, Makassarese built a stone mausoleum at the grave site, and when it was finished slaves and servants brought flowers, prayed, and placed smoking perfumes there for the duration of the mourning period, which also depended on the rank of the deceased. For a ruler of Gowa or his close kin Eerdmans reported this period lasted one hundred days, for other notables between seven and forty days, and for commoners but three to seven days.[12] At the end of the mourning period a great feast was held at the mosque or the home of the widow, a final chance for the family of the deceased to assert its status through the number and rank of the guests who arrived.

Cermonial occasions that marked status, such as weddings and funerals, were sporadic events punctuating social life. There were also innumerable signs of status visible in everyday life. Clothing and houses were perhaps the most malleable mediums in which to communicate status.[13] The richness of one's jewelry and clothing was perceived as a sign of rank, not wealth. Wherever the hero Andi Patunru journeyed in the epic *Sinrilikna Kappalak Tallumbatua,* rulers greeting him hastened to don their most magnificent clothes to signify their high rank.[14] Andi Patunru's own rank was always apparent from a distance because of his clothing and appearance. So too was the heavenly origin of *tumanurung* read in their splendid clothing and gold jewelry.[15] Gervaise wrote that the hilts of weapons, bucklers, and helmets of warriors were silver if the warrior was of high rank and gold if of very high rank.[16] A hat or *songkoq* had to be worn when one entered the yard of the ruler's palace.[17] As yellow was the color of royalty, only the ruler of Gowa or the very highest ranking nobles could wear yellow sarongs.[18] Surprisingly, given early modern Europe's own preoccupations with status and honor, European visitors did not recognize how clothing communicated rank in Makassar and felt that Gowa nobles wearing European-style cloth coats were ridiculous.[19] Hunting deer was a custom of the nobility, and Gervaise reported that no wild fowl were sold in markets because fowl hunting was also a sport reserved for the ruler and high-ranking nobles, and infractions were severely punished.[20]

There are dozens of similar examples. Throughout South Sulawesi a long lance was a prerogative of those of high rank.[21] Although the lances were often carried behind them by their followers, Eerdmans observed that only royalty could carry their lances upright against their shoulders; lesser nobles had to carry their lances sloping upward from under their arms.[22] During the mid-sixteenth-century reign of Karaeng

Tunibatta, when the Gallarrang Sudiang was raised in rank and made a member of the Bate Salapang, part of the oaths sworn by the two lords included the ritual phrase "I am not required to bear the ruler's lance." A ruler of Pattalassang stepped down from office because he felt insulted when a relative of Karaeng Gowa touched him with a lance.[23]

Where and when did this pervasive emphasis on status and status differentiation begin? A critical move enabling this vision of society as divided into an array of ranks, each of which possessed tokens indexing their rank, was the spread of what I call an ideology of white blood in early modern Makassar.[24] Here we must be careful. Just as the idea of social differentiation by rank was a common feature of Austronesian societies, so too the Makassarese belief that people were inherently unequal was not a new concept in the sixteenth century. There is every reason to believe that the modern Western notion of fundamental human equality would always have been alien to Makassarese. There was a deeply rooted perception among Makassarese that social inequality was natural, and not an artificial by-product of wealth and circumstance concealing a basic sameness shared by all humans.[25] Makassarese today, though certainly borrowing from the models of Dutch colonial ethnographers, describe "classical" Makassarese society in terms of an elaborate division by rank based upon blood descent (figure 7). What role did new ways of imagining and possessing the past in written histories play in shaping social hierarchicalization in early modern Makassar? What are the roots of "classical" Makassarese conceptions of society? When did Makassarese begin imagining society as divided into such finely demarcated layers? To answer these questions we need to return to the *Gowa Chronicle*.

The *Gowa Chronicle* set down in writing a myth that became the justification for the rule of Gowa's *karaengs*. It told of a heavenly being who appeared suddenly, married another stranger from afar, and founded the line of rulers who would henceforth govern Gowa. The *tumanurung* married Karaeng Bayo and before long gave birth to a child named Tumassalangga Barayang. In this history, quoted in the last chapter, the rulers of Gowa claimed to have a purity and nobility of descent surpassing that of all others. As descendants of the heavenly *tumanurung*, they have not red, but white blood flowing in their veins.

Makassarese oral traditions describe this event more elaborately, further emphasizing the godlike stature of the *tumanurung* and, by implication, of her descendants. One such tradition survives in a Dutch summary of a now-lost 1795 manuscript. It recounts the meeting of Karaeng

Bayo and the *tumanurung*. In this story, Karaeng Bayo was tracking down a source of water when he discovered an earthly paradise or garden of delights. In the center of this garden was a magnificent house that looked like a palace. Full of wonder and fear, Karaeng Bayo saw the *tumanurung* inside, sitting on a white throne of ivory beneath a multicolored roof sewn with gems that sparkled like the stars above. He was struck silent. Then the *tumanurung* spoke to him, saying that among mortals only he

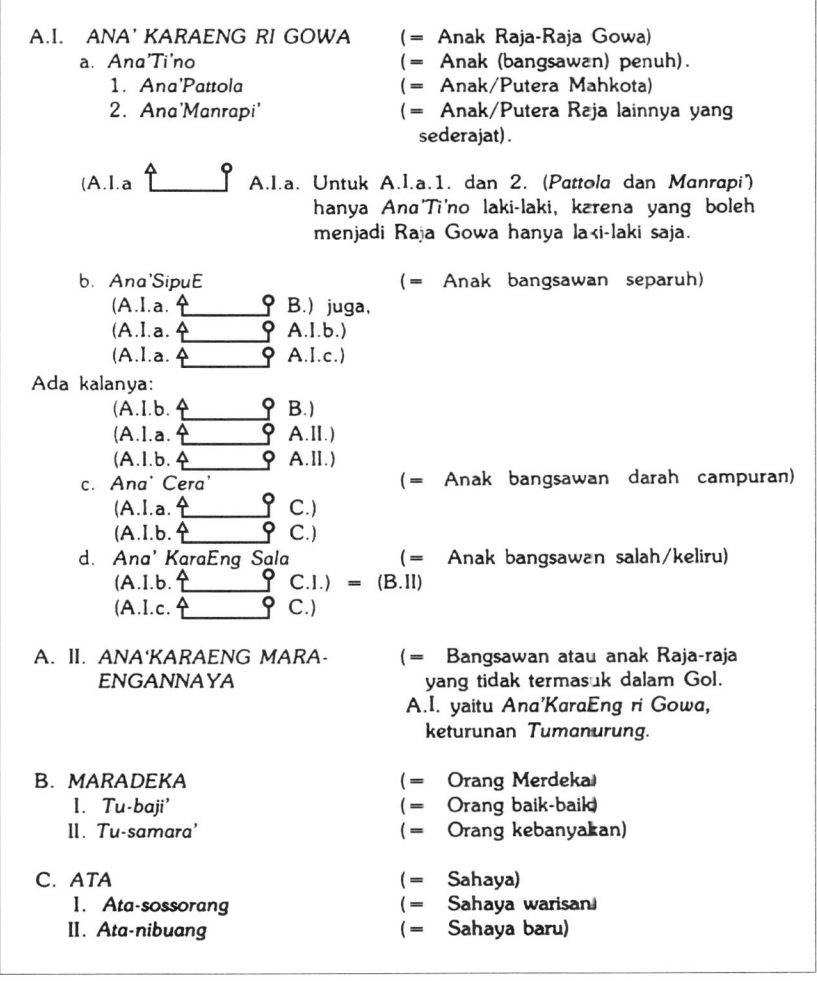

Figure 7. Social divisions in Makassarese society (Reprinted from Mattulada, *Latoa*, 1995, courtesy of Hasanuddin University Press)

was fit to be her mate and live in contentment. Not knowing what to say or do, with reverence he took her by the hand and before the gods, the manuscript records, they were joined.[26] The existence of many similar oral traditions attest to the widespread Makassarese acceptance of the claim made in the *Gowa Chronicle* about the heavenly origins of Gowa's rulers.

It is impossible to say if this *tumanurung* myth, now found in many places in South Sulawesi, in both oral and written histories, was newly minted in sixteenth-century Gowa. Perhaps so. Perhaps too it was one variety of common tales about beings of unknown origin who appeared and brought wondrous regalia or innovations before magically disappearing again. Certainly the perception that such beings have white rather than red blood is not confined to Makassar or South Sulawesi; it is common in many parts of Southeast Asia.[27] Similarly, the story of Karaeng Bayo, a lord from outside who establishes a line of rulers by marrying a woman there, is reminiscent of myths of "stranger-kings" that Marshall Sahlins identified throughout Polynesia, itself part of the larger Austronesian world.[28] On the other hand, the anthropologist Martin Rössler believes that the *tumanurung* myth spread from Gowa to other Makassarese polities once they were brought into the orbit of Gowa's expanding influence.[29]

Whatever its origins, the myth acquired a new status when it was incorporated into written *patturioloang*. No longer merely one oral tradition among many, the *tumanurung* myth became the authoritative history explaining and justifying a new social order created in sixteenth-century Gowa. Writing granted this story tremendous influence over how people in Gowa, and increasingly throughout Makassar, conceived of the distant past and of society in the present. As writers began to imitate the *Gowa Chronicle* and create *patturioloang* in Maros, Sanrabone, and elsewhere, a crucial element they borrowed was the *tumanurung* myth. In this Gowa was archetypical. This process of imitation is explored in greater detail, and its political significance discussed, in the next chapter.

The *tumanurung* myth did not simply act as a political justification for the rule of later *karaeng*s, however. It justified the establishment of an entirely new social order. It is the nature of this social order, and the role of written histories in its creation, that is vital to address. Another Makassarese text describes in detail the agreement made between the *tumanurung* and the local lords of Gowa, known as the Kasiang Salapang before the *tumanurung* arrived, as the Bate Salapang after her arrival, and led by an official known as the *pacalla*. It tells how the nine lords of

Gowa faced turmoil ranging from disagreements among themselves to outside invasion. When the *tumanurung* appeared, they approached and asked her to become their ruler.

After the Kasiang Salapang arrived, the kasiang *said to the* tumanurung, *"You we take as our* karaeng." *Then said the* tumanurung, *"You make me* karaeng, *yet I pound rice, I fetch water." Then said the Kasiang Salapang, "Our wives do not pound rice, do not fetch water, much less you our* karaeng." *After the* tumanurung *agreed to be* karaeng, *she was installed as Karaeng Gowa. She became* karaeng, *even though she was a woman. If there is a disagreement among the Bate Salapang, Karaeng Manurunga adjudicates. If something is decided wrongly, and one does not know, the other eight know. Then also the Bate Salapang and the* pacalla *servants gave seventy-five men and seventy-five women [to the new Karaeng Gowa]. The men were placed under a toappalili; the women were placed under a towappokoq. A palace was built in Takang Basi named Tamalate because the tree leaves were not withered: leafy trees were taken to make house poles. After a while [the* tumanurung*] became famous in other communities. It was said there was a divine person who descended in Gowa who was made* karaeng *by the people of Gowa. Many came to pay respects to the* karaeng tumanurung *among all the communities that had heard of her, including those communities not conquered by Gowa. After a while there were again worries among the Bate Salapang because the Karaeng Manurunga had not yet married. They said, "It is a problem our ruler has no children; our ruler may be without descendants [to rule after her]." A while later a person came from the uplands; his community was unknown, his position and where he came from was unknown. His mother and father were unknown also. It was only said that a person named Karaeng Bayo and a person named Lakipadada came from the uplands into the center of Gowa. The one named Lakipadada was the owner of a sword Sudanga. Karaeng Bayo was the owner of a sword Tanruq Ballanga.*[30] *It was lost. Karaeng Tunipalangga armed [with Tanruq Ballanga] his son named Karaeng Anaqmoncong. After the Kasiang Salapang and* pacalla *learned [of the arrivals in Gowa] they came to a decision. They agreed to go and bring Karaeng Bayo to marry Karaeng Manurunga. The Kasiang Salapang arrived [before Karaeng Bayo]. Then said the Kasiang to Karaeng Bayo, "You we take to marry with our* karaeng." *Then said Karaeng Bayo, "If you step that will crack the land. You are the owners of the community." We were simply silent. "Because you raise me to the top of the coconut tree, for that I am indeed very happy." Then Karaeng Manurunga was married by Karaeng Bayo. Then each of the Bate Salapang gave servants [to their rulers]. After some time Karaeng Bayo went out to Kalong-Kalong. Then he summoned the Kasiang*

Salapang and the pacalla. *The Kasiang arrived. Then said the* karaeng, *"For this I have summoned you, Kasiang. You take me as your Lord. I speak and you agree. I am the wind and you the leaves of the trees." Then said the Kasiang Salapang and the* pacalla, *"We take you as our Lord. You are our Lord and we are your servants. You are our hook, we are the container. If the hook breaks, the container breaks too. If the hook breaks and the container does not break, we will fight unto death." Then said also the Kasiang Salapang, "We are not attacked by your weapons, you are not attacked by our weapons. Later we will be given a normal death by Rewata, you will be given a normal death by Rewata. You speak and we agree. If we are carrying something on our head, we will not be made to carry something on our shoulders too. If we are carrying something on our shoulders, we will not be made to carry something on our head too. You are the wind and we the tree leaves, but you can blow only yellow leaves away. We are a floating log, but like the high tide you can wash us away. Although they be our children, although they be our wives, if any of them commit a crime,*[31] *we agree it is a crime." Then said again the Kasiang Salapang, "We take you as our lord. Only we ourselves make you our lord, not our possessions. You may not take chickens from our coops, take eggs out of our baskets. You may not take even one coconut or cluster of areca nuts. If you desire our possessions, you buy them at a fair price, you replace them with what should replace them, you request what is appropriate you request, and we will give it to you. You cannot just seize, just take our possessions." The* karaeng *agreed.*[32]

This manuscript describes in some detail the principles that would govern the new kingdom the *tumanurung*, Karaeng Bayo, and the lords of Gowa established. The Bate Salapang were careful to limit any arbitrary actions their ruler might commit, but they also acknowledged that they submitted to him as loyal servants eager to do his bidding. The Bate Salapang recognized the rank of the *tumanurung* and Karaeng Bayo as higher than their own, and as signs of their status surrendered part of their followers to serve the ruling couple. This is a crucial point: white-blooded rather than red-blooded, the new rulers were of a fundamentally different status from the lords of the Bate Salapang or any existing Makassarese ruler. This history elevated the rulers of Gowa above all others. Though the founding of Gowa described here purportedly took place in the fifteenth, fourteenth, or an even earlier century, its visible social effects date from when it was inscribed in writing. There was a fundamental difference between an oral *tumanurung* myth, similar in kind to dozens of such tales in South Sulawesi, and a history establishing and preserving that myth in a written, sacred manuscript.

The history of Gowa's founding at the hands of the *tumanurung* and Karaeng Bayo, and the belief in the white blood possessed by their descendants, gave the rulers of Gowa a claim to dominate the sixteenth-century present. The perhaps surprising and widespread acceptance of this claim among Makassarese stems, I believe, from the incontrovertible fact that it was contained in sacred manuscripts. The histories recounted within these manuscripts shared in that aura of power; being written made it so, however alien that seems to skeptical modern historians accustomed to adjudicating between fact and fiction. Moreover, as Gowa and Talloq grew in size and power beginning in the early sixteenth century, their very success and the increasing wealth and influence of their *karaengs* verified the truth of the history they had made.

The belief that Makassarese society was governed by a noble class who had inherited the white blood of the *tumanurung* was a conception of society that written histories created. A social order dividing Makassar into clearly demarcated commoner and noble classes, finer layers within the nobility, and presided over by the august rulers of Gowa and Talloq was made possible by the presence of new forms of written histories. To contemporary readers this may seem to claim too much for written manuscripts. But as earlier chapters described, Makassarese give manuscripts as spiritually powerful objects a significance that I, for example, do not. The cultural position that manuscripts occupy in early modern Makassar made them historical agents capable of effecting such social changes. So too the tremendous importance Makassarese placed on the past in general, and on origins in particular, further made written histories efficacious historical agents and the development and spread of written histories an important social force in early modern Makassar. This pride of place does not belong to *patturioloang* enshrining *tumanurung* tales alone, however. As significant in shaping social change and increasing social hierarchicalization in Makassar were written genealogies.

Making Nobles Noble

The ability of new ways of writing about the past to concretely effect how Makassarese imagined their society is most apparent in genealogies. As the previous chapter discussed, the creation of elaborate genealogies in Makassar stemmed from the period after literacy began. In contrast to many oral societies, apparently Makassarese did not orally compose, remember, or chant royal or clan genealogies. With the advent of literacy, however, increasing numbers of people clustered around Makassarese courts began to keep close track of genealogical information. The genealogical paring in *patturioloang* mentioned in chapter 2 is useful to recall here, for it provides an important clue about why Makassarese kept *patturioloang*. The concept of inherited rank, which became increasingly significant in early modern Makassarese life, meant that one's status derived from ancestors. Genealogies were vital because they allowed Makassarese to trace their ascent up to prominent ancestors. To have illustrious ancestors, according to Makassarese cultural logic, meant by definition that one had inherited some of their might and prestige. The increasing social hierarchicalization visible in sixteenth- and seventeenth-century Makassar was predicated on genealogical claims.

This section looks at three ways in which genealogies fueled increasing social hierarchicalization in early modern Makassar. First, and in conjunction with the ideology of white blood inherited from *tumanurung*, genealogies supported a more elaborate division into narrowly gradated social classes. Second, written genealogies encouraged a reconceptualization of kinship categories and relations, resulting in a more complex understanding of Makassar's social order. Third, the possession of manuscripts containing genealogies itself indexed rank and social privilege in Makassar.

The establishment in Gowa of the *tumanurung* myth was the founding charter explaining and justifying a new social order. It also provided the necessary ideology to reconceptualize all Makassarese as being naturally ranked depending on the amount of white blood they possessed, or on the lack of white blood in the case of those who can now be referred to as "commoners." This social reconceptualization, however, required the means to trace descent over many generations in order to track the flow of white blood. The proliferation among "nobles" of written genealogies enabled this reconceptualization to take place. Genealogies provided raw data about descent, marriages, and offspring, preserving a wealth of information with the precision necessary to distinguish reliably between, for example, third and fourth cousins of a prominent noble, or to discriminate between the grandchildren of a Makassarese noble by his noble and commoner wives. More significantly, it made it possible to give social meaning to these distinctions.

As figure 7 suggested, Makassarese came to see fundamental differences between social classes. Among the nobility, for example, there were four main classes: *anaq tiqno* or full white-blooded nobles; *anaq sipue* or "half" white-blooded nobles; *anaq ceraq* or nobles with mixed red and white blood; and *anaq karaeng sala* or "false" nobles. A given noble's rank was determined by the rank of his parents. Thus parents of *anaq tiqno* must themselves both have been *anaq tiqno; anaq sipue* were most commonly the offspring of one *anaq tiqno* and one *anaq sipue* or *anaq ceraq*, or an *anaq tiqno* and a commoner, but may also have been descended from one *anaq sipue* and one commoner or one *anaq tiqno* or *anaq sipue* and one *anaq karaeng maraennaya* (a local lord not descended from the *tumanurung*, such as one of the original Bate Salapang); *anaq ceraq* were the offspring of one *anaq tiqno* or *anaq sipue* and a commoner; *anaq karaeng sala* were the the offspring of an *anaq sipue* or *anaq ceraq* and a slave. Below this hierarchy of nobles was a class of local Makassarese lords, known as *anaq karaeng maraennaya*, who were descended from families who ruled before the coming of the white-blooded *tumanurung*. Below them were commoners *(maradeka)* and below them slaves *(ata)*. This complex calculus, though certainly more rigid and rule bound in this anthropological chart than was probably the case in Makassar, was a model of a society that depended upon genealogical information. The creation and acceptance of the ideology of white blood, coupled with the details genealogies provided, made envisioning this new social order possible. Its creation, of course, depended not only upon changing cultural evaluations and ideological values, but on the power and wealth to enforce them. Nevertheless, power and wealth alone do not lead to reimagining an entire social order, and the ideological changes that took place in early modern Makassar were not derived simply from economic forces.

A significant token of how successfully this ideology of white-blooded descent became in Makassar is the practice, still common today, of explaining unexpected success or accomplishment by reference to unknown ancestors. If by virtue of talent or diligence a Makassarese achieves a level of success or importance that exceeds what is typical for someone of his (rarely her) rank, especially among commoners, Makassarese cultural logic explains this by positing that the person in question undoubtedly inherited the blood of a forgotten but noble ancestor. In them this noble blood "surfaces." This explanation resolves anomalies, reinforcing the belief that social position derives from the quality of the blood individuals inherit.

Makassarese looked beyond their parents to more distant ancestors to define their social rank. The rank Makassarese could claim also depended on the renown of ancestors to whom links could be traced. Blood transmitted nobility, and the more far-flung and exquisite a genealogy, the more replete with links to rulers and nobles of Gowa, Talloq, and other major polities, the more impressive the social position of that Makassarese. Makassarese nobles striving to outdo their similarly ranked rivals became aggressive genealogists, eager to incorporate as many prominent Makassarese figures as possible as relatives. Predictably, this activity sometimes led to creative fabrications. Among the Bugis, powerful families throughout South Sulawesi incorporated childless Arung Palakka into their genealogies, thereby enhancing their social status by enhancing their descent.[33] In a *Maros Chronicle* written in the nineteenth century to provide Maros' rulers the same luster and pedigree as the rulers of Gowa and Talloq, not one but three *tumanurung* are incorporated into the tale. The first *tumanurung* appeared in Pakere, a small community within Maros. The second *tumanurung* appeared in Pasadang, another small Maros community, and was adopted by the first *tumanurung*. The third *tumanurung* appeared in Asaqang, a Maros community, but had previously descended in Luwuq, the most ancient and prestigious of all South Sulawesi kingdoms. This third *tumanurung* married the second, and their offspring became the rulers of Maros.[34] The *Maros Chronicle* not only incorporated the *tumanurung* tale leitmotif of the Gowa and Talloq *patturioloang,* but creatively incorporated an even more ancient and illustrious *tumanurung* from Luwuq into the rulers of Maros' ancestry.

Genealogical rivalry and positioning progressively shaped Makassarese politics. As the pace of commercial activity at Makassar increased over the course of the sixteenth and seventeenth centuries, the fruits of this activity enriched Makassarese society, but did so unequally. Along with the prestige that high rank brought, the profits and possibilities wealth brought sharpened Makassarese desires to maximize their social position. Competition between nobles of similar rank was keen as they jockeyed for advantage in the effort to achieve a higher status, itself the key to wealth and influence. For those who failed, the price was rapid social demotion, particularly evident in the next generation of offspring, whose rank often was defined by the combination of an unsuccessful and uninspiring father and the lower-ranking wife he was able to attract. For those who succeeded, the rewards included grants of titles, lands, wealth, and the likelihood of an excellent marriage that would enhance the rank of one's children. There was little room for lateral movement; with the finite rewards available, a few enjoyed the opportunity to rise, while most were consigned to social demotion.

In this developing social order, expanding one's links to the powerful in the present and the prestigious in the past was the foundation for political prominence. Makassarese created many ways to form links establishing or reinforcing social ties. Adoption by one family of the child of another created a strong bond between two sets of parents. Having children from different parents nursed by the same woman and thereby sharing her milk created a future tie between these "milk-siblings." Nobles lending their names or simply selecting names for the offspring of their clients strengthened the bond between nobles and their followers. All these created very real social ties, but none were as strong as blood. All were important mechanisms, in other words, but none were as important as marriage.

In this genealogically dependent social order, marriages became crucial. Through an analysis of the ranks and titles of offspring in the Gowa and Talloq *patturioloang,* David Bulbeck argued that both the father's and mother's rank played a part in determining the rank of a given person.[35] This argument, based on contemporary historical sources, matches well the formal description of Makassarese society depicted in figure 7. The father's rank seemed to be of slightly greater significance than the mother's, probably because it was more variable. Nevertheless, status rivalry in Makassar centered on the politics of marriage. Marriages in general, and women in particular, were key links in the chains between past and present through and along which white blood traveled.[36] It should come as no surprise, then, that early modern Makassarese created an elaborate body of guidelines and cultural beliefs surrounding this politically charged institution. Indeed, it is to this period of genealogical proliferation and social hierarchicalization that we can trace many of the "rules" anthropologists have identified as most consequential in guiding Makassarese social life. Two in which marriage plays a central role are of particular consequence: first, that women's rank is fixed; second, that important political positions are reserved for those of high rank.[37] In both cases these are better thought of as originating in what Christian Pelras calls "spontaneous patterns" and not "consciously articulated models."[38]

One of the most commonly encountered statements of anthropologists who have worked in South Sulawesi is that, unlike men, women cannot by accomplishment and ability raise their status beyond their birth rank. Men can achieve higher status; for women, rank is carefully ascribed. Moreover, whereas men can take wives who are either higher or lower than their putative rank, women cannot marry someone of lower rank. That is, accomplished men can raise their status and marry women of higher rank, while men of poor ability are likely to marry a woman of lower rank. Put still another way, wives mark the status of their husbands. Women and their ascribed rank became the stable measuring stick by which the deeds and status of men could be judged. An oral history from the Malay community in Makassar illustrates well how men were barred from marrying women of higher rank. In this story a Malay in Sanrabone named Datuq Panlautia fell in love with a noble Makassarese woman. He went to a Makassarese-Malay official, the translator and intermediary *(juru bahasa)* of the ruler of Sanrabone, to ask for his aid in securing the betrothal. But her father, Karaeng Agangjeqneq, and the other Sanrabone nobles forbade the marriage because he lacked noble Makassarese blood. Then one day Datuq Panlautia performed a great deed, proving, according to Makassarese logic, that he must indeed have had an unknown Makassarese noble ancestor. With this the Sanrabone council met and decided that according to their written laws, such an accomplishment proved his worth, and they were allowed to marry.[39]

The creation of a cultural "rule" that the status of women was fixed and that they could not marry men of lower rank clearly served noble Makassarese men well. It provided a fixed standard by which the success or failure of their status rivalries could be judged and acknowledged. In one modern example, a Makassarese man is allowed to hold a traditional office to which his wife has a genealogical claim. But at her death, or in the event of divorce, the husband loses that right and must abdicate.[40] Women, however, were never simply passive participants in the machinations of fathers and husbands. If the activities of men focused on the everyday world of political advance, social improvement, and economic profit, the activities of women focused on future generations. Women, it seems, manipulated marriage for their own purposes. The Gowa court *lontaraq bilang,* another important repository for genealogical information, contain abundant examples not only of marriages and offspring, but of divorces as well. No stigma was attached to divorces in Makassar; typically a neutral verb describes how the man and woman "split from each other" *(sipelaq).* The privileging of men and their desires that some might expect in an Islamic society is absent. Put simply, noble Makassarese women used marriages, divorces, and children to position themselves within future genealogies as critical links to renowned ancestors.

A recurring pattern in the *lontaraq bilang* is divorce and remarriage in rapid succession. One of the noblewomen about whom we know a substantial amount is Karaengta ri Bontojeqneq. The following entries from the *lontaraq bilang* recount her involvement in Makassarese marriage politics.

August 1628	Karaengta ri Bontojeqneq was born [to the ruler of Gowa Sultan Malikussaid and a commoner wife who also gave birth to a future ruler of Gowa, Sultan Hasanuddin].
3 September 1646	The ruler of Bima I Ambela married Karaeng Bontojeqneq.
13 December 1651	The future ruler of Bima Mappatabung Nuruddin was born [the son of I Ambela and Karaengta Bontojeqneq].
23 January 1653	Karaengta ri Bontojeqneq had a daughter named Sitti Aminah.
22 April 1654	Karaengta ri Bontopaqja Maemuna was born [the daughter of I Ambela and Karaeng Bontojeqneq].
8 December 1655	Karaengta ri Bontojeqneq arrived from Bima.
11 November 1656	Karaengta ri Bontojeqneq had a daughter named I Cinra.
27 March 1658	Karaengta ri Bontojeqneq and the ruler of Bima divorced.
20 June 1658	Karaengta ri Jarannika [the brother of Karaeng Lengkeseq] married Karaeng ri Bontojeqneq.
3 January 1660	Karaengta ri Jarannika and Karaengta ri Bontojeqneq divorced.
19 April 1661	Karaengta ri Jarannika and Karaengta ri Bontojeqneq divorced.[41]
4 June 1662	Karaengta ri Bontojeqneq was banished down to the house made of *kerasaq* wood.
18 September 1662	The ruler of Sumbawa married Karaengta ri Bontojeqneq.
3 February 1663	The ruler of Sumbawa and Karaengta ri Bontojeqneq divorced.
10 February 1663	Daengta Daeng Mattiro [a son of Karaeng Karunrung] married Padukka Dompu [a daughter of the ruler of Bima I Ambela and Karaengta Bontojeqneq].

25 November 1664	Tumamenang ri Lakiung [the future Sultan of Gowa Abdul Jalil] married Karaengta ri Bontomateqne [a daughter of I Ambela and Karaengta ri Bontojeqneq].
30 January 1665	Karaengta ri Jarannika and Karaengta ri Bontojeqneq divorced.
4 February 1669	Tumamenang ri Lakiung and Karaengta ri Bontomateqne [a daughter of Karaengta ri Bontojeqneq] divorced.
8 February 1669	Karaengta ri Bontojeqneq died at age forty-one.
10 May 1669	Tumamenang ri Lampana [the ruler of Gowa Sultan Harunarasyid] married Karaengta ri Bontomateqne [a daughter of Karaengta ri Bontojeqneq].

During her lifetime Karaengta ri Bontojeqneq married and divorced four times, twice to rulers of overseas kingdoms within Gowa's political ambit (Bima and Sumbawa) and twice to Karaengta ri Jarannika, one of the foremost nobles in Gowa. Although her motivations are not explained in the text, their overall effect is clear: they placed Karaengta ri Bontojeqneq along the lines linking future generations with powerful forebears. The rulers of Bima would trace their ascent through her, and had the marriage not failed, the same might have been true of later rulers of Sumbawa and even Gowa through her daughter's marriage to Tumamenang ri Lakiung. Though they produced no children, Karaengta ri Bontojeqneq's two marriages to Karaengta ri Jarannika were strategic and potentially of enormous significance. In fact, Karaengta ri Bontojeqneq was apparently active in court politics, forcing her brother Sultan Hasanuddin to temporarily exile her in 1662. Karaengta ri Bontojeqneq also supervised politically important marriages of her daughters from her first marriage. One married a son of Karaeng Karunrung, the dominant figure at the Gowa court and in Makassarese politics for more than two decades. Another daughter was married to a son of Karaengta ri Bontojeqneq's brother Sultan Hasanuddin. Offspring from this marriage of first cousins would have been influential and high-ranking figures at the Gowa court, but the marriage failed shortly before Karaengta ri Bontojeqneq died. Undaunted, her daughter married the ruler of Talloq three months later.

Karaengta ri Bontojeqneq was not the only Makassarese woman to manipulate the politics and possibilities of marriage, offspring, and divorce. The political aspirations and marriage of Karaeng Bontolangkasaq in the early eighteenth century were opposed by the wife of the ruler of Sumbawa, who first resisted giving her daughter in marriage to Karaeng Bontolangkasaq, then divorced the ruler of Sumbawa and married Karaeng Bontolangkasaq's archrival, Sultan Sirajuddin of Gowa. In the sixteenth century, the most famous example is a woman who became known as "the repeating widow" *(balu maqlonjoka)*. Balu Maqlonjoka was the daughter of Tunipasuruq, the ruler of Talloq, and his wife, Karaeng Makeqboka, a sister of Tumapaqrisiq Kallonna, the ruler of Gowa.[42] Tumapaqrisiq Kallonna's son Tunipalangga ran off with Balu Maqlonjoka without her father's consent, angering Tunipasuruq and eventually leading to war between Gowa and Talloq. Ultimately the two wed and produced six children. In 1565 Tunipalangga died invading Boné, and his brother Tunibatta became Karaeng Gowa. Seven nights after Tunipalangga died, Balu Maqlonjoka and Tunibatta married. He too marched off to war against Bone, only to be beheaded forty days after becoming ruler.[43] Although the repeating widow's tragic misfortune is emphasized in the *patturioloang*, we should acknowledge her political astuteness in first running off with Gowa's future ruler and certainly in marrying a second ruler of Gowa.

The expansion of a political and social order in which marriage and descent were critical shaped how noble Makassarese women sought influence both in the present and in the future by becoming ancestors linking later generations with influential forebears. As Nancy Florida reminds us, histories are often made with an eye toward how those in the future will read the past.[44] Central to these marriage politics was the cultural determination that the rank of women must be fixed and that noblewomen not marry men of lower status. The byzantine political machinations of early modern Makassar depended upon these decisions, which themselves became imaginable with the proliferation of genealogies beginning in the late sixteenth century.

A second Makassarese cultural "rule" based on ideas about white-blooded descent in which marriage was a vital factor reserved political positions within the expanding kingdom of Gowa for those of high rank. As Gowa began to extend its influence in the early sixteenth-century reign of Tumapaqrisiq Kallonna, and as commerce increasingly brought new trade goods and traders, new offices were created to manage the growing empire. Some, such as the position of harbormaster, were typically held by lower-ranking nobles and never became the preserve of high-ranking nobles. But as David Bulbeck has argued, several other offices did become the domain of nobles with *karaeng* titles.⁴⁵ The most important of these was *tumabicarabutta,* whose task it was to assist the ruler of Gowa as regent and chief adviser. When Tunijalloq became ruler in 1565, Tumamenang ri Makkoayang was appointed to be the first *tumabicarabutta.* According to the *Talloq Chronicle,* "With the death of Tunibatta, he [Tumamenang ri Makkoayang] was installed in Gowa as the speaker of the land by the people of Gowa alongside Tunijalloq."⁴⁶ As rulers of Gowa and Talloq, Tunijalloq and Tumamenang ri Makkoayang worked closely together. They are even described in the *Gowa Chronicle* as ruling jointly *(mabali gauq),* and during their reigns they established the foundation for the close partnership between Gowa and Talloq. This pattern of the ruler of Talloq advising the ruler of Gowa became the norm in the first part of the seventeenth century. The ruler of Gowa Tumamenang ri Gaukanna was assisted by the ruler of Talloq Karaeng Matoaya, and this relationship was perpetuated under their sons Tumamenang ri Papambatuna and Karaeng Pattingalloang.⁴⁷ Dutch records frequently refer to the ruler of Talloq as the "elder king" whose wisdom tempered the impetuous behavior of the younger Karaeng Gowa. With a few exceptions in which other powerful Gowa *karaeng* held the office, the ruler of Talloq or his son consistently served as *tumabicarabutta* for Gowa.

Another important office was the *tumailalang,* the trio of ministers (literally, "the person on the inside"). From the title it appears that the *tumailalang* were in charge of managing everyday affairs within Gowa. According to the *Gowa Chronicle,* there was a joint *tumailalang-sabannaraq* office during the reign of Tumapaqrisiq Kallonna. During the subsequent reign, Tunipalangga separated these offices, and by the reign of Tunijalloq there were two *tumailalang,* later known as the elder *tumailalang toa* and younger *tumailalang lolo.* The link between high rank and the *tumailalang* office apparently stemmed from an agreement forged between Tunijalloq and Tunikakasang, the ruler of Maros. As the *Gowa Chronicle* recounts, "There Tunijalloq and the Karaeng Maros swore oaths to each other. Spoke the Karaeng Maros to Tunijalloq, 'As long as your descendants become *karaeng* [of Gowa], so too you will raise my descendants to become *tumailalang.*'"⁴⁸ As Bulbeck notes, by the seventeenth century all holders of the *tumailalang* posts were high-ranking *karaengs.*⁴⁹ The creation of the positions of *tumabicarabutta* and *tumailalang* was not haphazard, but intimately tied to the developing logic that the ideology of white blood mandated. Makassarese believed that to hold one of these offices meant being of high rank and white-blooded descent, while to be of such high rank and pure descent qualified one to hold such an office.

Little to this point has been said about the expanding system of titles that ordered and ranked the Makassarese nobility. The variety of titles used by leaders of small polities is bewildering: *anrongguru, dampang, gallarrang, jannang, kare, kasuiang, lao, loqmoq, todo,* and more besides. All were local titles Makassarese used before the rise of Gowa. Gowa's expansion brought some systematic order to this variety. In more than one case, Gowa conquered a smaller Makassarese polity and "demoted" its ruler by taking away the title he had used and giving him another. For example, after Gowa conquered Parigi, to help prevent any resurgence of resistance to Gowa, the new ruler of Parigi was installed with the lower title *anrongguru* in place of the title *karaeng* borne by previous rulers.[50] Similarly, after Bontonompo was conquered, its ruling title was changed from the relatively prestigious *kare* to *anrongguru*.[51] On the other hand, Gowa could reward allied rulers by raising their titles and hence their status. Pattalassang, for example, originally ruled by a *kare*, came to be governed by a *karaeng*.[52]

Granting titles was an important method of establishing and recognizing a given person's and a given community's place within society. Ideally, but not always in fact, this hierarchy of titles corresponded to the natural hierarchy of white blood that nobles possessed. Distinguishing nobles from commoners, for example, was the right to have a royal or *daeng* name as well as a personal name. Distinguishing lower-ranking nobles such as *anaq ceraq* from higher-ranking nobles like *anaq tiqno* was the latter's right to a *karaeng* title. Granted by the ruler of Gowa, *karaeng* titles not only signified the bearer's accepted high status, but were often toponyms that gave the bearer the right to demand tribute and labor from the community of that name. When in 1669 Sultan Hasanuddin's son, later known as Sultan Abdul Jalil, ceremonially had a royal umbrella raised over his head in an installation rite in Sanrabone, he simultaneously became Karaeng Sanrabone and received that area as an appanage. The first ruler of Gowa whose daeng name and *karaeng* title is known was Tumapaqrisiq Kallonna (Daeng Matanre, Karaeng Manngutungi), whose reign was also the first extensively described in the *Gowa Chronicle*. The link between systematic use of *daeng* names and *karaeng* titles and the history of white-blooded rulers descended from the *tumanurung* in the *Gowa Chronicle* was not fortuitous. White blood, high rank, and having a *karaeng* title became isomorphic in early modern Makassar.

By that same time the Bate Salapang council of nine *gallarrang* who had originally installed the first Karaeng Gowa had all but disappeared. The position of *pacalla* or leader of the Bate Salapang had in fact been eliminated; in the twentieth century it was resurrected to mean a kind of sheriff. The *gallarrang* remained as local lords, but they had little or no role to play at Gowa's court or in the administration of the kingdom. White-blooded *karaeng*s now occupied those positions. In the Gowa court *lontaraq bilang,* a register of who's who in Makassar, only very rarely are *gallarrang* or other local lords mentioned, testament to their declining significance.

This close association between the prestigious descent that genealogies established and holding important positions within Gowa extended to the very peak of Makassarese society. At some point during this evolution the decision was made that only *anaq tiqno* could inherit the thrones of Gowa, Talloq, Maros, and other major polities. The *Maros Chronicle* frankly explains that in one case, "a person named I Mappasosong Daeng Pabunduq, he always wanted to be made *karaeng* by the Dutch, but it was forbidden by Maros *adat* and the seven *gallarrang*. Because I Mappasosong Daeng Pabunduq was not *anaq tino,* he could also not inherit the *karaeng*-ship of Maros."[53] In Gowa, and perhaps in Talloq and Maros as well, only male *anaq tiqno* could inherit the throne. The origins of this gender bias, so stark a contrast with Bugis Boné and its female rulers during the same era, is unknown. As a principle of inheritance, however, the determination that only *anaq tiqno* could become rulers of Gowa was well established by the seventeenth century. Ideally, it assured that a son of the ruler by his highest-ranking wife would inherit the throne. Indeed, at the installation ceremony of a new ruler, the custom began of formally recognizing and honoring his principal wife if she was of equally high rank. Circumstances arose, however, in which it was impossible to follow this principle governing who was *anaq tiqno* and who could inherit the throne. While Sultan Malikussaid, who ruled Gowa from 1639 to 1653, became ruler, "because he was the only child by a wife of equal rank [with Tumamenang ri Gaukanna, his father]," Sultan Malikussaid himself died without leaving children of *anaq tiqno* rank. Before his death, Sultan Malikussaid chose his son Karaeng Bontomangape as his heir. Thus the son inherited the throne not because of his pure descent, but "because he was the child that was entrusted [with the task of ruling]."[54] Among some Gowa nobles there was bitter opposition to being placed under the authority of a person with less pure white blood than their own. Some wanted the ruler of

Talloq, also a direct descendant of the *tumanurung,* to become the ruler of Gowa. The ruler of Talloq, Tumamenang ri Bontobiraeng, however, defended the choice of Karaeng Bontomangape, and with the former's weight behind the nomination, Karaeng Bontomangape was installed as Sultan Hasanuddin, the sixteenth ruler of Gowa. In the future the "rule" that only an *anaq tiqno* could become Karaeng Gowa faced other moments where a compromise with ideals was necessary. During the 1710s, for example, many Makassarese supported the noble but not *anaq tiqno* Karaeng Bontolangkasaq in his effort to usurp the throne of Gowa from Sultan Sirajuddin, another ruler whose claim to the throne was of dubious validity. Yet more telling than the compromises that historical circumstances forced upon Makassarese is the depth of this cultural belief that only those of the highest rank were appropriate and fit holders of the most important position in the land.

It is in the growing corpus of genealogies that the significance of historical literacy is most evident. Writing was not just a memory aid making it possible to record more information, as has so often been argued. The significance of writing was not in its capacity to supplement memory; oral specialists are capable of tremendous mnemonic feats. Rather, in Makassar genealogical writing created a new social role for the past. It created the reason to record more, and in more detail with ever more focused categories and definitions. Literacy does not mechanically and automatically lead to the rote recording of information for its own sake. Instead, literacy in Makassar changed how the past was first viewed and then put to use. It is from this novel perception and use of the past that social consequences flowed. Writing down histories changed the role the past played in the present. Important social changes in early modern Makassar were rooted in this change in historical consciousness. The establishment of a more elaborate division into narrowly gradated classes based on descent was thus one important change written genealogies effected, but it was not the only one.

Shifts in how Makassarese conceptualized kinship categories and relationships accompanied the development of the finely graded social hierarchy that *patturioloang* and genealogies encouraged. The nature of the shift from oral memory to written genealogies in Makassar can be seen most clearly in the category of *sampu* (cousin). Asked today, almost any Makassarese can name dozens of his or her cousins. The category is flexible and inclusive, capable of assimilating a host of relatives. But when asked about a particular cousin, that same Makassarese will typically have to think for a few moments, tracing mentally the kinship tie they share, and consult another relative before being able to pronounce with certainty that the cousin in question is a second, third, or fourth cousin. In the oral world of everyday life there is little need for precision; "cousin" is a handy catch-all category.

The contrast could not be stronger in the case of written, noble genealogies. Here the difference between a second or third cousin of a *karaeng* had important implications. The same was true of distinctions between full siblings and half siblings. The prerogatives one could claim as a full sibling of a ruling *karaeng*—in terms of gaining prestigious titles and desirable appanages and of influence in decision making and the range of available marriage partners—were significantly better than what was available to half siblings. So too with first, second, third, and fourth cousins. Closer kinship meant purer white blood, higher rank, and all the benefits that flowed from them.

With the advent of literacy and the proliferation of written genealogies, the oral world of "cousins" was increasingly replaced among the nobility by more carefully graded kinship categories. The ease with which written texts could preserve, order, and indeed create complex kinship relations was one of the gifts of literacy.

A text relating the first marriage ties between the ruling family of Gowa and the ruling family of Bima is an excellent example. The genealogy the text relates begins fairly simply. The ruler of Gowa Tumamenang ri Gaukanna (r. 1593 to 1639) ordered a noble from Bima to marry his sister-in-law. The noble did so and they had a son who married the niece of the noble's first cousin, the daughter of Tumamenang ri Papambatuna (r. 1639 to 1653). They had a daughter who had no children but who did have a half-sister who married four times in succession. The fourth marriage produced a daughter whose husband was related to her in three ways: she was simultaneously his second cousin, the third cousin of one of his parents, and his fourth cousin. In other words, depending on which path one traced through her genealogy, her husband could be located in at least three places. In fact, depending on which path one traced, she and her husband could be considered of the same or of different generational layers. The story continues with a son of theirs who married a woman who was simultaneously his second cousin, fourth cousin, and his father's second cousin. At this point the text ends with the admission, "There are other relationships too which are just not mentioned."[55]

Such a genealogical reckoning is likely to be impossible in an oral culture. As chapter 3 mentioned, Makassarese prefer broad kinship categories, in part because they are so much easier to use, in part because fine gradations serve no purpose among commoners, and in part because such a system allows Makassarese to easily include others and thereby expand their network of relations. Makassarese, for example, refer to everyone in the generation above them except their parents as *toa* and everyone in the generation below them except their children as *kamanakang*. Without exception, everyone in their grandparent's generational layer is referred to as *puri*, while everyone in their grandchildren's generational layer is known as *cucu*. Makassarese can navigate large networks of relatives using these broad conceptual categories.

With the evolution of written genealogies these categories become more refined. Makassarese today still use these broad terms, but when pressed to be more precise they can specify whether a given person is a second or third cousin, for example. This change, I believe, is produced when genealogical charts become the medium on which kinship relations are inscribed. Roger Chartier asked how material forms affect meaning.[56] How did words inscribed on paper for the first time begin to shape historical consciousness? What are the effects of the presence of this new medium? A genealogy written out as a tree or chart, as a vast web of individuals arranged by generations and linked by marriages and births, provided a novel way of conceptualizing one's relations. Being able to unroll a genealogy on the floor and trace relationships with such specificity created, I believe, a new way of thinking about social relations. Seeing one's kindred arranged on paper was vastly different, we must assume, from how nonliterate Makassarese thought about their kindred.

Conceptually, then, the proliferation of written genealogies among what would become the Makassarese nobility spurred the creation of a new way of envisioning social and kinship categories and relationships. Imagined in this way, society could become much more differentiated and relations between two individuals much more complex. This pattern may well resonate throughout the archipelago. Among the Gayo, Bowen identified a connection between political centralization and genealogically framed histories that legitimized authority by referring to the unbroken tie linking past and present. "Political centralization brought with it pressures to render genealogical and unequivocal the history of the ruling line."[57]

Most Makassarese, however, did not have genealogies and were not literate. This difference, as the last section on white blood suggested, erected and maintained a clear social barrier. Those below it had became commoners, those above it, nobles. Within the ranks of the nobility, the information in genealogies was crucial to distinguish between, say, *anaq sipue* and *anaq ceraq*. The fabric of Makassarese social life, and the political and economic opportunities that stemmed from high status, came to be based on these distinctions. For commoners, however, it mattered little whether a given noble was *anaq sipue* or *anaq ceraq*. This distinction had no practical meaning. What distinguished commoners from nobles was not the contents, but the possession of written genealogies. Like other manuscripts that contained the past and preserved it into the present, genealogies were spiritually powerful objects. Their existence conferred importance and prestige on their guardian owners. In those rare cases where commoners came to possess a written text, the manuscript was venerated and surrounded by rituals marking its separateness and acknowledging the power within it. Even if commoners did not own and could not read manuscripts, or perhaps in part because of these very facts, they knew that the manuscripts nobles possessed were powerful and granted their possession enormous social significance. Far more than with *patturioloang*, which were rare and rarely seen manuscripts, the proliferation of written genealogies was a tangible marker separating noble and commoner. The carefully limited and guarded presence of manuscripts policed the boundary between social classes, becoming a crucial instrument in the evolving social hierarchicalization that characterized early modern Makassar. However, it was not commoners alone who saw written texts as sacred objects. As the next section explores, nobles, too, increasingly sought to possess the past contained in objects, a practice that had remarkable social repercussions.

Possessing the Past

One of the more extraordinary effects of writing histories was that it objectified the past. What had hitherto been passed down and received in oral traditions was now codified and preserved in manuscripts. The past, incarnate in manuscripts, could now be held in the hand and seen with the eye. Significant again here is the Makassarese sense that written histories preserved the very past and brought it into the present, rather than merely representing a past that was forever removed. The past was not a foreign country. The idea that the past could be possessed reinforced interest in collecting the objects in which the past adhered. Manuscripts containing historical texts—*patturioloang*, genealogies, *rapang*, *lontaraq bilang*—were the most obvious repositories of the past that

Makassarese sought to collect. But as we saw in the oral histories presented in chapter 3, other sacred objects also acted as repositories for the past. This section considers the practice of collecting and possessing these objects of history in early modern Makassar, and in particular the overarching effects this had in elevating the social position of rulers.

There is debate among historians about the relative importance of rulers and regalia in South Sulawesi. Leonard Andaya argued that sacred stones *(gaukang)* were the objects around which communities formed and that sovereignty rested within these objects. Rulers were in fact guardians or custodians of the *gaukang,* on whose behalf they governed.[58] Campbell Macknight disputes this interpretation, maintaining that *gaukang* in particular and *kalompoang* in general should be considered popular magical objects rather than significant loci of political activity.[59] The most detailed anthropological investigation of *kalompoang* has been carried out by Martin Rössler. He concludes that in the face of the expansion of secular Indonesian administration, the role of regalia as the key legitimizing focus of rulers' political authority has declined, though on a personal level many Makassarese still have faith in the sacred power of *kalompoang.*[60] Part of the difficulty when considering Makassarese *kalompoang* may be the dehistoricized nature of the debate. Certainly the role of *kalompoang* and rulers could have changed over time. I argue that during the sixteenth and seventeenth centuries rulers eclipsed *kalompoang* as the anchors of Makassarese society. After the fall of Gowa in 1669, however, and in an era when Gowa was dramatically weakened and much of Makassar subject to Dutch colonial intrusions, *kalompoang* again surpassed rulers as the centers of Makassarese society. In other words, a persistent theme not only in scholarship about South Sulawesi but in Makassarese history itself is ambiguity about the relationship of rulers to regalia.

Imagining the mental landscape of fifteenth-century Makassar is a daunting task. There are no authoritative sources to cite, no definitive assertions that can be made. A valid starting point may be the recognition that early modern Makassarese did not share our modern view that human subjects dominate the world around them. Makassarese saw the need to ensure that their lives harmonized with the supernatural rhythms, the cycles of lucky and unlucky days, whose existence was a simple fact of the world. In Makassar, the physical landscape provided the anchors that framed people's lives. Like other Southeast Asians, Makassarese saw the landscape not as the inert backdrop that human subjects dominated and acted against, but as a world alive and with which they must reckon. A description of this veneration for the spirits of the land comes from Alfred Wallace's travels in Makassar. "At such times [stopping traveling to eat] my Macassar boys would put a minute fragment of rice and meat or fish on a leaf and lay it on a stone or stump as an offering to the deity of the spot."[61] Scattered across the Makassarese landscape were locations that held enormous power. Often marked by prominent trees, rivers, mountains, or other distinctive features, at these points dwelled spirits of the land who could, if angered or neglected, wreak havoc on humans. The world was not inanimate, but full of things that were alive. Many *kalompoang* were not manufactured krisses, banners, and spears, but stones, trees, and even unusually shaped tubers. Makassarese believed that unnatural human acts such as incest would invoke the wrath of the land itself, causing famine, epidemic, or other misfortunes. Other signs, including earthquakes and eclipses, were carefully watched as indicators of how the natural world judged human behavior; rulers in particular were sensitive to the fertility of harvests and animal life as indicators of the quality and continuing legitimacy of their rule.

In this world spiritual power was concentrated at certain locations and in certain objects. It is these objects, *kalompoang*, that concern us here. Often of heavenly origin, but in any case always found and never crafted by humans, these objects were repositories for mysterious spiritual power. Tales abound in Makassar about the supernatural behavior of *kalompoang*, such as banners that possess their bearers and force them to gyrate wildly, or *kalompoang* that move themselves from place to place.[62] This spiritual power derives from their origins, and in particular from their distant origins in place or time. Whether they came from far away (the Upperworld) or from the distant past (the foundation of the community), their presence as incarnations of those distant places or times made *kalompoang* the focus of ritual veneration.[63] To Makassarese, the links between wonder, strangeness, and power were evident. This sense is captured in an abandoned cannon on the grounds of the Gowa fort Somba Opu. Apparently one of the cannons used to defend the fort against the Dutch in the 1660s, the cannon is now considered a sacred presence from that distant past. Local inhabitants make offerings and burn candles on and next to it in an effort to tap the power present in the cannon. Originally, it seems, mere red-blooded humans had little power or significance compared to such objects. Made the focus of ritual, these objects bolstered the influence of ruling chiefs and were perceived as the legitimate political authority overseeing the welfare and autonomy of the community. Martin Rössler describes one community in highland Gowa today where the "*karaeng*'s house" is not the house of the *karaeng* ruling the community, but the house in which the *kalompoang* are kept. It is here in the *kalompoang* that the spirit of the local *tumanurung*, and real governing power, dwell; the *karaengs* who come and go over the centuries are earthly agents acting on behalf of the *kalompoang*.[64] It seems almost certain that *kalompoang* were regarded in the same way across Makassar's landscape of small polities before the rise of Gowa in the sixteenth century.

There is much in the investigations of Dutch colonial officials too suggesting that Makassarese at times treated *kalompoang* like sentient beings and as the center of authority within the community.[65] The use of objects as surrogates for people in general and rulers in particular is a practice found elsewhere in the archipelago.[66] The link between possession of regalia objects and social authority is also recurrent. On Bali, for example, Margaret Wiener describes powerful, named kris as "agents of social reproduction." The practices of caring for, venerating, and ritually handling these charged objects manifested, and through such display thereby produced, gender and rank hierarchy.[67]

In the case of Makassar, Dutch sources indicate that from early in their history Makassarese constructed and set aside rice fields, gardens, and fishponds for the support of these sacred objects. Farmers performed labor service for the *kalompoang,* and considered rulers to be the worldly caretakers of the *kalompoang* rather than the lords of these lands. Of course it was in Dutch interests to portray Makassarese rulers as despotic and rapacious, or as somehow illegitimate rulers who did not truly own the land to justify early twentieth-century Dutch plans to introduce a land-rent system that would systematize land rights and increase tax revenues. Nevertheless, there is no doubt that over the course of the sixteenth and seventeenth centuries, the rulers of Gowa gained power without precedent in Makassarese history and that an important pillar of their power was increasing the land and labor at their disposal. Forced resettlements and orders to perform services for the ruler were common occurrences during this period.

The two most revered *kalompoang* in Gowa had been brought by the founders of the kingdom. Tanisamaang, half of a golden chain, had been carried down from the Upperworld by the *tumanurung* when she appeared in Gowa. Sudanga, a sword, had been brought to Gowa by Karaeng Bayo's brother Lakipadada. Both were left behind for later rulers of Gowa. These two *kalompoang* typify the ability of regalia to make present distant places and times. Both came from far-off, unknown places, while their presence recalled the age of the *tumanurung* and Karaeng Bayo, when Gowa was founded. To possess these two items without being destroyed by them proved that one was of pure white blood and fit to govern Gowa. Indeed, one manuscript describing the split between Gowa and Talloq recounted that Tunatangkaqlopi had originally chosen Karaeng Loe ri Sero rather than his brother Batara Gowa to inherit the throne. Batara Gowa, however, seized the *kalompoang* while Karaeng Loe was hunting. When he returned, Karaeng Loe left Gowa in frustration and sadness at this irrefutable proof that he had lost the favor of the *kalompoang*. By seizing the Tanisamaang and Sudanga, Batara Gowa usurped the throne without bloodshed and was accepted as their lord by the people of Gowa.[68] Originally at least, the *kalompoang* were greater than any single ruler of Gowa, though white blood from the *tumanurung* flowed in his veins.

Although the most powerful of all the regalia, Tanisamaang and Sudanga were far from the only *kalompoang* in Gowa. Dutch scholars catalogued dozens of krisses, swords, spears, banners, and other objects held at the Gowa court that were believed to have varying degrees of sacredness and spiritual power.[69] Most had names, and often the history of each and how it came into Gowa was remembered. To this archive of objects Makassarese added written historical manuscripts. As powerful objects, written texts encapsulated, to use Drakard's phrase, the authority and presence of an absent ruler, "providing a material link with the divine powers" the ruler emitted.[70]

Written histories—genealogies, *patturioloang, lontaraq bilang, rapang*—also conveyed the past to the present. More than simple accounts of former times, Makassarese viewed these manuscripts as physical incarnations of the past, as past origins objectified. To this day many Makassarese jealously possess and guard these relics from the past. The contents may be of little note, or even completely unknown, but manuscripts written in *jangang-jangang, lontaraq beru,* or *serang* script and handed down through the generations are considered a sacred inheritance equivalent to the *kalompoang* preserved by noble families. In addition to this, however, the way in which written histories explicitly made it possible to hold words from the past in one's hands prompted the desire to possess the objects manifesting distant times and far-off places. Written histories changed how the past was viewed and available in the present. Put succinctly, collections of manuscripts spurred collecting other objects in which the past resided.[71]

A common lineament in the process of Gowa's political and military expansion in the sixteenth and seventeenth centuries was the seizure of other communities' *kalompoang*. The *Gowa Chronicle* records several instances. During the reign of Tunipalangga, for example, Gowa conquered and took the *kalompoang* of Lamuru. Tunipalangga "mastered Lamuru up to the edge of the Walanaya, then took *saqbu katti* [72] from them, took the sword of the ancestors of the people of Lamuru called I Lapasasri."[73] Histories, both written and oral, from many other communities describe the same fate. A manuscript recording an oral history from Bontonompo recalls the following events.

During the time of Kare Useng Daeng Malikai, the ruler of Gowa wanted Bontonompo to follow Gowa, but the people of Bontonompo did not follow. This caused a quarrel between the ruler of Gowa and Kare Useng Daeng Mailikai. A war took place. This was called the War of Mangasaya, the war between Kare Useng Daeng Malikai and the Karaeng Gowa. At the time of the War of Mangasaya, [Bontonompo] was conquered by the ruler of Gowa and the kalompoang *and the history "book" of Bontonompo were taken. At this time Kare Useng Daeng Malikai died, and the* kalompoang *and book were taken. Now Bontonompo followed Gowa.*[74]

A crucial element in Gowa's policy of expansion was to take the *kalompoang* of conquered communities back to Gowa to become part of the court regalia. In doing so, Gowa progressively gathered in one location the Makassarese sacred objects linking distant times and places to the present.

The cultural significance of collecting *kalompoang* went beyond the simple accumulation of sacred power. This theme is found throughout Southeast Asia.[75] In Makassar, the collecting of *kalompoang* taken from others by white-blooded nobles in Gowa and Talloq in particular had political and social dimensions. Culturally, the importance of the past for Makassarese identity, and the tremendous weight given to the words of the ancestors, meant that the accumulation of written histories and historical objects contributed to the fundamental redefinition of society taking place during the early modern era. Possessing the past became the distinctive hallmark for the new nobility. Possessing the past distinguished and elevated the rulers of Makassar's most powerful polities: most notably Gowa and Talloq, but also communities such as Maros, which grow in importance during the seventeenth century. Like the passage from oral to literate history-making discussed in chapter 3, changing ways of perceiving and organizing the past contributed to the rapid social hierarchicalization that took place in early modern Makassar.

By the seventeenth century, the rulers of Gowa and Talloq had gone far beyond acting as guardians and caretakers ruling on behalf of Tanisamaang, Sudanga, and the impressive collections of *kalompoang* each court had collected. The *kalompoang* were the possessions of these rulers, augmenting their sacredness and social position in the eyes of Makassarese. Rulers, in a sense, had become the foremost of the *kalompoang*. To commoners, their persons were sacred beyond measure, a perception originating in the ideology of white blood and continuously buttressed by rituals that constructed social reality in accordance with this perception. Rulers had eclipsed *kalompoang* as the most sacred objects in the land and as the central focus of social and political life. *Kalompoang,* as the possessions of rulers, very nearly approached the apt but unwitting translation of Dutch scholars describing them as "ornaments." Socially, rulers had become beings vastly different from and far above commoners. With this and their control and dominion over the past, rulers within Gowa and Talloq overshadowed sacred *kalompoang* as objects of veneration. This shift in where Makassarese looked to define the center of their social world was facilitated in critical ways by the objectification of the past in written texts and the urge to collect and possess the past that this objectification made possible. Yet this perception of rulers as the anchors of Makassarese society did not last.[76]

The Dutch and Bugis conquest and occupation of Gowa in 1669 had repercussions that went far beyond political and military defeat. In later imaginations and memories, particularly as Makassarese recognized that the events of 1669 were not the temporary setback that earlier defeats had been, the war became a watershed retrospectively separating a glorious golden age from a period of debasing colonial subjugation. It became, I believe, easy to contrast the political impotence of Gowa's rulers under Dutch and Bugis overlordship with undiminished faith in the power of *kalompoang*. The supremacy of Gowa's august *karaengs* gave way to an ambivalence in which rulers and regalia competed for the allegiance of the Makassarese people. One *lontaraq bilang* describes a series of meetings between not the rulers, but the regalia swords of Boné and Gowa in which the two were "laid side by side" five times between 1706 and 1730.[77] These acts were metaphoric and symbolic, but literal as well. *Kalompoang* among the Makassarese were regaining the centrality that Gowa's powerful rulers had usurped in the past two centuries. During the rebellion of Karaeng Bontolangkasaq, possession of the Gowa *kalompoang* was vital to gaining popular support in an era where no direct descendant of Sultan Hasanuddin held the throne. Messianic movements beginning in the middle of the eighteenth century focused on a series of figures of purportedly unknown origin who possessed Gowa's *kalompoang*.[78] By the end of the eighteenth century, the struggle for control of Gowa fought between the Dutch and Batara Gowa I Sangkilang, the leader of one such messianic movement, centered on control of the *kalompoang*, particularly Sudanga, as the source of sovereignty over Gowa.

The final chapter in this history of the changing places of rulers and regalia began with the death of the last *karaeng* of Gowa, Andi Ijo or Sultan Muhammad Abdul Kadir Aidid, in 1960. For those who are still connected to the palace and that lost social world, efforts to recall and preserve its values and customs are tinged with sadness and nostalgia. In this context, the events reported about a Friday night in the early 1970s take on a poignant meaning. At that time one of the last *karaeng*'s sisters died and was buried. That very night, a Friday, a small iron kris mysteriously appeared in the palace. Like the *tumanurung*, its origins were unknown but its sacredness undoubted. With no one to reveal its name, the kris is known only as Basi Manurung (the blade that descended), and it is now part of the Gowa royal *kalompoang*, kept in a safe, behind red curtains, on an elevated platform, in the innermost room of the palace. Bereft of their rulers, Makassarese at the Gowa royal palace today attach even greater significance to the *kalompoang*. Annual commemorations at Idul Fitri include an elaborate washing of the *kalompoang* by descendants of members of the royal family. One family member explained that even the *karaeng* did not sleep on an elevated platform, because then he would have been as high as or higher than the *kalompoang*, something inconceivable since Gowa's golden age in the seventeenth century. In the absence of living *karaengs*, *kalompoang* are the last remaining tangible incarnation of the illustrious past surviving in the present.

Conclusion

This chapter takes the position that written manuscripts are not simply inert reflections of changes and developments whose true causes lie elsewhere. Instead, I believe that written manuscripts, particularly in a culture, such as Makassar, that grants them such a prominent and potent place, have the power to effect changes in their own right. Makassarese manuscripts are not simply sources for historians to use, but agents whose nature and effects must be explored. In general, written *patturioloang* and genealogies influenced Makassarese society in three ways. First, the very presence of written manuscripts in a society where they were viewed as sacred and powerful objects ensured that they had tangible effects. Because Makassarese grant them such significance, those who possessed the past incarnate in texts possessed a legacy and fount of authority denied to those who did not. Second, the setting down on paper or palm leaf of histories that had hitherto been orally transmitted changed how people view the past and the present. To see genealogical relationships, to spatially reimagine Makassarese society, was itself a significant change in mentality and a transformation that altered social behavior. The volatile politics of marriage, offspring, and divorce so often identified as typifying Makassarese society, and the cultural guidelines governing these practices, stemmed from this period of historical literacy. Third, the presence of the past in written histories enhanced a disposition to view the past as something that could be possessed, whether in manuscripts or other sacred objects. Rulers in particular expanded their influence and further elevated their lofty social position by gathering these objects to themselves, turning the past into something over which they had dominion.

Cumulatively, these changes extended and refined the social hierarchy that would later be considered the definitive, "classical" social formation of premodern Makassar. Makassarese society had certainly never been egalitarian, but the differences separating rulers such as the nine *gallarrang* in the original Bate Salapang and their subjects was a matter of degree rather than kind. Most important, all shared red blood. The political landscape of pre-sixteenth-century Makassar witnessed the rise and fall of numerous small polities and federations. Their relatively small size and impermanence suggest that successful and ambitious men could attract followers and carve out domains of their own. The codifications and ideology of white blood in Gowa's written histories changed this landscape. Those of red blood were relegated to a lower social status, while those of white blood formed a new nobility far more elevated than earlier Makassarese rulers.

The ability of manuscripts to create and sustain particular visions of social relationships is a theme that resonates throughout the archipelago. Among the Minangkabau, for example, royal letters contained seals that graphically mapped relations between the ruler and subordinate lords, while the words within the manuscripts depicted the Minangkabau ruler as the wellspring from whom justice, blessings, and greatness flowed.[79]

On Bali princes composing court chronicles often referred to or borrowed from the *Babad Dalem* chronicle of the court of Klungkung. So too the *Babad Dalem* textually situated the island's main political actors in relation to the Klungkung dynasty. Both of these practices aided in "affirming that dynasty's centrality in constituting the order of society" by the nineteenth century.[80] Earlier still, O. W. Wolters has interpreted the *Sejarah Melayu* as, in part, an effort to textually link the new rulers of Melaka with the more ancient and prestigious kingdom of Srivijaya.[81] Further examples could certainly be cited, but the essential point is that the advent of literacy provided novel means with which to construct and buttress new social orders across the archipelago.

Against this theme can be juxtaposed a tendency in Southeast Asian historiography to explain social hierarchicalization as a process propelled by rising commerce and the opportunities it brought to new shores. This mechanical model of state formation and political centralization privileges economic forces as those most responsible for driving historical change, discounting other forces as derivative and secondary. Certainly it would be equally partial to regard economic forces as ephemeral, but room should be made in our historical imaginations for other views of historical change. This chapter, examining a society that placed importance on the past, emphasizes the concrete historical effects that resulted from the advent of written histories and the changes in mentality it catalyzed. The following chapter, focusing on the increasing political centralization in Makassar, considers a process parallel to the social hierarchicalization that marked early modern Makassar.

∞ 5 ∞

Historical Literacy and Gowa as the Center of Makassar

One of the great themes historians have found useful in explaining social and political change in early modern Southeast Asia concerns the catalytic events of expanding international commerce.[1] Put simply, ambitious rulers and would-be rulers along maritime trade routes benefited from a surge in world trade beginning perhaps in the fifteenth century. By providing facilities and controlling access to valued goods, these rulers grew wealthy in a way unavailable to their less strategically positioned rivals. From this new wealth flowed advantages as obvious as the ability to attract or pay large armies equipped with imported firearms and as subtle as the prestige that accrued to rulers of entrepôts frequented by Asian, Middle Eastern, and European traders. Across maritime Southeast Asia new states flourished that were more powerful, centralized, and larger than their predecessors. Toungoo Burma, Ayuthya, Melaka, Aceh, Mataram, Gowa, and others all flourished. But far more was involved in the creation of what many now consider "classical" states of Southeast Asia than simple military supremacy or political centralization.[2]

This chapter offers another interpretation of how one of these new states, Gowa, established itself in Makassarese minds as the center of Makassar. It is not the process of political centralization and its mechanics that concern us here, but a process we might call "centerization." Makassarese understandings of their world shifted from seeing it as a landscape of autonomous communities to one divided into a core and periphery. It is the naturalization of this perception that is at issue. How did Makassarese come to see Gowa as the natural center of the Makassarese world? Behind the word "Makassar" always looms the presence, the example, and the standard of Gowa. How this shift in perception came about is the focus of this chapter. Rather than tracing chronologically how Gowa became the politically dominant polity, I consider how Gowa became recognized as exemplary.

Clifford Geertz coined the term "exemplary center" to describe the way that Southeast Asian courts used ritual and pageantry in an act of cosmological self-fashioning by which they impressed themselves upon people's minds as the centers of societies.[3] Among Bugis the example is Luwuq, considered the land closest to the ancient origins and mythical beginning of Bugis history and culture. During the sixteenth and especially the seventeenth centuries Gowa came to be seen by most if not all Makassarese as the exemplary center of Makassar. As with Luwuq, this culturally based perception of Gowa as the locus of Makassar far outlasted Gowa's period of political, military, and economic dominance. To this day, Gowa is seen as the heartland of Makassar, while other communities are envisioned as peripheries in orbit around Gowa. Exemplary centers are not found, but constructed at particular historical moments, and this chapter explores the role of written histories in establishing and reinforcing this cultural perception.

At the dawn of the sixteenth century no single community dominated the Makassarese landscape. Nor did Makassarese see one community as its ancient homeland or as the location of their sacred origins, unlike the Bugis, who revered Luwuq. Yet two centuries later in Makassarese minds Gowa had clearly become the center by which other communities judged themselves and to whom they desired prestigious links. It is temptingly easy to assume that the creation of this perception was the simple by-product of Gowa's unprecedented military and economic might, which by the mid-seventeenth century had encompassed much of Makassar within its ambit. Certainly this might was not irrelevant, but establishing an exemplary center involved changes in mentality and in perceptions of the historical landscape of Makassar. In a world where the past was not distant and severed from the present, but an intimate and consciously acknowledged partner in present-day social arrangements, the battle for cultural centrality was a battle for control of the past.

This chapter argues that the advent, then manipulation of written histories offered Gowa an extraordinary opportunity to reshape how Makassarese viewed their political and cultural landscape. It did so in three ways. First, Gowa made explicit efforts to control how the past was interpreted and recollected in other Makassarese communities, especially the sacred objects that embodied that past, and these efforts had political ramifications. Second, the spread of written historical genres and motifs outward from Gowa prompted Makassarese to view Gowa as the measuring stick for other communities' histories. Third, the ability of Gowa to dominate and direct Islamic practices in Makassar, and in particular the historical interpretation of Islam's origins in South Sulawesi, further contributed to the perception that Gowa was the unique, exemplary center of Makassar.

CONTROLLING THE PAST

Chapter 4 alluded to the political implications and cultural meanings Makassarese attached to seizing and collecting *kalompoang*. It was argued that this activity helped heighten the social hierarchy in early modern Makassar, elevating the rulers of Gowa and Talloq in particular above other Makassarese. This section examines how seizing and collecting *kalompoang* also helped establish a political hierarchy across the landscape of Makassar. To understand this process it is necessary to grasp not only the sacred power that Makassarese saw in their *kalompoang,* but the way in which these objects became potent currency in rivalries between polities.

In an illuminating study, Richard Parmentier discusses how objects on Belau functioned as signs *of* history and signs *in* history. By signs of history he means those objects that by their iconic, indexical, or symbolic properties stand as markers recording or classifying the past as history. For example, postage stamps explicitly commemorate past events in the United States, while in Belau a rock or knife that was present at a past ritual or event brings to mind, when viewed or invoked, certain associations, feelings, and stories linked to that time. These objects of history, like *kalompoang* in Makassar, are conceptual anchors for history-making. Signs in history refer to those signs of history involved in contemporary social life. Modified, manipulated, contested, and concealed, contemporary signs in history are possessed and used to make political claims about the present based on the precedents and events of the past that these objects signify. As Parmentier puts it, on Belau, "physical objects, rather than linguistic discourse, function as both signs of history and signs in history." In contemporary Belauan political life, "ownership of these valuables and esoteric knowledge of their names, classes, and exchange histories are essential to the maintenance of the pervasive social stratification between high-ranking or chiefly families and low-ranking commoner families."[4]

Two extended and illuminating examples of how Makassarese *kalompoang*—signs of history—became signs in history asserting Gowa's centrality come from Bajeng and Baku. Bajeng, say its inhabitants, once was a polity as large and powerful as Gowa. Its might dated to the day a farmer named I Panai burned down a grove of trees so that whenever he awoke from a nap he could gaze unobstructed to locate his wandering water buffalo.[5]

He came awake from his nap and looked again toward that which had been burned. He was startled to see there was a small clump in the middle not consumed by fire. Then I Panai went to see. He saw in the middle a straight piece of black wood leaning there. It had a hole in the center from the bottom to the top. There was also a piece of black iron damasked with gold located close by on top of a stone. It was a hand span in length. He took those things and put the iron inside the hole. It fit perfectly. There appeared in I Panai's heart the feeling that perhaps it should be made into a blowpipe. Then he tried to shoot the blowpipe dart toward a heron. He was surprised and pleased because completely without aiming the heron was struck, and moreover the blowpipe dart returned into the center of that wood.

After the afternoon [had passed, I Panai] returned leading his water buffalo and carrying the sacred blowpipe. After tying up his water buffalo, he went to wash his feet, then ascended into the palace. He told Karaeng Loe of Bajeng, "I have found a sacred blowpipe." After hearing I Panai tell his tale, [Karaeng Loe] asked for the blowpipe and then went down in front of his dwelling to try it. Karaeng Loe of Bajeng too shot birds flying, frogs jumping, lizards running. All were struck when shot. Then he asked for that blowpipe from Panai. And it was given. The blowpipe was named I Buqle. The blowpipe dart never ran untrue. It struck everything.

Armed with the magical weapon I Buqle, Bajeng was invincible in battle. Karaeng Loe rewarded I Panai by making him the *karaeng* of Galesong.

Karaeng Loe had a daughter named I Naima, who grew up renowned for her beauty. Hearing of her, Tumapaqrisiq Kallonna, the ruler of Gowa, asked for her hand in marriage, but he was refused because Karaeng Loe did not want Gowa to absorb Bajeng. Angered, Tumapaqrisiq Kallonna and his warriors marched into battle against Bajeng but were defeated by the bravery of Bajeng's champions and the power of I Buqle.

Thus died one by one the people of Gowa. Sombaya [Tumapaqrisiq Kallonna] was routed. Those people of Gowa who still lived ran tumbling like chicks abandoned by their mother. Hundreds of people from Gowa died in the battle. If they had stayed, clearly all would have died too, because I Buqle did not shoot people in error. All were cut down. Of those people who returned from the battle, each told of the potency of the missile-weapon of the people of Bajeng called I Buqle.

Ashamed of this defeat but determined to triumph, Tumapaqrisiq Kallonna gathered his forces and attacked again, but with the same result.

The dead sprawled over each other, the wounded lay stacked against each other. The people of Gowa were pursued all the way to Bontonompo. In the battle in fact hundreds of people of Gowa were destroyed, killed when hit by I Buqle. After the people of Bajeng returned up to their community, Sombaya ordered that the dead be gathered there in a forest east of Bontonompo. The way people buried the dead was disorganized because they buried them hastily, fearing the return of the people of Bajeng.

Three more times Gowa attacked and was routed by Bajeng and I Buqle. Finally, with the counsel of his soothsayer, Boto Lempangang, Tumapaqrisiq Kallonna devised a scheme to defeat Bajeng. Pretending to be under a death sentence from Tumapaqrisiq Kallonna, Boto Lempangang fled to Bajeng and was given sanctuary. Karaeng Loe came to trust Boto Lempangang, and thus Karaeng Loe's fate was sealed. Though an ally of Bajeng, the ruler of Galesong (I Panai) secretly sided with Tumapaqrisiq Kallonna because Galesong was closer to Gowa than Bajeng. Karaeng Galesong invited Karaeng Loe to a feast and got him so drunk from palm wine that Karaeng Loe could barely move. At that moment Gowa feigned an attack on Galesong, and I Panai persuaded Karaeng Loe to lend him I Buqle to fight off the attack. Incapacitated himself, Karaeng Loe acquiesced but spoke these words:

"Only to you I lend this, but return it. If it is not returned here after you use it, forever down to your descendants may your lives deteriorate and come to misery, may you be without offspring, may you eat shit, may you wear fishing nets for clothes, may your homes be overturned, may you be cursed by the gods." But I Panai did not heed the curse of his former karaeng. *Karaeng Loe of Bajeng gave I Buqle to Karaeng Galesong. Immediately he mounted his horse and made off straight down to Sombaya of Gowa. Arriving before Sombaya, he went to pay homage and present I Buqle too.*

Possessing I Buqle, Gowa now easily had the power to defeat Bajeng in war. Karaeng Loe, however, knew that with the loss of I Buqle there was no reason to struggle against Gowa any longer, and he summoned his chiefs to counsel.

Now knew Karaeng Loe of Bajeng that he had been tricked by his former subject. He called all the Anrongtau. Then he told them, "Just now I Panai has made off with I Buqle. Sombaya of Gowa has been given it. Therefore it is no longer my kalompoang. *Bajeng has no* kalompoang. *All of you, you followed me precisely because you followed I Buqle. Now because it is now in Gowa, it is best if you all go down to Gowa and pay homage to I Buqle, because I will go far away: I will not return."* [6]

Commanded to follow Gowa because it possessed their *kalompoang*, Bajeng submitted to Gowa without further warfare. As suggested in the previous chapter, Makassarese considered *kalompoang* the sacred locus of their community, identity, and history. I Buqle was the cohesive force that held the people of Bajeng together, and it more than Karaeng Loe was considered the ruling force to which they owed allegiance. It was this loss that compelled the people of Bajeng to submit to Gowa and recognize its ruler as the lawful bearer of I Buqle and as their overlord.

A similar story explains how the people of Baku lost their *kalompoang* and with it their autonomy to Gowa. The community of Baku was founded after people from the area encountered a mysterious couple whose origins were unknown. The people installed them as the rulers of Baku and honored them with the title of *somba*. The new rulers settled in Baku and as the years passed had four daughters.

These rulers had several magnificent things, usually called by people kalompoang. *There was a sword, a trident, a crown, a* cinde *named Ularaq Tasampena Mamampang.*[7] *It was purportedly extremely potent, that* cinde. *If the* sombaya *was threatened it became a huge snake and ran amok. There were also warriors following [the* sombaya*], very brave and strong, who pulled out large trees like grass if they were clearing a path.*

This sombaya *had no quarrels and there were also no wars, because there were no communities they argued with. Crops flourished; so too did the animals. The people of the land were healthy and safe. There were no thieves in the community. There were no people who quarreled within the community. This community governed by* sombaya *of Baku was not very great in extent. It included Lappara, Datarang, Tomboloq, Pao, Mamampang, Bentengiya, Cengkong, Suka, and Balasuka.*

After [he ruled] some time, livelihoods were given to [his] children. They were four, all girls. The oldest was called Turilenrang. The second was named I Nagaulang. The third was called I Nela Daeng Lino. The fourth was named I Bunga Daeng Ngingtang.

Each of the four daughters grew up and married men from other communities. Each was then raised to become the karaeng *of that community and given one of the Baku* kalompoang *by their* tumanurung *parents. The four daughters became the rulers of Mamampang, Salassaq, Sapolambere, and Sapotanga.*

One day, [the sombaya*] gathered all four of his children and his sons-in-law, and too the people of the land, then said to each of his children, "Now all of you can each rule alone, even if I do not help you, because I have seen for each your manner of shepherding your subjects. I want now to go abroad to another community." Then [the* sombaya*] stood on top of a large stone; there [he] gave advice. He said, "O, my descendants, O my people of the land. If later suddenly I am gone, then after you must establish a ruler. If so, choose one of my descendants or someone bringing a character like me: with my prowess, my honesty, my justice, my bravery." Then there was a huge clap of thunder. The* sombaya *had disappeared. That place where [he] disappeared was named kampung Sombaya. The wife of the* sombaya *disappeared too. Then all the people of the community mourned for forty days and forty nights.*

After the people had mourned for some time came news to Mamampang, to Salassaq, to Sapolambere, to Sapotanga, to Pao, that there was purportedly a person found sleeping in a boat on the edge of the sea at Barombong. He was called Karaeng Bayo. Then Karaeng Mamampang, Karaeng Sapotanga, Karaeng Sapolambere, Karaeng Pao each ordered people to go see Karaeng Bayo. "Who knows? Perhaps he is really Sombaya of Baku." A portion of the people of Mamampang arrived at Barombong. They saw that it was indeed their karaeng *who had disappeared. They asked [Karaeng Bayo] if he would want to return to Baku. But he did not want to return. Then [Karaeng Bayo] was brought by the people of Barombong to Lakiung[8] because the Bate Salapang [of Gowa] wanted to join him with the* tumanurung. *After being joined together, [the Bate Salapang] wanted to install and make him* karaeng *of the people of Gowa. [Karaeng Bayo] said to the people of Gowa, "Wait first, because there is something I want to command taken from these people who have come." Then the people of Baku were ordered to return and bring their crown, trident, the two* cinde, *the sword. Then went back the people of Baku to bring all that they were ordered to bring. In seven days' time the people of Baku arrived bringing their* kalompoang. *Said [Karaeng Bayo] to the people of Baku, "Dwell here, you." But already sad-hearted they asked leave to go back to Baku. Then [Karaeng Bayo] was installed by the people of Gowa to become* somba. *This* somba *was the first in Gowa. The* kalompoang *stayed in Gowa.*[9]

Like the history from Bajeng, this history is about the loss of Baku's *kalompoang*, and indeed their founding lord, to Gowa. Significantly, this history of loss does not mention warfare and conquest. In both these stories it is not military conquest that leads to submission and recognition of Gowa's superiority, but the passage of sacred objects from one community to another. These histories communicate well both the central place *kalompoang* occupied as objects of history and their significance as objects in history.

The histories from Bajeng and Baku are not unique in Makassar. To return to the oral history of Pattalassang discussed in chapter 3, the Cinde there too functioned as both a sign of and a sign in history. As a sign of history the Cinde was the focus for historical recollection and ritual commemoration of the origins of the community. It brought the remains of the past into the present. As a sign in history, the Cinde was manipulated to create a close political alliance between Gowa and Pattalassang. The ruler of Gowa asked for and was given the Cinde, and in return he gave a banner named Alakaya to be Pattalassang's *kalompoang*. More than a ceremonial or symbolic nicety, this exchange of regalia bonded the two communities together. Through this exchange, the history of Pattalassang and the identity of its people became inextricably tied to Gowa. The two became, as Makassarese say, "of one *siriq* and one *pacce*." Other histories recall similiar events. Some, such as those telling of the regalia sword of Lamuru and the *kalompoang* of Bontonompo, describe Gowa's conquest and seizure of the *kalompoang* of Makassarese communities. In some, Gowa granted *kalompoang* to express kinship and create a lasting emotional bond with another community. Oral histories from Parigi, for example, recalled that Tumapaqrisiq Kallonna gave a peculiarly formed tuber named Lasikapa to a ruler of Malewang in thanks for his aid in defeating Parigi and Sapaya. To this tuber belonged a flag, also named Lasikapa after the tuber was lost, considered the foremost *kalompoang* of the area.[10] In addition to seizing *kalompoang* by force to subdue communities and create relations of master and servant, then, Gowa also manipulated *kalompoang* through exchanges with other communities to create bonds that approximated kinship. More like patron and client than master and servant, these links too established Gowa's importance and centrality in the minds of many Makassarese.

The connections examined here among sacred objects, sovereignty, identity, and history resonate throughout the archipelago. Margaret Wiener's description of the intimate connections between kris as objects and historical chronicles detailing the origins of a kin group shows important similarities with that of early modern Makassar. Similarly, the words of I Wayan Rekan, a Balinese historian, would surely have been understood by Makassarese: "When a lord conquered a neighboring area, he not only confiscated the *sawah* and the women, but the history as well."[11]

Individually, the loss of *kalompoang* to Gowa established a clear hierarchy of dominant and subordinate. For most communities, defeat in battle by Gowa and the subsequent surrender of tribute was ignominious, but it did not entail an absolute loss of sovereignty, identity, or self-worth. Certainly it did not mean permanent acknowledgment of Gowa's suzerainty. As entries in the Gowa and Talloq *patturioloang* make clear, rulers of Gowa had to conquer some areas two or three times. Military defeat was regrettable, but inherently fragile and subject to reversal. This process of defeat and revolt, of shifting alliances and sudden changes of fortune, is an apt description of much of South Sulawesi's past, where there was a constant ebb and flow of political power as polities sought to triumph over their rivals. Dominating historical memory in a very different way was the loss of *kalompoang,* an event likely to be irreversible. The loss of *kalompoang,* which was the locus for a community's identity and an object far surpassing gold in value, signaled and symbolized the

Figure 8. Offerings to *kalompoang* at the Gowa royal palace

community's subordinate status. Gowa, the possessor of the community's past, became the center to its periphery, the place where its past was located (figure 8). It was from the creation of this consciousness of loss and inferiority that Gowa's centrality grew. Collectively, the loss of *kalompoang* by so many communities established on a wider stage Gowa's centrality and claim to preeminence within Makassar. It is from such actions and realizations that exemplary centers are made. Yet as significant as *kalompoang* were as objects in history, Gowa built its new centrality on the spread of other kinds of history-making as well. It is to these that I now turn.

From "history" to "History"

This section explores the process by which Gowa and its history came to be acknowledged by other Makassarese as the measuring stick by which their communities and histories would be judged. In Dipesh Chakrabarty's words, Gowa became the "silent referent" or "master narrative" for all Makassarese history.[12] Gowa's "history" was turned into "History." This process of centerization had several components. First, genres of history-making, notably *patturioloang,* spread outward from Gowa, making Gowa's chronicle the archetype after which other communities would model their histories. Second, historical manuscripts spread outward from Gowa, a process that made Gowa the main geographical source for the sacred words of the ancestors. Third, Makassarese adopted motifs found in the *Gowa Chronicle* as the key tropes oral communities used to make histories from the past, again conferring on Gowa the recognition that it was the cultural center and most important polity in Makassar.

The *Gowa Chronicle* was the first Makassarese chronicle. The important polities that preceded Gowa's sixteenth-century rise—Siang, Bantaeng, Bajeng—did not write *patturioloang* or, from what we can determine, write at all.[13] By the late sixteenth century, Gowa, Talloq, then other Makassarese communities began to compose *patturioloang*. Their model and inspiration was the *Gowa Chronicle.* As chapters 2 and 3 argued, written historical *patturioloang* had a particular form that contrasted markedly with orally composed histories. With few exceptions, most *patturioloang* composed in Makassarese communities were pale imitations of the *Gowa Chronicle,* but they did share the form and concerns of that written history. In Bangkalaq, Binamuq, Camba, Cenrana, Galesong, Maros, Sanrabone, and possibly in other communities that came under Gowa's influence, Makassarese composed *patturioloang* that cast their past into the form first used in the *Gowa Chronicle*. To understand this development, I present translations of *patturioloang* from three of these polities: Sanrabone, Maros, and Binamuq. We begin with the *Sanrabone Chronicle*.

This is the story of the ancestors of the people of Sanrabone.[14] *Karampang Cambelo, he was also called Karampang Matowa. He was the* karaeng *who first established the settlement of Sanrabone. Before doing so he lived to the north in Majapai. Karampang Cambelo had a child named Tunilonjoq Kaparaqna. Tunilonjoq Kaparaqna made a treaty with Karaeng Tunipalangga [r. 1546 to 1565]. Tunilonjoq Kaparaqna had a child named Karaeng Masawayang. Karaeng Masawayang had a child named Karaeng Tunibatta. Karaeng Tunibatta had a child named Tumamenang ri Paralakenna. He was the* karaeng *for whom drums were beaten when he descended to the ground [from his palace]. He was the rich* karaeng *but he was killed. Karaeng Tunibatta was killed. He too was killed. Tumamenang ri Paralakenna had a child named Tumamenang ri Campagana. Tumamenang ri Campagana had a child named Tumamenang ri Batanna. Tumamenang ri Batanna had a child named Karaeng Puanna Ijenalaq. This ruler was deposed. He went over to Bali. Over there he died a death from disease. His personal name was I Kase. His royal name was I Daeng Talebang. These are the words about Karaeng Bambang. He was called I Pareqbawang. His royal name was I Daeng Tanitu. These are the answers that were given by Puanna Ijenalaq. This Karaeng Bambanga had a child named Tumamenang ri Paralakenna. Tumamenang ri Campagana left as an heirloom for descendants a quantity of gold: thirty-five kattis of gold. This* karaeng *was said to have seventy bearers for his golden crown. Tumamenang ri Paralakenna had a "Javanese" mother. Jawa Barusu was the name of her homeland. She was named I Gannaqbilang. This Tumamenang ri Paralakenna married a sister of Tunijalloq [r. Gowa 1565 to 1590]. She was called Karaeng Mapedaka. Her personal name, may I not be cursed, was I Tamakeqboq. They had as children [these sons]: Tumamenang ri Campagana, Karaeng Kassuwarang, Karaeng Tamaqdagang, Karaeng Manilingi, Karaeng Pasaraka, I Daeng Mani, I Daeng Mamempo, I Daeng Manyiko, Karaeng Bambanga.*[15] *Their daughter was named Karaeng Tajameng. Her mother was the grandparent of I Jamali. He was called Karaeng Manjalleng. His wives were named I Daeng Masiang, I Daeng Tojeng. He became the grandparent of I Tulung. Tumamenang ri Paralakenna died. Tumamenang ri Campagana inherited the throne. His personal name, may I not be cursed, was Manasurang. His royal name was I Daeng Maqnassa. He was the* karaeng *who married the full sister of Tumamenang ri Gaukanna [r.*

Gowa 1593 to 1639]. She was called Karaeng ri Tabaringang. Her personal name was I Calaqna. They had a child named Tumamenang ri Batanna. His personal name was I Bara. His royal name was I Kare Bandang. His sibling was named Karaeng Tamananga. His personal name was I Yanteng. His royal name was I Kare Daeng. His wife was Karaeng Bungaya. He was called the grandparent of I Mappasepe. He was the grandparent of Karaeng Balloq and I Tanicini. They had a child named Karaeng Bulo-Bulo, called I Banang. He [Tumamenang ri Campagana] also married again a child of Tumamenang ri Makkoayang [r. Talloq 1540 or 1543 to 1576] named I Kune Marusuq. They had two children. A daughter was named I Pucu. I Pucu was married by Karaeng Taipa, the first cousin of Tumamenang ri Campagana. They had a child named Karaeng Banyuwanyaraq, also called I Tanicini. Their son was the father of I Daeng Mabela. He [Tumamenang ri Campagana] also married again down in Segeri. Tumamenang ri Campagana was the brother of Karaeng Segeri The woman he married was called I Daeng Saraba. They had nine children: Karaeng Unti, he became the grandparent of Karaeng Bontotangga; I Daeng Mangalle; I Daeng Manjakala, the father of I Daeng Tuna; Daeng Manggapa; I Daeng Kombong, he became the grandparent of Karaeng Manilingi; I Bissu Karaeng; I Daeng Kalling; I Daeng Nicala; I Wantenaku, Patanu Biliq.

This chronicle describes the successive rulers of Sanrabone from the early sixteenth to the mid-seventeenth century. Unlike the *Gowa Chronicle*, the *Sanrabone Chronicle* does not begin with a *tumanurung* tale, nor does it include the extensive oral histories that the Gowa chronicler incorporated into his work. In fact there are virtually no traces of the themes and concerns that gave meaning and shape to oral histories: no mention of *kalompoang*, no story about how the community was founded. The *Sanrabone Chronicle* does evince the two most important hallmarks of Makassarese written histories: the past is structured by the lives of rulers, and there is an emphasis on recording genealogical information. Noteworthy too is that the chronicle begins and ends with Gowa. One of the earliest pieces of information the chronicle recalls is that the second ruler of Sanrabone, Tunilonjoq Kaparaqna, made a treaty with the ruler of Gowa, Tunipalangga. More significantly, the time period the chronicle covers closes with the deposition of Puanna Ijenalaq in 1658. The chronicle ends short of the reign of the next ruler of Sanrabone, Abdul Jalil, the son of Sultan Hasanuddin who became Karaeng Sanrabone in 1668 and Karaeng Gowa in 1677.[16] These same patterns of written composition and focus on Gowa are evident in the *Maros Chronicle* as well.

> *This is the story of the ancestors of the people of Maros. There was no wife, no children. It consists of Gallarrang Pakere and Daeng Masiang telling how Karaeng Loe of Pakere was the first ruler in Maros. He found a female* tumanurung *in Pasadang. He took and cared for her. Later a story was heard that the* tumanurung *in Luwuq had disappeared, descended in Asaang, and had two children. The youngest, he was married to the* tumanurung *in Pasadang. They had a son. He was named Sanggaji Gaddong. Sanggaji Gaddong had four children. The oldest was a daughter. She was named Karaeng Kasikeqboq. [The other three were named] Karaeng Loe; Karaeng Tapiye; Karaeng Loe of Marimisi, he was a transvestite. Sanggaji Gaddong died. Karaeng Loe became Karaeng of Maros. Karaeng Loe had a child Patanna Langkana. Patanna Langkana was a sibling of Tumammaliang ri Talloq. His mother was Karaeng Barasaq. Tumammaliang ri Talloq married Tunipasuruq [r. Talloq 1500s to 1540 or 1543]. They had a child named Tumamenang ri Makkoayang [r. Talloq 1540 or 1543 to 1576]. He it is told was said to have had twenty children. We do not know their names. Karaeng Loe the ruler of Maros died. Patanna Langkana became* karaeng *of Maros. Patanna Langkana had a child named Tunikakasang. Patanna Langkana died. His personal name, may I not be cursed, was I Mappasomba. His royal name was Daeng Uraga. He built Langkana.*[17] *It had twelve sections between rows of house poles. Patanna Langkana died. Tunikakasang became* karaeng *of Maros. Tunikakasang died. Tunipasuluq [r. 1590 to 1593] became* karaeng *of Maros. Now he Tunikakasang adopted Karaeng Tumamenang ri Gaukanna [r. Gowa 1593 to 1639] while Tumamenang ri Gaukanna was still small.*[18] *Tunikakasang died. A wife from Layu was also taken. He also went down to Gowa to marry. He married a daughter of Karaeng Patteqne. They had children I Daeng Kanite and the mother of Karaeng Banyuwanyaraq, I Maninrori.*

In both these two short texts, and in the third, the phrase "the story of the ancestors of the people of . . ." is an awkward translation of the Makassarese word for chronicle: *patturioloang*. Both begin, then, by stating clearly that they are *patturioloang*, like those from Gowa and Talloq. Unlike the *Sanrabone Chronicle*, but like the *Gowa Chronicle*, this *patturioloang* begins with a *tumanurung* episode. In this case, no fewer than three such heavenly beings are involved in the establishment of Maros. After this foundation the chronicle describes the unbroken line of ruling, white-blooded *karaeng*s. It also mentions politically and socially important marriages and ties to prominent nobles in Talloq and Gowa. For all intents and purposes the chronicle ends after the brief but turbulent reign of Tunipasuluq, deposed as ruler of Gowa, Talloq, and Maros in

1593. His successor is only alluded to, and the extensive information available about his descendants in the *Gowa Chronicle* is not mentioned.[19] Both the Maros and Sanrabone *patturioloang*, I believe, were composed shortly before or after Gowa nobles assumed their *karaeng*-ships. In the case of the *Maros Chronicle*, this probably took place at the beginning of the seventeenth century. The *Sanrabone Chronicle* probably dates from the decade between 1658 and 1668, when Abdul Jalil became ruler of Sanrabone. Less easy to date, and less impressive, is the *Binamuq Chronicle*.

This is the story of the ancestors of the people of Turatea in Binamuq. Karaeng Binamuq Pesoka, he had four children. One was called I Daeng Riolo. One was called I Daeng Bilusu. One was called I Daeng Tanga. One was called I Daeng Sarang. He had a child I Daeng Binamuq. His wife descended from Gallarrang Manngasa. He was the one who had a child Karaeng Malangkasaka. Descended from I Loqmoq ri Manngepe, he was the ancestor of Karaeng Empowa. He had a child Daeng Matayang, personal name I Tinggi. Katepaja was the ancestor of Gallarrang Pao. Karaenga Basanigaya, a child of Karaeng Loe ri Bantaeng, went down to establish a settlement at Binamuq. He had a child I Daeng Laisi, who had a child named Palakiparanga and the one called Babalaraukanga. Palakiparanga was called I Daeng Matamu. He went down to Talloq to marry. He married a child of Karaeng Tunipasuluq [r. 1590 to 1593]. They had a child I Mantakepayung. He aided Gowa [in war]. The one called Babalaraukanga, he was named I Daeng Manyere. He did not have any children. This is all.

Even shorter than the *Maros Chronicle*, this is the briefest *patturioloang* I have encountered. The only dateable reference is to a marriage with a presumably low-ranking daughter of Tunipasuluq who ruled Talloq, Gowa, and Maros in the early 1590s. The account was probably written in the early seventeenth century, then, but it is impossible to be certain. In any case, the writer may only have had a vague idea of what a chronicle was; this text in fact is little more than a king list that has been titled *patturioloang*. What is significant is certainly not the sparse historical and genealogical information it contains, but the effort at mimicry that it represents. Binamuq was never a prominent Makassarese polity and had little significance within Gowa's domain. Unlike in Sanrabone, which was closer to Gowa and more politically and economically important, in Binamuq what seems to have spread was not the chronicle genre of which the *Gowa Chronicle* was the archetype, but the *idea* of a chronicle. Peripheral though Binamuq was, marriage links to members of the Gowa and Talloq nobility must have provided the example and impetus to compose this "chronicle" in imitation of Gowa's. The reasons for doing so, however, were local.

The *Gowa Chronicle* reimagined the past in a way that emphasized the central place and importance of rulers, accentuating social hierarchy and contributing to a clearly demarcated social division between red-blooded commoners and white-blooded nobles. Within Gowa this way of perceiving and preserving the past in written manuscripts had social effects benefiting the new nobility in general and the rulers of Gowa in particular. The attraction beyond Gowa of this way of conceptualizing the past and making its implications manifest in the present must have been the recognition that possessing a chronicle modeled on Gowa's could have similar benefits in local communities. Wielded in local political rivalries, the claims made in *patturioloang* marked out local rulers as distinct, thereby elevating their social position above that of other claimants. The narrative efforts in each of the three short *patturioloang* to create an unbroken chain of rulers linking the origins of the community to the present represented the foundation for these political claims. Moreover, the physical possession of new, sacred *kalompoang* itself established these rulers as exceptional.

Eager to use Gowa's example to elevate their own social position, rulers in these smaller polities also benefited from forging closer ties to Gowa. This benefit surely helps account for the fact that all three short *patturioloang* record historical links with Gowa, and sometimes Talloq as well. There was, however, a deep ambivalence among Makassarese about relationships with larger and more powerful neighbors. On the one hand, Makassarese frequently saw relations between communities in terms of sexual rivalry, and they feared the loss of status and prominence that surrendering women to men from another community culturally implied. Furthermore, although marriage to white-blooded Gowa nobles raised the status of the offspring from these marriages, such ties made the community vulnerable to absorption if a powerful noble from Gowa later claimed the throne through such kinship links.[20] On the other hand, reluctance and fear were counterbalanced by the desire to form links with and thereby share in the obvious potency of prominent people, places, and objects. In this context, links with Gowa were prestigious and sought after.

As anthropologists have noted throughout South Sulawesi, the desire and attraction of highland groups in particular to the material goods and cultural embellishments that lowland polities offer is equaled only by their suspicion and desire to remain autonomous. This ambivalence often centered on the politics of marriage. Bugis rulers historically used marriages to solidify their influence over subordinate domains.[21] So important were marriages that a Bugis noble was described as having "three points" *(tellu cappaq)* with which to extend his influence: the point of his dagger, his tongue, and his penis.[22]

These three *patturioloang* evidence how local Makassarese created written histories of their own modeled after Gowa's *patturioloang*. Two other short *patturioloang* were apparently written as Gowa expanded and consolidated its hold over new regions. *Patturioloang* from Bangkalaq and Cenrana also follow in the footsteps of the *Gowa Chronicle,* but they were composed after these areas became *karaeng*-ships within Gowa.

This discusses the ancestors of the people of Bangkalaq.[23] It was the people of Kalimporoq who were the roots of these ancestors. It was the child of the Karaeng Kalimporoq who established a settlement in Mamampang He had two children, one daughter, one son. The daughter was named Batara Langiq. The son was named Saupalinge. Batara Langiq had a child Tunibatta. Tunibatta had a child Tumakajiang, and Tumakajiang established a settlement in Bangkalaq. He was called Latena Bangkalaq. Latena Bangkalaq had a child Tumalompoa Battanna. Tumalompoa Battanna married down in Gowa a daughter of Tunipalangga by Karaenga ri Biliq Tanngaya. The woman he married was named Daeng Mangamu. They had two children: one son, one female child. The male child, he was titled Karaeng Bangkalaq. The female child, she was Karaeng ri Garassiq. Because he was widowed by the child of Tunipalangga, Tumalompoa Battanna went up to Layu and married. They had one son. He was Karaeng ri Layu. He was the father of I Daeng Mangalle and I Repu. He [Tumalompoa Battanna] was widowed again by his wife from Layu. He went down to Gowa again and married a daughter of Karaenga Patteqne. They had children I Daeng Katite and I Maninrori, the mother of Karaeng Banyuwanyaraq.

This *Bangkalaq Chronicle,* which discusses six generations, is most concerned to locate the offspring of local people from Bangkalaq and two nobles from Gowa, a daughter of Tunipalangga and a daughter of Karaeng Patteqne. The genealogical information presented here, while briefly recalling an ancient movement from Kalimporoq, culminates in the creation of a new *karaeng*-ship as a result of intermarriage between this local family and the rulers of Gowa. The first Karaeng Bangkalaq was the son of the Bangkalaq lord Tumalompoa Battanna ("the person with the large stomach") and the daughter of the ruler of Gowa Tunipalangga (r. 1546 to 1565). As Gowa expanded in the middle of the sixteenth century, through intermarriage it elevated and in doing so incorporated this local lord into the evolving social and political hierarchy taking shape in Gowa. A similar process emerges in the *Cenrana Chronicle*.

This discusses the ancestors of the karaengs of Cenrana.[24] *To have a* karaeng *was desired by the people of Barasaq. A woman came up from Makassar and established a settlement. She was married by Dampang Darana. They had four sons; one was called I Langase; his royal name was I Loqmoq ri Marana. He married the sister of Tunikakasang [of Maros]. Her* karaeng *title was Karaeng Asekeqboq. They had four children: three daughters, one son. He was called I Daeng ri Ballaq Bulowa. He had a child I Lipo. One daughter, she had a child I Daeng ri Betaang. She became the grandparent of I Simibu. Another daughter had four children: three sons, one daughter. One was called I Daeng Manyampang. One was called I Daeng Maewa. One was called I Daeng Mapala; he had a child I Kare Suro. One daughter was called I Jaria. Her* karaeng *title was Karaeng Marana. She had a child Karaenga ri Cenrana. She married Karaeng Pakkaleballaka and had four children. One son, he was called I Daeng ri Mangkasaraq. One daughter was called the mother of I Marusuq. Another, she became the mother of Karaeng Bengo. Another daughter, she was married by Karaeng Buttatowa named Daeng Mangamara. She [I Jaria, Karaeng Marana] was divorced by Karaeng Pakkaleballaka. She married again with Karaeng Lekoqbodong, his personal name was I Sabali. He was a person from Gowa. They had two children: one daughter, one son. The daughter was called I Bissu Sunganga. The son was called I Mallewai. His royal name was I Daeng Maqnassa. His* karaeng *title was Karaeng Cenrana.*

The *Cenrana Chronicle* similarly tells of the ancestry of the first Karaeng Cenrana, who was descended from a Gowa noble (Karaeng Lekoqbodong) and a local woman from the Barasaq area. The chronicle spans five generations and represents a second example of Gowa's creating a *karaeng*-ship outside the Gowa heartland via marriage. As in the *Bangkalaq Chronicle,* here too a local lord was both elevated and incorporated into Gowa through marriage and the establishment of a new *karaeng* title. Both *patturioloang* provided for these areas what already existed in Gowa: a history made to answer the questions the chronicle genre posed about the past. The *Bangkalaq Chronicle* is equivalent in this sense to the *Gowa Chronicle,* but inherently subordinate too. The Gowa example, and the fact that Gowa nobles were asking these kinds of questions, prompted the writing of this "chronicle." It thus had different concerns from oral histories. It is not about the origins of the community, but the origins of a new *karaeng*-ship. It is the social fact of the existence of such a text that is most vital. It may signify the perception that part of being a ruling *karaeng* meant possessing just such a written history. In this important sense *patturioloang* resemble the Balinese histories that Henk Schulte Nordholt termed *"negara*-building texts."[25] Here too, then, written *patturioloang* emerged as objects in history entangled in political claims and contests.

In the case of the Sanrabone, Maros, and Binamuq *patturioloang,* local rulers eager for the benefits that links with Gowa might bring mimicked the *Gowa Chronicle*'s socially and politically useful reconceptualization of the past. In the case of Bangkalaq and Cenrana, it seems that Gowa played a more insistent role in providing the impetus for the writing of a chronicle in areas newly incorporated into Gowa's expanding empire. In both situations, given that the model or in some cases the idea of a chronicle did spread beyond Gowa and that it was a desirable tool in the hands of local rulers, the question is what concrete effects did this change in the perception and use of the past have?

A difficult but essential point to grasp is that the narrative vision of written *patturioloang* had the power to shape thought and lives in early modern Makassar. In the Malay world, Amin Sweeney has argued, writers did not sit down before blank pages free to write what they wished; instead they were constrained and guided by patterns and expectations that reassembled events to fit these schematic structures.[26] Literary models shaped how the past was perceived and organized, helping to bring about an albeit imperfect correspondence of fact and concept. The influence of such schemes need not be conscious or even remarked upon. Indeed, as through marriage local Makassarese communities became acquainted with the history of the past that Gowa's rulers had made, and as they adopted it to enhance their own standing in local political contests, local rulers implicitly but irrevocably made Gowa the center to their periphery.

Mimicry by definition establishes a hierarchical relationship of superior and inferior. Adopting the idea of a chronicle, and even imitating its narrative form, aided local rulers in domestic political rivalries by giving them an innovative and prestigious claim on the past. It also meant recognizing the *Gowa Chronicle* as the archetypal (even if unread) model for their own past and Gowa as the preeminent polity by which they would be judged. Seeing the past in a new light meant revising perceptions of the present. Gowa, for example, is the one community present in the histories these five *patturioloang* recount. Part of the significance of the past in other Makassarese communities now derived from the presence of Gowa. Furthermore, acknowledging Gowa as the master referent for their past meant acknowledging Gowa's centrality in the social and political landscape of Makassar. Texts do not simply reflect, but actively create the worlds of which they are part. In this context, Pierre Bourdieu's comments about the symbolic power of words applies equally well to the symbolic power and social currency of *patturioloang*. "The symbolic efficacy of words is exercised only in so far as the person subjected to it recognizes the person who exercises it as authorized to do so, or, what amounts to the same thing, only in so far as he fails to realize that, in submitting to it, he himself has contributed, through his recognition, to its establishment."[27] More colloquially, by conceding the playing field established by Gowa, other communities accepted the guidelines of how the past should be construed, and of what a polity should be, that Gowa determined.

A critical measure of the degree to which other Makassarese communities established the authority and preeminence of Gowa is the cessation of chronicle writing that accompanied the Makassar war. Not only did chroniclers cease adding reigns to the Gowa and Talloq *patturioloang* after the 1669 catastrophe, but chroniclers outside Gowa and Talloq ceased as well. Both the Sanrabone and Maros *patturioloang,* for example, end before this defeat, even though both areas lay outside the areas immediately under Dutch control after the war. In these communities too, an era had passed and with it the social order that *patturioloang* envisioned and upheld. What should we make of this fact? The contention here is that this narrative correspondence between the *Gowa Chronicle* and *patturioloang* from other communities was not mere literary device or coincidence, but a social fact indicative of changes in how Makassarese perceived their own social and political world. This world was now anchored in Gowa.

Patturioloang were not the only literary historical product that spread outward from Gowa and in so doing encouraged acknowledging Gowa as the center of Makassar. In addition to the idea or model of *patturioloang,* physical manuscripts dispersed outward as well, and to similar effect. An extraordinary story of how Gowa provided other communities with manuscripts comes from beyond Makassar. A Makassarese version of a Mandarese history describes—from a viewpoint clearly favorable to Gowa—how the Mandarese community of Balanipa borrowed the written customs and laws of Gowa. The text tells of a Mandarese champion, later known as Tudilaling or "the person who brought," who as a young man journeyed to Gowa and took service with the Karaeng Gowa. After living there for many years and distinguishing himself in battle, he took leave and returned to Balanipa. Shocked by the cruelty of Mandarese customs after his long presence in Gowa, he sent an envoy to ask the ruler of Gowa to give Balanipa Gowa's customs and laws. In this excerpt, the Karaeng Gowa instructs the Gowa *gallarrang* to record this information for Balanipa.

Spoke the karaeng *of Gowa to the* gallarrang, *"It is not wrong if you provide him with what has already been written so that nothing is forgotten." Answered the* gallarrang, *"Good,* karaeng*." The* kajaowa *took paper and wrote all that the* karaeng *related to the* gallarrang. *Said also the* karaeng, *"It is better if we provide paper containing the* adat *that is customary in Gowa; so too the laws and customs of Gowa, so that it too becomes the heritage of the people of Balanipa." Then instructions were given to the* gallarrang: *the* adat, *laws, and customs of the people of Gowa that are written [should be copied]. The* lontaraq *was written and given by the* gallarrang *to the* karaeng. *After receiving the* lontaraq *the* karaeng *of Gowa asked, "Is absolutely all of the customary* adat *of the people of Gowa inside?" Answered the* gallarrang, *"Yes,* karaeng, *it is." Asked again the* karaeng, *"Are also the laws inside?" Answered the* gallarrang, *"They are,* karaeng*." Then spoke the* karaeng *to the nephew of I Puang ri Pojosang, "Bring this letter to your* puang, *Mandar. It is all inside. This is the compass day and night of the people of Gowa. This letter is called* lontaraq*."*[28]

The "*adat*, laws, and customs of the people of Gowa that are written" refers to what Makassarese called *rapang* and *parakara*. *Rapang* were compilations of the words of revered ancestors, especially rulers, advising their descendants how to behave. *Parakara* were legal guidelines that most commonly concerned inheritance rights, property protection, and criminal penalties. Their authority derived from the fact that they were considered to set forth in writing the most ancient practices of the community. They defined what behavior was demanded of Makassarese, spelled out what constituted an infraction, and prescribed punishments for violators. *Parakara* established guidelines describing how the property and children of divorcing parents was distributed, how debts must be handled upon someone's death, and the like. They began to be written in the seventeenth century, but would have their heyday in the eighteenth and nineteenth centuries.

Together, *rapang* and *parakara* are among the most common types of text found in Makassarese historical codices. Short and separated into individual articles, they were easily and frequently copied. In his *Makassaarsche Chrestomathie* Matthes gave samples of each, but these are in fact only the tip of the textual iceberg.[29] Particularly when it comes to *rapang*, hundreds of different articles can be found in Makassarese historical manuscripts. Two impressive collections are found in a pair of late-eighteenth-century manuscripts. The first, ANRI 62/1, contains more than three hundred *rapang* and *parakara* articles. The second, ANRI 8/16, contains more than forty large folio pages of *rapang*. As mentioned in chapter 2, even a cursory examination of several different *rapang* manuscripts displays the same pattern. Composed cumulatively, Makassarese added the sayings and advice of local ancestors and renowned figures to the "core" *rapang* articles copied from other manuscripts. If they are read side by side, a picture quickly emerges of just whose advice and guidelines constituted this core. Without exception, every *rapang* manuscript I consulted contains the words of Gallarrang Manngasa of Gowa, Karaeng Matoaya (r. Talloq 1593 to 1623), Tumamenang ri Bontobiraeng (r. Talloq 1641 to 1654), and the Islamic *syekh* (Sufi adept) Tuanta ri Dima. Nearly every manuscript contains the words of Tumamenang ri Taenga (Karaeng Bontosunggu, the brother of Karaeng Karunrung and a powerful noble in the mid-seventeenth century), Tumamenang ri Lakiung (r. 1677 to 1709), Tumamenang ri Ujung Tana (a Gowa noble), and Karaeng Sumannaq (another powerful mid-seventeenth-century Gowa noble). A variety of other figures appear, and many *rapang* are attributed only to "the ancestors" or "the learned one" or are "something I heard." But without exception, the words of this small group of renowned leaders from Gowa and Talloq were recorded. Not only were seventeenth-century Gowa and Talloq the focal point of a cultural dynamism that other scholars have noted,[30] but the guidelines and advice seen as particularly valuable and forged during this period reverberated across the Makassarese landscape. As much as anything, the words of its foremost nobles made Gowa exceptional.

The results are similiar, if less dramatic, for *parakara* manuscripts. In the same manner, a body of regulations first written in Gowa seems to have been copied from manuscript to manuscript and made its way with slight emendations across the landscape of Makassar. The significant point here is not only that written manuscript traditions spread outward from Gowa, but also that Makassarese came to see Gowa as the heartland for what the Mandarese text calls "*adat,* laws, and customs."[31] Whether or not these regulations and guidelines were followed is beside the point; certainly the spread of these texts did little to reduce the local variety and cultural particularities that characterized early modern Makassar. Gowa's customs were not adopted wholesale. What is significant is the recognition in other Makassarese communities that Gowa's historical legacy was somehow unique or privileged and that it possessed a resource or represented a locus of cultural values and ideas. It is from such recognitions that Gowa gained its position as an exemplary center.

In addition to inspiring historical *patturioloang* modeled on its own, and in addition to becoming the focal point for the production and spread of *rapang* that carried the past into the present, Gowa provided motifs for oral history-making that further conferred on Gowa the recognition that it was the center of Makassar. Of the many oral histories available in Makassar, a surprising number bear the unmistakable imprint of historical tropes and themes elaborated in the *Gowa Chronicle*.

The most evident feature of the *Gowa Chronicle* that became widespread throughout Makassar was the motif of a *tumanurung* descending and founding a new kingdom. As suggested in chapter 4, this myth may have been a local oral tradition enshrined in writing when the *Gowa Chronicle* was first written, but it belongs to a large family of similar oral traditions and beliefs in South Sulawesi. Stories of mysterious beings who descend from the Upperworld or, among the Bugis, ascend from the Lowerworld, are common throughout the peninsula. The chief features of the *tumanurung* tale in the *Gowa Chronicle*— appearing suddenly, bearing magical objects, marrying a local lord, having offspring who become the first rulers of new kingdoms, disappearing suddenly— appear in a wide array of variations in South Sulawesi oral traditions. Indeed, the general theme of a mysterious stranger coming from afar, marrying into the local nobility, and founding a new line of rulers is common far beyond South Sulawesi and may be, as Marshall Sahlins suggested, a narrative plot describing the origins of kingship in many human societies.[32] To cite but one Indonesian example, the *Hikayat Aceh* incorporates two such tales, with one brother marrying a princess he finds in a clump of bamboo, a second brother marrying the youngest of seven sisters who descend from heaven.[33] In the case of Makassar, this motif may have been borrowed from Luwuq, generally regarded as the oldest major polity in South Sulawesi and one whose rulers claimed descent from a *tumanurung*. Whatever the ultimate origins of the myth, what is at issue is how this narrative trope, once objectified in sacred manuscripts in Gowa, gained a new status and currency in Makassar.

That the version of this common tale written down in Gowa did indeed spread to other communities is beyond doubt. Martin Rössler has argued that the idea of the *tumanurung* as the fount of political legitimacy spread from Gowa to the Makassar highlands.[34] In Kasepekang it became an important pillar of political legitimation, granting a unique social position and authority to one favored descent group. Not only the *tumanurung* motif spread and became useful, however: the title *karaeng*, the veneration of *kalompoang* bequeathed by the *tumanurung*, and the belief that *kalompoang* were the social center of the community took root as well.[35] Rössler believes that Kasepekang incorporated this form of history-making into the fabric of social life because the area was integrated into Gowa's empire. In this Kasepekang resembles Bangkalaq and Cenrana, two *karaeng*-ships Gowa established. By way of contrast, the more distant area of Kajang was never similarly integrated, and there different founding myths, titles, and the comparatively minor political significance of *kalompoang* suggest that this part of Makassar remained largely beyond Gowa's influence.[36]

Ambitious local Makassarese leaders found that the *tumanurung* motif, like *patturioloang*, provided an interpretation of the past that helped distinguish and elevate them above others. As Rössler writes,

Especially in Kasepekang, the rise of a new kind of political authority which, as in Gowa or other kingdoms in South Sulawesi, was legitimated by sacred heirlooms, obviously resulted in a general increase in social differentiation, since it fostered the rise of a nobility as well as the development of bilateral descent groups among commoners, which not only are ranked, but also are internally differentiated as regards 'degrees' of descent. That these developments were stimulated by external influences is in the main corroborated by the fact that, aside from some rather vaguely worded legends about the alleged local origin of kalompoang *and political leadership, there are many traditions indicating that both of these institutions were widespread in the highlands because of a close relationship between Kasepekang and Gowa.*[37]

The *tumanurung* motif provided what Pierre Bourdieu called "symbolic capital."[38] Perceptions are the building blocks of social and political reality, and the way in which the *tumanurung* motif offered a construction of the past was instrumental in effecting social change. As with the idea and model of the chronicle and manuscripts themselves, this motif almost certainly spread along the paths that marriage links established.

This spread did not take place evenly, but happened as Gowa's political and economic influence spread and was cemented by kinship ties.

The evidence Rössler collected about the Gowa highlands may help explain the historical background behind the widespread proliferation of oral histories throughout Makassar about the origins of the *tumanurung*. Two good examples come from Bisampole, near Bantaeng, and from the Kajang highlands in eastern Makassar. The first tells of how fisherman from Bisampole saw an unknown person of noble countenance whose magnificent gold medallion blinded their eyes. The fisherman took the stranger to the house of Bisampole's lord, the Dampang Bisampole. The stranger reported that he was one of three brothers and that the other two had gone to Gowa and Boné. Shortly afterward the stranger disappeared, but he left behind as *kalompoang* a variety of statues, banners, and weapons. The people of Bisampole decided these were left behind to become the *kalompoang* of the kingdom of Bantaeng: whoever held and cared for them would be considered the ruler. The Dampang Bisampole therefore became the first Karaeng Bantaeng.[39] This story contains the essential elements of the *tumanurung* motif: a mysterious person of unknown origins appears, brings sacred objects that become the *kalompoang* of a new kingdom, then disappears from the earth. Like nearly all the *tumanurung* stories from Makassar, it also contains a link or reference to the *tumanurung* or to another ruler from Gowa.

In Kajang, a story tells of a childless couple who found a large piece of bamboo while fishing. It seemed empty, but after drinking water began to mysteriously disappear from their house when they were working in the fields, they discovered that a beautiful young *tumanurung* lived in the bamboo.[40] Eventually the husband married the *tumanurung* and had four misshapen children with her. Disheartened, the *tumanurung* left her husband and children and went to Sinjai, apparently married again, and had three children who became rulers of small communities. She left Sinjai and next appeared in Pallangisang, where again she had three children who became rulers of small communities. Finally, the *tumanurung* appeared in Gowa, where the ruler of Gowa was struck by her beauty and married her. They had nine children who grew up and became the Bate Salapang council ruling Gowa. Meanwhile, her first four children in Kajang also became rulers of communities.[41] While omitting the *kalompoang*, this story too tells how a mysterious being appeared, had children who became rulers, then disappeared. The first four misshapen children are reminiscent of Tumassalangga Barayang, the misshapen child of Karaeng Bayo and the *tumanurung* in Gowa who nevertheless became *karaeng*.[42] Like the *tumanurung* who first descended in Luwuq before appearing in Maros described in the *Maros Chronicle,* in the Kajang tale a *tumanurung* is "borrowed" from a powerful community, in this case Gowa. In Kajang, it seems, not only did the *tumanurung* motif spread from Gowa, so did the *tumanurung* herself. In short, I argue that the *tumanurung* motif gained social and symbolic currency throughout Makassar as Gowa's influence and might increased during the sixteenth and seventeenth centuries. For their own purposes Makassarese from other communities embraced this motif and made it part of their histories. The *tumanurung* motif was in fact easily appended onto or incorporated into Makassarese oral schemata as a stock element, one firmly linked in people's minds to Gowa.

In an interesting parallel, Ian Caldwell argued that Bugis writers attached the idea of a sacred *tumanurung* apical ancestor to existing written king lists, transforming what may have been historical figures in the early fourteenth century into legendary *tumanurung*.[43] In both Bugis and Makassarese polities, histories beginning with a *tumanurung* founding the kingdom became the dominant way of claiming prestigious origins. Among Makassarese, it appears there was a corresponding change in many communities in the kind of myth that provided political legitimacy. In communities without oral histories containing *tumanurung,* tales of origins often focused on the deeds of usually three or seven siblings, each of whom founded a given community and are remembered as its foremost ancestor. Together, the communities share a special sense of identity. A story from Bantaeng tells of seven sisters, the youngest of whom was responsible for collecting wood for the kitchen after their parents died. Burying the bones of a fish she had fed, but which her sisters ate, the youngest sang, "Grow up into a tree, may your leaves fall on Java and be picked up by the king of Java." This indeed happened, and the king of Java came and married the youngest sister. All seven, however, sought their own places to dwell and thus established seven communities near Bantaeng.[44] This history implies that the seven communities are themselves siblings and should cooperate as siblings. Another oral tradition from Bantaeng tells of seven brothers who became the rulers of Bajeng, Katingang, Barasaq, Jipang, Powang, Sapaya, and Kalimporo; this history again stresses the special bond the inhabitants of these seven communities share.[45] In a slightly different version, the *Gowa Chronicle* records the belief that before they were incorporated into Gowa, seven communities in Polombangkeng saw themselves as descended from ancestors who were brothers: Bajeng, Sanrabone, Lengkeseq, Katingang, Jamarang, Jipang, and Mandalleq.[46]

These histories, and many more like them, were an expression of solidarity aptly suited to the federations of communities that rose and fell across Makassar before the expansion of Gowa, an event that necessitated the different origin story the *tumanurung* motif provided. First in Gowa, and then elsewhere, *tumanurung* myths emphasizing social hierarchy and exclusivity overshadowed myths of siblingship emphasizing cooperation and equality.[47] *Tumanurung* tales did not simply elide this cultural substratum of siblingship tales. In at least one case the two tale types are combined. In an unusual admixture, what is described as a *patturioloang* from Camba uses elements from both. It tells of three brothers, each of whom founded a community, their close cooperation, and the intermarriage of their descendants. But the account describes these three as children of a *tumanurung*. Furthermore, the youngest wins a contest by being the only brother able to climb up into the house of another beautiful, mysterious stranger he discovered inside a thick piece of bamboo. They marry, and their descendants become the rulers of Camba.[48] The story tacks back and forth between these two poles, first emphasizing the equality and kinship of the three brothers, then stressing the social hierarchicalization commonly expressed in *tumanurung* tales. *Tumanurung* tales represented a history of the past that provided a new kind of political legitimacy.

The reasons behind these adaptations of Gowa's *tumanurung* motif are probably diverse. Some surely are efforts to tap into or appropriate a share of Gowa's potency to create a link with that polity; others are attempts to localize an outside idea to further claims in political rivalries, while still others are efforts to assert local identities that contested Gowa's claims to preeminence. But for the moment it is not the veracity of the stories that is at issue, nor the diverse reasons why this motif spread, but the unstated yet unavoidable implication that unequally defined the course of future interaction. As Pierre Bourdieu's earlier statement suggested, simply by accepting or making use of a form of history-making derived from Gowa they established its efficacy and its truth. Like ripples in a pond, the spread of the *tumanurung* trope and the beliefs associated with it progressively created the perception that Gowa was the archetype for other Makassarese polities, the source of much of the significance in their own past, and the natural center of the Makassarese world.

Making History of Islam in South Sulawesi

The rulers of Talloq and Gowa formally converted to Islam on Friday, 22 September 1605 (9 Jumad al-awwal 1014).[49] By 1611 in what were called "wars of Islamization" *(bunduq kasallannganna)* they had through pressure and conquest carried the new faith throughout South Sulawesi and were preparing to carry it overseas as well. The histories made of Islam in Makassar during the first half of the seventeenth century are among the most illuminating cases of how Gowa's efforts to control the interpretation and remembering of that past helped first establish and later perpetuate its status as an exemplary center. Islam was crucial in making Gowa the center to which other Makassarese communities looked and by which they gauged themselves. In particular, Gowa's possession of ancient, sacred Islamic manuscripts—the newest form of *kalompoang* in Makassar—bolstered the perception that Islam was centered in Gowa. Simultaneously, Gowa's claim to precedence as the first to convert to the new faith was effective in shaping the perception that Gowa was the locus of Islam in Makassar.

The importance of Islamic texts as sacred objects in history derived from how Makassarese first perceived and understood Islam itself. Examinations of the acceptance of Islam in South Sulawesi often focus on the practical benefits rulers derived from becoming part of the larger Islamic world.[50] Less remarked upon is how Makassarese perceived Islam. Put succinctly, Makassarese viewed Islam as a new form of sacred writing. Versions of the popular oral tradition about the coming of Islam to Talloq stressed how a stranger, perhaps even the prophet Muhammad himself, inscribed with his finger either the *syahadat* confession of faith or the sura Al-Fatihah on the palm or fingernail of Karaeng Matoaya.[51] Manuscript N17, which I collected during fieldwork in Makassar, contains an even more elaborate oral tradition about the miraculous events that brought or, more precisely, renewed Islam in Sanrabone. Although it describes events that supposedly took place in the eighteenth century, it is noteworthy because it conveys that accepting Islam meant accepting the Arabic Qur'an.

This tells about the descent of a garuda in Sanrabone. Of this descent of the garuda in Sanrabone, one story tells that Nabi Muhammad made himself into a garuda bird and descended in Sanrabone. Another story says that Gabriel made himself into a garuda bird and was ordered by Allah Ta'ala to descend in Sanrabone to plant the truths called Islam. This garuda descended in Sanrabone on a Friday when people where coming out from Friday prayer at the mosque. This was in year 1175 Hijra. The garuda descended on the south side of Lajalajaya in Bantilang Biseang, above a campagaya tree in Sanrabone That garuda had two heads, a large one on the right, a small one on the left. All its feathers were covered in Arabic writing. It was there, alighted on a broken campagaya branch, but it kept hovering just a little, touching its claws to a large branch of the campagaya tree. The one who described the garuda was Tuang Abdul Gaffar, Daeng Janggoq. The one who copied the Arabic letters that were on the garuda's body, he was I Daeng Daeng Ngawong. The one who spoke with the garuda, he was I Johoro Daeng Ngena. The garuda was there from when he came at lururu [lohor, *the midday prayer] until after* asaraq [asar, *the late-afternoon prayer], then he left, flying up. When people went to* magrib pra*y*er [*the sunset prayer*] *he could no longer be seen. This was the coming of the garuda when it was in Sanrabone.*

Islam in this story *is* the written Qur'an. Beyond lowland Makassar even today Islam is perceived as sacred writing. Among the Mandar, one account describes Islam as a book moving threateningly from the lowlands to the uplands.[52] Certainly for the vast majority of seventeenth-century Makassarese, Islam was not conceived of as a body of abstract religious doctrines, or simply adopted because of the pragmatic benefits conversion brought. Islam was viewed and had an intrinsic appeal as strange and powerful writing, though of course this was not Islam's only appeal. Not surprisingly, then, the social and political implications of possessing Arabic-language Islamic texts were significant. One of the most striking examples of how Islamic texts occupied a vital place in Makassarese social life comes from the Dutch scholar Friedericy's report about Antang, Lassuloro, and Ujung Bori, three small settlements in Tomboloq. Originally the three were a single community led by a lord, titled Anrongguru Tumatenea, living in Antang. In the seventeenth century a disciple of Syekh Yusuf named Loqmoq ri Antang bequeathed to this community an Islamic volume that had been given to him, inhabitants related, by Syekh Yusuf himself. Written partly in Makassarese and partly in Bugis, it contained what Friedericy called "laudatory poems" *(lofdicht)* praising Allah and Muhammad. The book was considered sacred by the three settlements and passed down in a certain family as an heirloom. Kept in a special house, it was read aloud twice each month. At each such occasion, inhabitants made offerings of incense to the spirit of the book; then the reciter read aloud from it in melodious tones. The assembled crowd would join in, having memorized passages from the text. Friedericy believed that this was done to honor the memory of Syekh Yusuf. Remarkably, these three settlements celebrated Idul Fitri at the end of Ramadan one day before surrounding communities, perhaps to demonstrate their superiority, their uniqueness, and to recall that they had once had their own lord not subject to Tomboloq.[53] Veneration of this ancient Islamic text, a *kalompoang* shared by Antang, Lassuloro, and Ujung Bori, became the practice that most affirmed and expressed their distinctive identity. Like other objects of history, it had become an object in history with tangible social implications.

One of the institutional arrangements most responsible for concentrating Islamic texts at Gowa was the creation of a network of mosques that centered on Gowa. The wealth and patronage of the rulers of Gowa and Talloq were essential in building the infrastructure that Islamization required. Foremost among this infrastructure were mosques. Moreover, mosques were not simply scattered about the Makassarese countryside, but organized in a hierarchy that linked local, community mosques and prayer houses to the grand mosques built near the Gowa court. The *lontaraq bilang*, for example, record that on November 10, 1635, the mosque at Bontoalaq was built. Many Makassarese to this day consider Bontoalaq and the nearby but slightly newer mosque at Katangka the seat of Islam in Makassar. It was within this network of mosques that Islamic texts were preserved, protected, and recited. The religious hierarchy of *ulama* staffing these mosques was similarly organized. In his account of Makassarese religious life, Nicholas Gervaise described three levels of *ulama* charged with bringing Islam to Makassarese. Those of the highest rank, known as *touan*, were theoretically equal, but in reality their influence depended on the size and importance of their mosque; the one who had the honor to be closest to the ruler of Gowa was considered a sort of patriarch for the whole kingdom. The second tier, *santari*, appointed by the rulers of Gowa, had the duty to keep the sacred books, to care for the mosque, and to beat brass drums summoning people to prayer.[54] The sacred Islamic texts, therefore, were distributed along institutional lines that were established by Gowa and that emphasized Gowa as the place where Islamic potency was most concentrated.

Another institution centerizing Gowa in Makassarese minds was the office of *mokkeng*. From the Arabic word *"muqim,"* meaning "inhabitant," *"mokkeng"* in Makassarese referred to people the ruler of Gowa appointed to attend the Friday service to ensure that the minimum forty people demanded by *shafi'ite* doctrine for the service to be valid were present. Not only was the ruler of Gowa thus active in promoting Islamic religious observances among Makassarese, but he was also in a position to officially recognize certain Makassarese as the most devout and admirable of Muslims. The ruler of Gowa also appointed a leader of the *mokkeng* known as the *anrongguru mokkeng*. In Gowa this functionary was active in Islamic ceremonies (there was a similar position in Sanrabone).[55] When Gowa conquered Bima and Sumbawa it established *mokkeng* there as well. As one text relates, "He [Karaeng Matoaya] instituted the Friday service in those overseas countries. He desired heavenly reward by appointing *mokkings* and then setting them free. So the people called *mokking* were free, and the commoners were slaves."[56]

The rulers of Gowa established a system of Islamic education that paralleled this hierarchy of *ulama*, mosques, and *mokkeng*; it too centered Islamic devotion and Islamic texts at Gowa. In his discussion of Islamic education on Java, Mark Woodward characterizes *pesantren* education as a "process of text production as well as of memorization" because of the emphasis on writing down recited texts in *pesantren*.[57] Makassarese nobles provided Gervaise an account of text-centered education at the Gowa court during the mid-seventeenth century. He reported that noble boys at age five or six were sent to live with relatives or friends so that they did not "become soft" under their mothers' care. Noble girls were simply kept at home and taught by their mothers what they needed to know. At age seven or eight the boys were then sent to live at a school run by Islamic teachers known as *agguys (hajis)*. There they learned to read and write, to recite the Qur'an, and to perform the religious observances of a good Muslim. Such schooling lasted about two years.[58] Some added further, more-intensive study to this basic education, seeking out itinerant Islamic teachers, who first came to South Sulawesi in the seventeenth century. The *Story of Syekh Yusuf* describes Yusuf's religious education in Makassar along this pattern. "After being cared for for some time, he grew up. He was ordered to go learn to recite with a teacher named I Daeng ri Tasammeng. After some time he became proficient in reciting the Qur'an. [He then] mastered *syaraf, nahwu*, reciting holy books, *minhaj, tafsir,* and *mantiq*."[59] After completing this thorough but orthodox education, Syekh Yusuf set off to acquire the mystical knowledge that only Sufi *tarekat* masters could provide, ultimately spending years in Mekka before returning to the archipelago.[60]

The rulers of Gowa and Talloq created a network of *madrasahs* to educate and thereby disseminate Islamic practices and teachings throughout Makassar. In this the Malay community in Makassar played an important role.[61] Malay texts often mediated Islam to Makassarese. More than two dozen such seventeenth-century manuscripts exist in Makassar today. Typically a mixture of Arabic, Malay, and Makassarese, these manuscripts conveyed the Qur'an and other texts of Islamic doctrine and religious instruction to Makassar. For example, an Arabic text may have been translated into Makassarese and provided with a Malay commentary. In addition, Makassarese in Gowa and Talloq engaged Malays as teachers and mosque officials because of their knowledge of Islam and Arabic. The Malay presence in Makassar, coupled with the active role played by the rulers of Gowa and Talloq, made Gowa into the main center of Islamic learning in Makassar and thus the main repository of sacred religious manuscripts.

Like the Malays, the Arab and Indian Muslim traders who served as conduits for Islamic texts entering Makassar were themselves concentrated at Gowa and Talloq. Nevertheless, this point should not be exaggerated. Many foreign traders lived in other coastal communities in Makassar. The community of Cikoang, for example, is still renowned among Makassarese as a center of Islamic learning because of Arab sayyids (a title given to those descended from the Prophet) who purportedly settled there in the seventeenth century. Similarly, in the *Story of Syekh Yusuf,* the young Yusuf studied in Gowa but then journeyed to study with a *wali* (a semilegendary apostle of Islam in the archipelago) who lived outside Gowa on Mount Bawakaraeng. It was there that Yusuf gained "all the mystical knowledge in the land of Makassar."[62] As the story from Tomboloq further suggests, Islamic texts were not confined, even in this early period, to major courts. Collections of religious texts could be found wherever Makassarese built mosques. These caveats are important: Gowa should not be considered the only haven for Muslim visitors and settlers in Makassar, nor as the only place where Islamic texts were kept.

Makassarese in Gowa did, however, possess more Islamic texts than those in any other Makassarese community. It was at the Gowa and Talloq courts that Muslim tutors were engaged, large mosques built, wealth made available to patronize Islamic scholarship, and religious holidays celebrated in impressive public commemorations. Nowhere else in Makassar, for example, did rulers receive gifts such as the Qur'an that Nawab Mir Jumla of Golconda gave Sultan Malikussaid and Karaeng Pattingalloang.[63] Nowhere else could Makassarese nobles request from foreigners other sacred religious texts such as the Hebrew Bible, or receive as a gift Psalms translated into Malay.[64] Nowhere else did Makassarese rulers accumulate a library of books, manuscripts, globes, and other exotic objects devoted to the pursuit of knowledge.[65] Finally, nowhere else in Makassar was there a center of literary production of the letters, missives, and treaties that sustained diplomacy in the early modern Southeast Asian world. To an impressive degree, Makassarese literary production and consumption were concentrated in Gowa (figure 9).

Islamic texts were valuable *kalompoang* because they, like historical texts and other regalia, made distant places and times manifest in the present. The equivalence in Makassarese minds of the Qur'an to other *kalompoang* is indicated in this sentence about Karaeng Matoaya: "He was the *karaeng* who first swore oaths on the Qur'an, who first swore oaths on Sudanga."[66] This parallelism is significant, for it offered Makassarese a ready-made framework within which to make sense of Islam. Makassarese viewed Mekka as similar to places within Makassar: as a location laden with spiritual potency.[67] Arabic texts brought that potency to Makassar. So too they carried into the present the stories and words that were uttered when Islam was founded. A Makassarese Muslim in the seventeenth century could hold in his hands the words of Allah, relayed a millennium before through the Archangel Gabriel to the prophet Muhammad, that became the holy Qur'an. It is very likely that the importance Islamic practice placed on the written Qur'an contributed to the perception in Makassar that written language was superior to or had authority over spoken language, a perception of tremendous social significance. Although such a perception cannot be quantitatively measured, the proliferation of Islamic manuscripts and

Figure 9. Recitation of Islamic text at the Gowa royal palace

the institutions designed to compose, preserve, and teach them was centered at Gowa. This social fact did much to establish Gowa's centrality, adding Islam's luster to Gowa's own. But the accumulation of these sacred objects of history was not the only development that benefited Gowa. In addition, Gowa asserted its position as the first to convert to the faith and based its claim to leadership of the Islamic society on its taking root in Gowa.

As mentioned above, the Gowa and Talloq *patturioloang* record that their rulers, Karaeng Matoaya of Talloq and Tumamenang ri Gaukanna of Gowa, were the first Makassarese to convert to Islam in 1605. As the *Gowa Chronicle* relates of Tumamenang ri Gaukanna,

His Arabic name was Sultan Ala'uddin. After ruling twelve years he entered Islam. A Minangkabau led him in the syahadat [confession of faith]; the settlement of Wanga was the name of his homeland. Katib Tunggal was his personal name. Living at the tip of Pammatoang, in that land he was called I Datoq ri Bandang. The karaeng *entered Islam on the ninth night of the month of Jumadilawal, on the day of Friday in the Christian calendar, September 22, Islamic calendar* sallallahu alaihi wasallang.[68]

This entry notes that Tumamenang ri Gaukanna was the first in Gowa to enter Islam. The *Talloq Chronicle* did the same for Karaeng Matoaya, but also took special pains to emphasize his exceptional piety. "He was adept at reading and writing Arabic and well read in Islamic literature. From the time he embraced Islam until his death he never once missed the ritual prayer. Only at the time when he had a swollen foot and an Englishman treated him by giving him liquor did he omit to pray. He performed many additional prayers, such as *rawatib, witr, adduha, tasabih,* and *tahajjud.*"[69] Karaeng Matoaya took for himself the title Sultan Abdullah Awwal-al-Islam, meaning Sultan Abdullah "the first in Islam." The oral tradition about the Prophet's appearing and writing Arabic on the palm or fingernail of Karaeng Matoaya similarly emphasized that Gowa and Talloq were the first among Makassarese communities to embrace the new faith. Another version of this oral tradition omits the meeting with the Prophet, instead telling that Karaeng Matoaya greeted a stranger at the palace gate after the stranger stepped ashore. Without being taught, Karaeng Matoaya welcomed the stranger with the customary Islamic greeting, *Assalamu Alaikum Wahrahmatullahi Wabarakatuh.* For many Makassarese this story proves that Islam was already present in South Sulawesi before the arrival of missionaries.[70] Furthermore, ries, and guidelines that Makassarese will refer when asked to account for, measure, and judge behavior both good and bad.

Fascinating in itself, neither this body of what Makassarese today consider their core cultural values, their compass *(pedomang)*, nor contemporary constructions of "culture" *(kebudayaan)* in Indonesia are the focus of this chapter. Instead, we focus on the fact that Makassarese *refer* to this collection, and on the historical developments that led to this practice. I argue that writing enabled Makassarese to first conceive of their culture as having a core to which they could refer, as being something against which behavior could be measured, and that this mental shift was one of the most profound changes taking place in early modern Makassar. This chapter describes the corpus of written guidelines for behavior, the effects of committing these guidelines to paper, and some of the social changes to which the creation of these five pillars contributed.

Written Texts and the Idea of "Culture"

"Culture," like "society" or "ritual," is a mental construct that allows scholars to examine something that has no objective existence as if it were firm and self-evident.[2] This is not to say there are no cultures, societies, or rituals, but simply to acknowledge that these eminently useful constructions were conceived of at a particular time; they are historical products that allow us to define and find evidence for what previously was not envisioned in such abstract terms. There is, for example, no good reason to assume that early modern Southeast Asians conceptualized the world around them in terms of cultures and societies or that they understood their religious activities as rituals in the sense modern scholars intend. To argue in this chapter, as I do, that Makassarese first explicitly conceptualized of and then codified their beliefs and values after the advent of literacy is not to say that before this period Makassarese had nothing we can call culture. It is simply that they did not call it culture.

There is, of course, a dilemma here. How can we, who are so accustomed to seeing the world in terms of societies, cultures, rituals, and more, possibly expect to understand how the world might look without these concepts? Cast in a more immediate form, how can we literates gain a sense of how customs, values, and beliefs were perceived and preserved in oral communities? As members of a literate society we cannot simply peel away the mental processes of how we think that have been fundamentally shaped by literacy. As Walter Ong noted, "Though words are grounded in oral speech, writing tyrannically locks them into a visual field forever.... That is to say, a literate person cannot fully recover a sense of what the word is to purely oral people."[3]

There are no assured ways out of this quandary. Nevertheless, there is a significant body of work that has tried to provide answers to these questions. Walter Ong himself has written perceptively about oral societies and about the conceptual transformations that literacy engenders. Ong argues that in oral societies, words are discrete events that take place in an instant and are then gone, leaving no visual trace; that speech is highly rhythmic and based on balanced patterns to facilitate remembering; that its grammar is typically additive rather than complex and subordinate, as well as aggregative rather than analytic and terse; that orations are likely to be repetitive or redundant; that knowledge in general is conservative and aimed at preservation rather than innovation and experimentation; that it is concerned with the immediate world rather than abstractions and possibilities, situational rather than categorical and schematic; that speech is agonistic and dramatic more than it is removed and interior, and empathetic and participatory rather than aloof and distanced; and that knowledge is subject unwittingly to an economy of forgetting as events and memories from the past lose contemporary relevance.[4] Ong presents further ideas about the nature of oral societies that result from these characteristics, but these need not detain us here. Instead, these features of oral communities that Ong identifies offer a fruitful perspective from which to approach Southeast Asia.

In Southeast Asian history, recent work by Barbara Andaya (herself much influenced by Ong) discussing custom and memory in early modern southeast Sumatra provides a useful point of departure. As she writes, "The vast body of custom regulating social relations was retained in the communal memory in the form of rhymed proverbs, metered aphorisms, and inherited traditions in turn justified by reference to the authority of some long-dead ancestors." Furthermore, "With the community's implicit agreement, details extraneous to the present slipped away from legend to be replaced by newly relevant elements that were incorporated as ancestral lore, thus rendering the past continually meaningful."[5] With some latitude for local particulars, these statements probably represent fairly the play of custom and memory in many early modern Southeast Asian oral communities.

It is also useful to recall here the distinctions made in chapter 3 about the differences between oral and written histories in Makassar. Oral histories focused on the origins of a community, its sacred *kalompoang,* and its links with Gowa. The cultural importance placed on origins and the frailty of memory gave oral histories a teardrop or barbell shape: a great deal of attention was given to the distant past, some attention to recent generations, but very little to the decades or centuries in between. History was not conceived of as a continuous account or chain linking the past and the present; instead, these oral histories commemorated foundational events. Thus the histories placed little attention on genealogy, stressed some periods rather than others and some topics rather than others; they did not attempt to be comprehensive or systematic accounts the past. By way of contrast, Makassarese written histories replaced the teardrops and barbells of oral memory with linked narrative blocks, chronologically contiguous and standardized in format. In the case of *patturioloang,* there was a clear conception of the rules guiding how this genre should be composed. Written histories placed a particular emphasis on detailing genealogical relationships; above all, they privileged rulers as the anchors and source of significance in the past.

What, then, might we safely say about Makassarese conceptions of custom before the advent of literacy? From my reading of the anthropological and historical literature available about Makassar, my experiences in South Sulawesi, and my engagement with what other scholars have written about orality and literacy, I believe that two characteristics surface as both probable and significant for the discussion that follows. First, custom was contextual. Second, it was malleable. Custom—broadly defined as what behaviors were considered appropriate and what actions socially valuable—was not abstract. Behavior was not measured against an absolute and theoretical standard. There were of course general exhortations such as those in the oral history from Baku in which the *tumanurung* urged the people to find another ruler with "my prowess, my honesty, my justice, my bravery." But here the life of a specific person (the *tumanurung*) was the guide that others were encouraged to emulate. There was no reference to an abstract set of codes, no exemplar whose life was not derived from a particular historical and social context.[6] The behavior considered appropriate was based on analogies and directed at specific situations. In other situations, with other conditions and other participants, what was appropriate changed. That is, the stories and examples people mustered and brought to bear in evaluating the present were variable. The comments of Amin Sweeney about the inability of those in an oral culture to separate themselves from their speech are particularly relevant here: "The evanescent nature of the spoken word makes it impossible for the speaker to detach himself from his speech and contemplate it as an object."[7]

In addition to being contextual, custom in Makassar before the spread of written texts was malleable. Not abstract, neither was it absolute. The activities that were valuable and the behavior that was appropriate changed over time, though these customs were remembered as unchanging. The source of custom—stories and examples from the past—was community elders. As Jack Goody puts it, "All beliefs and values, all forms of knowledge are communicated between individuals in face-to-face contact; and they are stored only in human memory."[8] It was elders whose experience was longest and whose memory reached the furthest back. By asking the elders for their opinion, the community tapped into memories from the distant past, particularly the past of the community's origins. The actions of the community's founders provided the example of what behavior and activities were most important to the identity of the community and thus most vital to imitate and preserve in the present.

But though regarded as eternal and unchanging, customs were continuously altered to fit the occasion. And as valuable as memories might be, they were equally delicate and pliant. Memory, we know, is as dependent upon the occasion and context of its remembering as it is upon the time when what is recalled took place. Memories are not snapshots imprinted upon our brains, but fragile constellations of associations easily disturbed or transformed by later experiences.[9] "In this orally suspended transmission of knowledge," Hendrik Maier writes of Malay oral culture,

> tradition was a vague and fragmentary corpus of forms and themes which expressed itself also in every proverb or oration, every narration or recitation, every discussion of talk. Speakers and their audience resorted to tradition in order to have rules and concepts confirmed which they had all to rely on in their struggle to make sense of the world. In this constant renewal, the tradition's contours were hazy, its content indefinite.[10]

Though believed to be fixed, custom could not but change over time.

It was into this world that written texts spread. The depth of the transformation is illustrated in an episode from the *Story of Syekh Yusuf,* originally an oral tradition but one composed after the advent of literacy. It tells that a daughter of the ruler of Gowa fell in love with and wanted to marry Yusuf before he left Makassar but that he believed that such a union was impossible.

Spoke Yusuf, "O young one, that simply cannot happen. There are several [reasons] that action is not appropriate. First, you are a karaeng *and I am a subject. Second, we have been made siblings by the* karaeng *[of Gowa]. Third, I am a bearer of the* karaeng's *sirih box. Thus I am afraid and ashamed before my fellow man and Allah." Then said the* karaeng's *child, "It is for this you must be called a man of knowledge and you must become wise." Said Tuanta [Yusuf], "Though you speak so, young one, I am afraid."*

Later, after becoming well versed in Islamic theology, Yusuf too falls in love with the ruler of Gowa's daughter. Like the tale related in chapter 4, of the Malay in Sanrabone who fell in love with a noble Makassarese woman, initially Syekh Yusuf's desire is rejected because of his comparatively low rank. Then the ruler of Gowa consults written texts to see if this decision is correct.

Then spoke the karaeng, *"Open the* lontaraq, *you, look at them and read them." After this the* lontaraq *were opened and read by Gallarrang Manngasa. After this were encountered three reasons permitting a man to marry a woman above him [in rank]. First, if he was knowledgeable. Second, if he was brave. Third, if he was rich and used his money for the land of Gowa.*[11]

Realizing his error, the ruler of Gowa sent word that Yusuf could indeed marry his daughter.

Whether an accurate portrayal of historical events or not, this story is illuminating for the depth of change it registers in how Makassarese conceived of custom. Most importantly, custom now was depicted as residing not in the memories of elders, or even in the decisions and feelings of rulers, but in written manuscripts. Memory and opinion gave way to what had been recorded and preserved on paper. A second feature worth noting is that written manuscripts are described as containers. *Lontaraq* are opened and read for what lies within them. This is not an incidental change in terminology; Roger Chartier notes that the book in Western Europe has been one of the most powerful metaphors capable of shaping thought about the cosmos, nature, history, and the human body.[12] To conceive of *lontaraq* as containers in which sacred words are stored was an important step in the Makassarese reconceptualization of culture that the presence of manuscripts promoted. Of further significance is that the written words the ruler of Gowa consulted were absolute and abstract; these regulations transcended the particularities of individual situations. In this articulation of cultural values, stories and examples that shed instructive light on a given situation were not recalled; instead, all situations were made answerable to this set of rules. Finally, the ruler of Gowa engaged in a self-conscious act of referring to these objects as the location where cultural values could be found. This practice of explicit reference carried with it the belief that custom was now objectified in material form rather than stored in the precarious memories of elders.

The story of Tudilaling bringing the *"adat,* laws, and customs of the people of Gowa that are written" to Balanipa in Mandar is another suggestive example of the effects writing had on the concept of custom. In this account, orally preserved Mandarese customs appeared cruel indeed. The text begins with a description of how trial by ordeal resolved disputes.[13]

These were the Mandarese customs of the people of Balanipa at the arrival of Tudilaling; at that time they did not yet have adat. *If there were men who quarreled with men, the chiefs sat watching as the two were put inside an arena ringed with stone. Once inside the two faced off toe to toe and dueled with knives. The chiefs watched. Whoever was wounded first was defeated. If both were wounded, and one of them died, the one killed was defeated. Then his corpse was rolled down into a ravine. Normally each person got to stab only once, then they were separated. If a woman quarreled with a woman, the way the chiefs adjudicated here was this: it was commanded that water be boiled. Once it boiled, each disputant was ordered to put her hands into the boiling water. Whoever more quickly pulled out her hands, she was declared wrong. These were the practices of the people of Balanipa at the arrival of Tudilaling.*

The account is retrospective: composed long after these events bringing literacy to Balanipa purportedly took place, the text, perhaps not surprisingly, disparages these ancient practices. More important for our purposes is the depth of the transformation this account describes. The arrival of written customs was perceived as something that fundamentally changed both Mandarese society and Mandarese conception of traditional values and practices.[14] When Tudilaling brought the *lontaraq* back from the *karaeng* of Gowa to Balanipa, he invited his Mandarese lord to consult with him on what to do with the manuscript.[15]

I Puang ri Pojosang was ordered invited by Tudilaling. I Puang ri Pojosang arrived. Spoke Tudilaling, "For this I ordered you invited here: so that we together can study this lontaraq *given by the* karaeng of Gowa.*" Answered I Puang ri Pojosang, "Good, Daeng, but perhaps it is better if we summon too the Four Great Communities so that all hear the contents of this* lontaraq.*" Then the Four Great Communities were summoned by Tudilaling as well. All of the Four Great Communities arrived. Spoke Tudilaling, "I have summoned all of you here because I want this* lontaraq *read. The contents of the* lontaraq *will bring happiness and satisfaction to us." Answered the Four Great Communities, "Good, Daeng. Hopefully this will bring good fortune to us, the people of Balanipa, and become an heirloom of great value." Then said I Puang ri Pojosang, "Good. Perhaps if Daeng begins to read then we from the Four Great Communities will listen." Answered Tudilaling, "Yes, Puang. Listen well and I will begin to read."*

Tudilaling read the lontaraq. *All the Four Great Communities and I Puang ri Pojosang were silent listening. After reading the* lontaraq, *Tudilaling said to Puang ri Pojosang and the Four Great Communities, "This, Puang, will become that which we latch onto in each life of the people of the land in all of Balanipa." Answered I Puang ri Pojosang, "Yes, Daeng." Spoke again Tudilaling to Puang ri Pojosang, "Perhaps it is best if the* lontaraq *is taken in procession in a palanquin to the Four Great Communities." Answered I Puang ri Pojosang, "Yet I may not accompany [the* lontaraq*] on procession because usually I am taken on procession to the Four Great Communities, Daeng." Answered Tudilaling, "It cannot be so, Puang. It is best if [the* lontaraq*] is taken in procession by us together because we will later be installed here to oversee the good fortune and journey of the* lontaraq.*" Answered again I Puang ri Pojosang, "Yes, Daeng, that is very true. This I ask just because I want the* lontaraq *quickly confirmed [as our guide]." The Four Great Communities agreed.*

This account too is illuminating for what it indicates about the perception and effects of written guidelines for behavior and activity. The *lontaraq* became a sacred *kalompoang* guaranteeing good fortune and prosperity in Balanipa. Moreover, it was described as replacing the ruler as that which was most honored in the community by being carried in procession in the palanquin formerly reserved for I Puang ri Pojosang. In this the *lontaraq* acts much like any other *kalompoang*. But the *lontaraq* also plays a unique and novel role in Balanipa society: its words become the compass, "that which we latch onto." The *lontaraq* is installed as the people's guide; they will look to it for direction, not to elders and their memories, not to rulers and their commands. It is this heirloom that will now be consulted and whose dictates will provide guidance and act as the core determinant of Mandarese social life, activities, and behavior.

Both of these accounts are evocative narratives that describe what we can perhaps define as a shift from custom to culture in early modern Makassar. Written manuscripts containing the words of the ancestors signified a new object: "culture." The presence of written texts bringing the past into the present made it possible to conceive of a collection of texts as that which holds the absolute principles that should govern society (figure 10). Capable of being referred to, pointed at, held, and reverenced, manuscripts enabled the conceptualization that there was a body of guidelines or prescriptions that people should strive to imitate and against which people should judge human actions, motives, and choices. Custom, that shifting body of parables and stories from the memories of elders, gave way to culture, the codified, unchanging, and consultable guidelines for appropriate behavior and social norms.

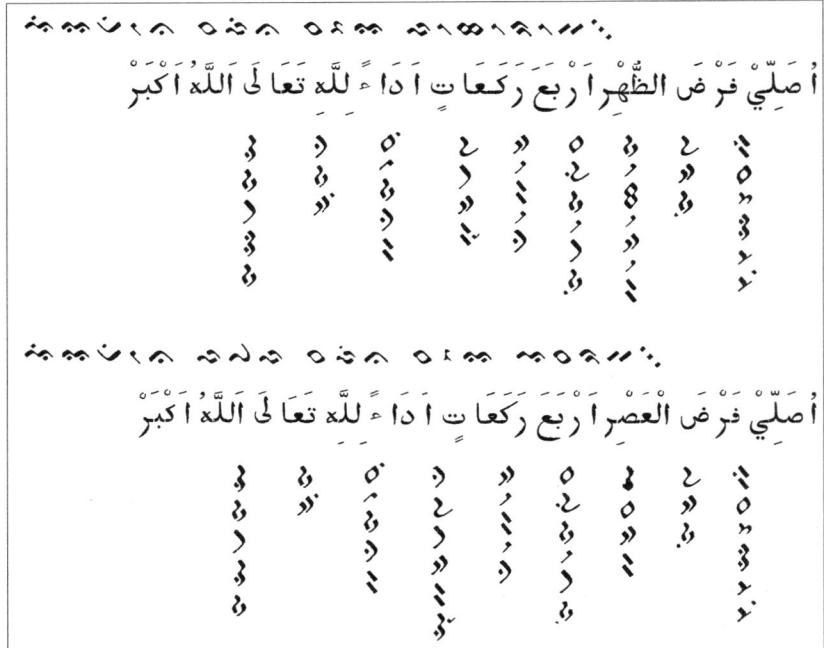

Figure 10. Makassarese Islamic prayer instruction manual

What caused this turn toward written texts as the authoritative source for Makassarese culture? One answer is that such transformations are inherent in the very adoption and spread of even a socially restricted literacy. Another answer is that Makassarese in the sixteenth century drew inspiration from contact with Malays, Europeans, and perhaps Arabs as well, three groups with established written traditions. Walter Ong and Jack Goody are among those who, though from different perspectives, argue that literacy produces fundamental mental changes. Ong argues that writing, by making visible and permanent what had previously been oral and fleeting, induces reconceptualizations of knowledge, the world, and oneself. These reconceptualizations range far beyond the mundane ability to store and preserve a greater volume of information, encompassing developments such as introspection. As Ong puts it, "Writing restructures consciousness."[16] Goody cautions against arguments claiming that on a physiological level literacy transforms the human brain, producing new mental abilities hitherto lacking. Rather, literacy makes possible new kinds of mental operations and conceptualizations because of the tools, the capacity to view the world in a new way, that literacy provides.[17] Is it, in other words, the very presence of written manuscripts that caused Makassarese to envision and then codify an abstract realm of "culture"?

But perhaps literacy was not the cause of these changes. Makassarese society during the sixteenth and seventeenth centuries was not isolated, but inundated with exposure to the merchants and products of literate cultures. Arab, Malay, and European traders are the most important to consider here. Were Makassarese exposed to and inspired by Portuguese or Dutch written law codes? We do know that Portuguese calendars influenced and may have been the impetus behind Makassarese *lontaraq bilang*. Did Arabic "mirror of princes" texts advising rulers how to govern well accompany the flow of Islamic manuscripts into seventeenth-century Makassar? We should at least note the similarity of these texts to Makassarese *rapang*. Did the Malay *Melaka Maritime Laws* encourage Makassarese to set down in writing what principles did or should govern their society? We do know that a maritime law code was written in Makassar at the beginning of the eighteenth century.[18] In fact, during the seventeenth century, there were strong links between the Islamic states of the archipelago, particularly Aceh, Banten, and Gowa, and it is almost certain that Makassarese could have consulted or collected such texts. Finally, these two centuries were a period of nearly constant competition and interaction with neighboring Bugis communities. Certainly these exchanges were the occasion for both borrowing and self-conscious acts of differentiation on both sides.

Choosing between these two positions might be a mistake. The impetus among Makassarese to write, and perhaps some of the models of how to write, was almost certainly affected by the waves of foreign, literate merchants who began to make Makassar their home in the sixteenth century. Surely their presence, and the mysterious but potent writings they carried with them, influenced and encouraged Makassarese to write. Yet the conceptual transformations, the capacity and inclination to view the world in novel ways—and the effects this novel view wrought—just as surely stemmed from the presence, accumulation, and veneration of Makassarese written manuscripts. It was this new social presence that transformed customs, malleable and remembered, into culture, enduring and consulted. No other form of writing was more instrumental in effecting this transformation than *rapang*.

R*apang* and the Codification of Culture

Among the nine foundations I Tuang Syekh ri Dima elucidated for behavior in this world was the dictate "Make your actions truly in accordance with the guidelines of *adat*."[19] Another manuscript repeatedly concluded discussions of what was not proper or what must not be done by declaring flatly, "That is not allowed by *rapang*."[20] A third text stated, "This is the place of patient behavior: to follow what you must obey. Thus by acting on the guidelines [you] avoid what is prohibited."[21] These three *rapang* from three different manuscripts are at the heart of the process under consideration. *Rapang* were not simply customs collected and recorded for easier preservation. Rather, *rapang* through their admonitions and because of the social force written texts possessed created the idea that there was a set of guidelines that constituted the core of something called Makassarese culture and by which Makassarese must judge their behavior. *Rapang* texts asserted with conviction, "This is our *adat*."[22]

Rapang—compilations of proscriptions and prescriptions for behavior—were one of the earliest of Makassarese genres of historical writing. As chapter 2 discussed, by the 1570s Makassarese may have been recording *rapang* spoken by the rulers of Gowa and Talloq. Makassarese judged behavior in the present by ideals established in the past. The guidelines and advice of renowned ancestors in general, and of the foremost nobles and rulers of Gowa and Talloq in particular, came to be seen as the authoritative benchmark to which actions and choices were compared. As noted in the previous chapter, the most frequently cited *rapang* came from the following Gowa and Talloq nobles: Gallarrang Manngasa of Gowa, Karaeng Matoaya, Tumamenang ri Bontobiraeng, Tumamenang ri Taenga, Tumamenang ri Lakiung, Tumamenang ri Ujung Tana, and Karaeng Sumannaq.

The written exhortations that all Makassarese should bring their behavior into line with what is set out in *rapang* had their origins in an earlier oral tradition of advice for rulers. Much of this advice was incorporated into written *rapang*. Here are two representative examples from one *rapang* text advising or cautioning rulers about their actions.

These are purportedly the words of Karaeng ri Ujung Tana. He said these are the three things that cannot be eaten, cannot be worn when you act because the negative consequences are too great: injustice, jealousy, and envy. Because these are unjust. They are like a stone dropped into a pool. Justice is like bamboo lying on the water: if the head at one end is pushed down, the tail at the other end rises. If the tail is pushed down, the head rises.

If his word is broken, it is no longer proper for him to be ruler. He will ruin the land, overturn the rice mortar, hang up the rice winnower, put away the rice pounder. Grass will grow in the kitchen, people will die of starvation, and the community will be consumed by fire. Women will not become pregnant; water buffalo will not give birth; the crops will not ripen; fruit from trees will fall in the garden. If correct decisions are made, the crops will thrive, the rulers will live long lives, the people will flourish, the inhabitants of the community will become rich.[23]

The first passage reminds rulers of the inevitable consequences of injustice, jealousy, and envy, which rise like one end of a stick when the other is pushed into the water. The second has its origins in the widespread Southeast Asian belief that the health and prosperity of the community hinged on the behavior of its ruler: an immoral or rapacious ruler, or simply one who by some act has lost the favor of the guardian spirits of the land, will bring about the famine, disease, infertility, and destruction of the community described in this *rapang*. A similar curse in Minangkabau royal letters was known as the *besi kawi* (the term is a conjunction of "iron" and "obligatory force"). It threatened those who disobeyed the actions authorized by the ruler's words with calamity and promised to reward those who obeyed the letter's royal words with prosperity.[24]

Written *rapang* became more than general guidelines, however. *Rapang* assumed a central place in the self-definition of what it meant to be Makassarese. Several texts describe *rapang* as one of the four fences protecting the community, and following *rapang* one of the three types of behavior people must cultivate.[25] *Rapang* moved beyond advice to rulers to become an essential component and guide to Makassarese culture. The consequences of ignoring *rapang* similarly moved from concerning rulers alone to concerning the entire community. The following asks that everyone turn to *rapang* or face the consequences: "Spoke Karaengta ri Sumannaq to Karaengta Tumamenang ri Taenga, 'Karaeng Matoaya said whoever's land is conquered, if people no longer know the *adat* of the ancestors the land will not return to normal.'"[26] *Rapang* texts speak of the need to "accustom yourself" *(ampakabiasai kalenu)* to the dictates of *rapang*. They urge Makassarese to "obey" *rapang,* using the verb "to fear" *(mallaki)* to mean "obey."

The reach of these texts codifying culture should not be exaggerated. Most obviously, while in theory *rapang* urged all Makassarese to follow their guidelines and to make *rapang* the compass for their lives, most Makassarese in the seventeenth century would never have seen or heard *rapang*. Like other Makassarese manuscripts, they were the preserve of nobles and indexed high rank. Only in later centuries, particularly the twentieth century, have these become more generally known. Nor did *rapang* spread evenly throughout Makassar. In some cases, there were *rapang* that referred to specific areas—for example, "This is a *rapang* that applies to the following vassals of Gowa: Sanrabone, Jipang, and Borisallo. If a man and woman do not marry but sleep together and have children, then separate, she gets all the children and he gets all their commonly held property [*cakkaraqna*]."[27] The best example of how the demands outlined in *rapang* were introduced gradually concerns Islam, both the requirements of religious observances and the prohibitions of *shari'a*. Contrast the following two *rapang,* the first of which demands compliance, the second of which recognizes that such a change can be made only gradually.

Follow the path of the Prophet. May you be well and do what is ordered by Allah: the proper Friday prayer of all Muslims. Those who cannot perform Friday prayer [at the mosque], you shall do it then at a prayer house. You pray: it is a sign that together we shall enjoy the atmosphere that is in a place of prayer. You should accept also anrongguru [ulama] *because later what you had will be destroyed: the customs of old will be replaced.*[28]

Spoke Karaengta Tumamenang ri Taenga to us, "Said Karaengta Tumamenang ri Bontobiraeng, *'If governing is inserted into the laws of shari'a,'* the karaeng said, *'do it just as was done by Karaengta Matoaya, who feared the people would be startled [if this was done too suddenly] and thus he slowly moved toward* shari'a *law.'"* 29

The introduction of Islamic *shari'a* law and the duty to perform daily prayer and the other requirements of the faith were incorporated into what Makassarese came to consider the "fifth pillar" of their culture. It is likely too that the introduction of such a clearly defined set of behaviors and demands sharpened the Makassarese codification of their custom into culture. In one regulation a clear distinction was made between the laws governing Arabs and those governing Makassarese: "The share of commonly held property of people who divorce is two shares for the man and one share for the woman in Arab lands, but among us in Makassar it is divided evenly in two."30 Makassarese culture formed both by adopting and by defining itself in terms of differences with the strictures of *shari'a* law.

Despite these caveats, however, *rapang* did exert a significant influence over Makassarese that went beyond the confines of a literate nobility. As Goody concluded, "But even the nonliterate groups are influenced by the existence of literates in their midst."31 In the case of Makassar, whether they could consult them or not, commoners found themselves subjected to the guidelines of *rapang* when their rulers made decisions concerning the community. One *rapang* prefaces the arrangements it contains with the statement "This was commanded by Tunisombaya: the instruction of the grandparent of I Kaqba to me concerning all people who do not uphold their tasks."32 Another *rapang* declared that if people marry and make a treaty beforehand that children will be divided evenly in the case of divorce, and this then happens, "whoever does not hold to the treaty is to be brought to the ruler and charged before the terms of the treaty."33 Similarly, another says, "This *rapang* is if people marry and they agree that if they have children, they will be divided in two [if they later divorce]. After they truly have children, if there is one who wants to cast down this agreement, they are brought to the ruler and he is the one who judges."34 Though unable to read *rapang*, Makassarese surely became aware that these potent manuscripts were the source of the guidelines and behavior being demanded of them. So too, as Jane Drakard notes in her analysis of the link between language and power among the early modern Minangkabau, the very display of written manuscripts would have had an extraordinary impact in a largely preliterate, rural society (figure 11).[35] Thus, the presence of *rapang* and their social deployment by rulers gave them force even over nonliterate Makassarese. This deployment significantly shaped what was permitted in Makassar and thereby influenced the social changes taking place during the early modern era.

Chapter 4 introduced two cultural "rules" that were codified in early modern Makassar: first, that women's ranks were fixed and that women could not dilute that rank by marrying men of lower status; second, that important political positions were reserved for those of high rank, thereby making the political hierarchy parallel or, better yet, instantiating an ideological and social hierarchy based on white-blooded descent. *Rapang* reinforced these principles. Consider two *rapang* addressed to noblewomen: in a list of what will bring catastrophe to the land, one text declared that incest was the sixth danger to be avoided. Among the definitions for incest it listed was, "People are called incestuous if a female *anaq karaeng* marries a male slave." Another *rapang* stated that a

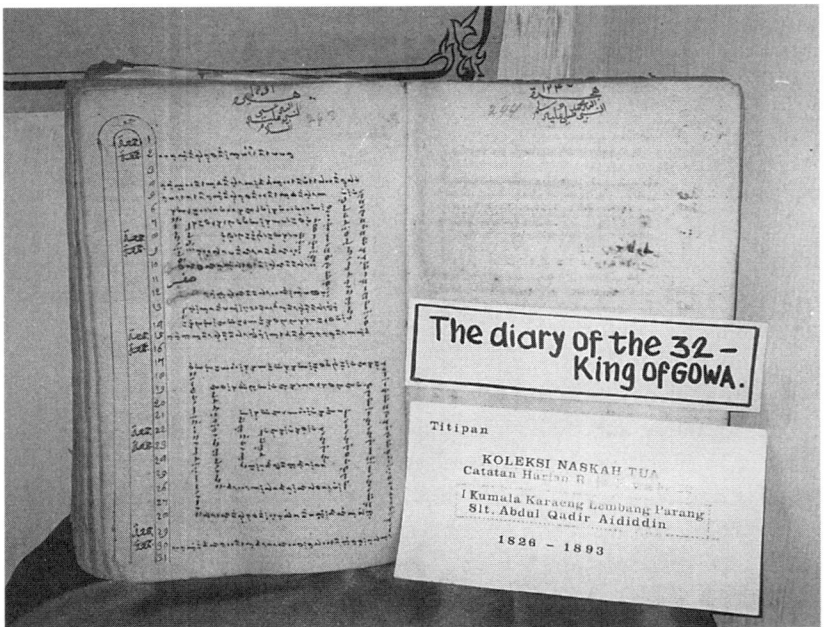

Figure 11. Manuscripts on display at Gowa's royal palace

male *karaeng* may take slaves as wives, but a female *karaeng* may not take slaves as husbands.³⁶ Alongside these specific admonitions were *rapang* that conveyed the importance of blood as the source of rank and the concomitant need to legislate matters involving children.

*Said Gallarrang Manngasa I Kare Mangalle, "It is most bad for men if they divorce, then go marry a woman when they already have children, to divorce their children. One's children must be taken and cared for. He said also, do not disregard your descent, those who are of noble origins. Those who do are bad."*³⁷

If a woman marries one of the tumakkajannangang *and he pays no brideprice and they have children, then [they] divorce, then she marries another* tumakajannangang *and they have children, the woman gets the children from both marriages and the first husband gets none. Made by Karaengta Mateya ri Dima.*³⁸

Rapang reinforced a growing sense of difference between the social position and activities appropriate to men and women. They also underlined the importance of blood as the provider of rank and the need therefore to regulate the mixture of red and white blood.

Numerous *rapang* aided Makassarese efforts to align blood rank and political position. One common *rapang* made a general statement that positions within Gowa should be reserved for those of the appropriate status.

*One other message [from Karaeng Matoaya]: do not choose as rulers of the land people [who] are not truly descendants of rulers. Do not install as envoys people [who] are not truly descendants of envoys. If you install as rulers those who are not indeed descendants of rulers, the land will be ruined. If you install as rulers those who are not indeed descendants of rulers you will be conquered in war.*³⁹

This association between position and rank not only elevated certain social groups, but also defended the boundaries between them. *Gallarrang*—originally the lords of the land before the coming of the *tumanurung*—occupied a mediating position between commoners and nobles. The following *rapang* recognized this position and defended it by protecting *gallarrang* from rapacious higher-ranking nobles.

Spoke Karaengta Tumamenang ri Taenga, "These children of gallarrang, *some are not of* anaq karaeng *rank. If one dies without issue, their possessions may not just be taken and seized by those of* anaq karaeng *rank and [their followers or family] made slaves. Though they are* karaengs *they must return to what has been willed [as inheritance by the deceased* gallarrang*]."*⁴⁰

Some Makassarese who held *gallarrang* titles were of high noble birth; others were not. *Gallarrang* could come from above or from below, and this *rapang* guarded the privileges of lower-status *gallarrang* by making sure their possessions were not seized by their *karaeng* if they died without issue: their inheritance instructions had to be followed. Indeed, inheritance rights were one arena in which written texts helped define social groups and relationships, giving substance to what at heart was an imagined, ideological differentiation based on white-blooded descent. As this *rapang* suggests, the highest-ranking nobles were not free to act arbitrarily, but were held accountable to the guidelines of behavior *rapang* established.⁴¹

Yet, like all cultural products, we should ask who created them, in what social context, and to whose benefit. Although the answer must be obvious by now, one *rapang*'s blunt declaration that the duty of subjects was to pay homage and the duty of rulers was to receive homage is a clear sign that nobles were in the position to shape and benefit from the codification of culture that *rapang* and other manuscripts encouraged.⁴² As has been stated repeatedly, ruling nobles were the most common source of *rapang*. One *rapang* described governing itself as "giving *adat* and custom."⁴³ Another *rapang* related that the first of the seven types of people who commonly visit their rulers are "those who want to know *adat*."⁴⁴ Still another *rapang* recorded the oaths rulers swore to keep to the path set by previous rulers: "I hold strongly, I do not forget the words invoked by Tumamenang ri Makkoayang in the great hall. I hold strongly, I do not forget the words invoked by Tunijalloq. I hold strongly, I do not forget the words invoked by the two brother rulers in the great hall in Somba Opu." Another *rapang* similarly declared, "We say this too: hold to the path of Karaeng Tumapaqrisiq Kallonna."⁴⁵ As a final example of the sources and transmission of *rapang*, one text described how Karaeng Lakiung summoned Gallarrang Manngasa to hear the *adat* he had heard once from Karaeng ri Ujung Tana telling how to act if Karaeng Lakiung died.⁴⁶

Manuscripts often attested to exactly who proclaimed or "made" a given *rapang*. One, for example, said, "This is what Gallarrang Manngasa was asked by Karaengta ri Bontosunggu," while another stated, "Gallarranga I Kare Manngaliki reported the words of Karaengta Tumamenang ri Ujung Tana."⁴⁷ Another *rapang* asserted, "The guidelines of the *tumakajannangang* have been established by Karaengta ri Popoq [and given] to Karaengta ri Bontomanompo this day, this month. The *rapang* guidelines [contain] what normally had been done before."⁴⁸ Sometimes not only is the noble who made the *rapang* known, but so is the precise event that led to its creation. For instance, "A slave of the wife of I Daengta Saju was killed and then this *rapang* was made."⁴⁹ Another *rapang* saying that a slave involved in a knife fight with a noble should be captured, tied up, then executed once the *karaeng* arrived was created when a friend of Karaeng Bontopatongko was involved in just such a fight on the grounds of the *karaeng*'s palace.⁵⁰ Another manuscript noted "Sitting together Karaeng Arumpone and Karaengta ri Ballaka made this *rapang* in Paqbineang: If there is an *anaq karaeng* or *anaq gallarrang* that impregnates a female *anaq karaeng* in a household, he is fined five tai, and they cannot marry." This is one of several regulations that appear to have been aimed at curbing the behavior of positionless young nobles whose marauding and wanton actions became a growing concern in Makassar in the late seventeenth century. The *rapang* closed with the words "This we desire to take as an agreement."⁵¹

Certainly too the contents of *rapang* corresponded to a social order favoring those of high rank. Some of these *rapang* resemble the *parakara* discussed in the next section. One read, "This is the fine according to law. If just the same in rank as the one wronged, he pays a fine. If the one he wronged was a person above him in rank, he pays two fines."⁵² In the same vein another *rapang* emphasized that people harming those of higher rank should not merely be punished, but shamed and desecrated. In this *rapang*, I Kare Kanjara Gallarrang Cambaya stated that someone who kills a person of higher rank is not only to be put to death but the corpse is to be "tossed away like a piece of wood" *(nibuangbatangi)*. Another *rapang*, dated 1700, anticipated future violations of nobles' prerogatives, beginning with the phrase "This *rapang* was made in case a person . . ." It declared that if someone's water buffalo strayed into the rice fields or gardens of a *karaeng*, the owner was to be punished. If much damage was done, the water buffalo was to be slaughtered at once and surrendered to the *karaeng*. If the fields or gardens were not too damaged, only half the slaughtered water buffalo was to be given. If no damage was done, the owner was to prepare an offering of respect consisting of various foods and present it to the *karaeng (kakaqdodomapapolei)*.⁵³ Also concerning water buffalo, another *rapang* declared that if a water buffalo of the *karaeng* was stolen and eaten, all who ate part of it were to be punished, including wives, children, and others in the house of the thief.[54]

More often, however, *rapang* set out guidelines for behavior that favored Makassarese nobles in a more symbolic—though not thereby less real or significant—manner. For example, one short *rapang* said that if a *karaeng* boarded a ship he could either lie down and sleep or move about at will. These two actions were normally forbidden, as everyone was required both to be alert and to not endanger the stability of the ship by moving.[55] Another *rapang* stated, "Purportedly said Gallarrang I Kare Parapa, 'It is not *adat* to wear yellow clothing when visiting the *karaeng*.'" A second *rapang* added, "If you go to the palace of the ruling *karaeng* do not roll up your *gaduq* though you are before [the *karaeng*]. If you want to tuck in your *limagaduq,* then tuck them in; it does not matter."[56] These seemingly trivial matters—being able to sleep or to move aboard ship or being prevented from wearing yellow—appear trivial, but in fact it was from such prohibitions that the distinctions and barriers of the social world were created. Recall, for example, all the visible signs of status permeating Makassarese everyday life introduced in chapter 4. In these symbolic acts reality was constructed. As David Kertzer puts it, "If symbols and rituals are used to build political reality, it is because, as humans, we can do it no other way."[57] In *rapang* and other written manuscripts, in both their contents and their social life as badges of status, the differences between social classes and the prerogatives that belonged to each were codified as part of Makassarese culture.

Rapang, then, had the power to effect a new way of thinking. They created an absolute, external, and consultable measure of behavior that Makassarese should strive to attain. In one meeting, Karaeng Tumamenang ri Lakiung and Tumamenang ri Taenga declared that fitting decisions based on *rapang* would never be destroyed.[58] Similarly, another *rapang* equated the unchanging guidelines governing Makassarese culture with the unalterable truths of Islam. "Said also the honored one from Sungguminasa, 'The three actions that cannot be bargained for are of three types: first, the *adat* guidelines governing the *karaeng*-ship cannot be purchased; second, the words of the Prophet cannot be purchased; third, if the hour of one's death has arrived, it cannot be negotiated.'"[59] One *rapang* even described this act of reference to written texts with the metaphor of a mirror: a *rapang* dated 1621 that concerned blood shed in a feud between two important Gowa nobles declared that to resolve this dispute, "people make a mirror [of whether their actions] were true to the agreement at Bungaya."[60] *Rapang* transcended both the whims of rulers and the memories of elders. *Rapang* also transcended the customs of individual communities, establishing a standard by which all Makassarese should be judged. In this respect, Makassarese attitudes toward written texts resemble Mark Woodward's description of Javanese: "Texts are considered to be important by, and are often referred to by, Javanese of all social classes and religious persuasions. They are thought of as repositories of cultural and religious knowledge that can be referred to when need arises."[61] Perhaps the surest indication of the importance Makassarese came to place on the guidelines *rapang* established as the core of Makassarese culture is this statement: "Purportedly said Karaengta ri Bantang, 'I do not call a person whose mother and father are dead an orphan. Only a person without *adat*, homeland, and *rapang*: I call that person an orphan.'"[62]

Parakara, Punishment, and the Social Order

Rapang were not the only form of written texts that helped codify Makassarese culture and transform Makassarese society. Often found with *rapang* in Makassarese codices are *parakara*: laws that defined principles governing social life and punished their violation. The rulers of Gowa presided over the administration of justice in areas under their influence, and European sources provide some glimpses of how this took place in the seventeenth century. With the Dutch there was often conflict. One source of tension with the VOC was their refusal to allow employees to be subject to the ruler of Gowa's authority while in Makassar, both because they feared the harsh penalties he might impose and because they were unwilling to submit in any way to his authority.[63] On one occasion, the ruler of Gowa declined to deliver to the VOC an ally of his whom the VOC accused of crimes; instead the ruler had him escorted back to his land with four or five ships, "according to Islamic law."[64]

The fate of those Makassarese who committed crimes lay with the ruler of Gowa. European travelers reported with morbid fascination the most shocking cases and punishments that they heard of or witnessed. Gervaise reported that after a man had run amok aboard ship, killing the ruler (Tunijalloq) and then jumping overboard to his death, "His nearest relations and dearest friends were seized and thrown into cauldrons of boiling water until dead as punishment." Elsewhere Gervaise remarked that in public executions, the condemned was tied up and shot at playfully with arrows. The ruler of Gowa often gave prizes to those able to hit a specific part of the body, while an earlier ruler skillfully shot and hit a condemned man's toe with a poisoned arrow, killing him.⁶⁵ The Englishman John Jourdain reported similarly in 1613 that

> if any offend and hath deserved death, he is brought before him, and with a truncke the Kinge will shute him with a little poysonned arrowe. If he will have him live halfe an houre, till hee come to his howse, he will shute him in the arme or legge, butt if hee will have him dye presentlie he will shute him in the breast neere the harte, and then he falleth downe presentlie before him. Others are presentlie crised without any farther tyrall of the cause."⁶⁶

In 1658 Friar Domingo Navarrete wrote,

> About this time the Sumbane commanded two Portugueses should be apprehended for a Murder they had committed, and condemn'd them to death. At the place of Execution he offer'd them their Lives if they would turn Mohametans. The first would not consent, so they ript him up with a sort of Dagger they call Clis [kris]. The other was so daunted at the sight, that he immediately abjur'd Christianity.⁶⁷

These seventeenth-century Europeans appear eager to portray Muslim rulers in distant lands as cruel and exotic, lovers of poisons and purveyors of cruelty. In some, such as Navarrete, this urge derived from a wider context of Muslim-Christian rivalry and the firm conviction that these rulers were both despotic and damned. Others, such as Gervaise and Jourdain, had much to gain by titillating and shocking their reading publics back home by reporting extreme or grotesque events. This is not to say that these reports were fabricated, for this kind of sanctioned violence by the rulers of Gowa was an important tool in maintaining the social order. But what these accounts do not report is the complexity of the law codes and punishments developed in early modern Makassar. Deprived of context, these acts are indeed not only cruel and grotesque, but meaningless. Yet viewed from another perspective, these executions appear calculated and meaningful rather than simply wanton. Thus we should note that Gervaise mentions that a commoner was punished for desertion before battle by exile and during battle by death, while a noble convicted of desertion during battle was not killed, but lost his position and lands, then was exiled. He remarks that exile was the usual punishment meted out to nobles. For commoners, however, death was a far more likely sentence. Only in cases of treason were nobles sentenced to death: boiled alive or thrown into the sea with a heavy stone tied to their neck.⁶⁸ Here we can begin to see how *parakara* spelled out gradations of punishment and the sense in which these penalties inscribed a social order based on class.

Dating *parakara* is problemmatic. From the tenor and contents of some articles it appears that they began to be composed during the seventeenth century. Their heyday, however, came in the eighteenth and possibly in the nineteenth centuries, when Makassarese ideas about "law"—much like their ideas about "culture"—were influenced by and developed against a background of growing experience with the Dutch laws of their colonial overlords. Certainly too the presence of written codifications of Islamic law was an important reference point. Acehnese were compiling Islamic laws in the seventeenth century, though when such compilations reached Makassar or when a parallel development began is difficult to determine. In any case, the process addressed in this section began during the early modern period, but in a sense it "belongs" to the early colonial era. Nevertheless, we should not be bound by artificial periodizations; more critical is that the developments discussed here were part of the family of transformations engendered by the presence of written texts whose authority and origins derived from the past. The penultimate stage in this development of Makassarese "laws" is represented by a collection of twenty-eight *parakara* (circa 1910) listed under the Dutch title *Wetten* (laws).⁶⁹ With this and the persistent early-twentieth-century efforts of Dutch scholars to investigate *"adat* law" throughout the archipelago, Makassarese increasingly conceptualized *parakara* in terms of Western ideas about lawful order and individual rights. Today, Makassarese often describe these ancient *parakara* as analogous to or naturally supportive of contemporary laws in the Republic of Indonesia.

The *parakara* discussed here are taken from a collection of ninety-eight articles published by Matthes in his *Makassaarsche Chrestomathie*. Unlike the *rapang* Matthes published, this collection seems to have been a coherent work that already existed before his arrival; several other nineteenth-century manuscripts contain the same collection of ninety-eight articles. Furthermore, *parakara* texts show far less variation than *rapang* texts, where nothing that can remotely be considered a "standard" version exists. It is from these ninety-eight *parakara* that this section takes its material.

One of the fundamental tenets *parakara* recorded and thereby established was the belief that appropriate punishment depended on social class. The same trend toward social hierarchicalization and naturalization of the authority of white-blooded nobles visible in the creation of *rapang* is apparent in *parakara* as well. More concretely than *rapang*, *parakara* dictated, policed, and in so doing ingrained in Makassarese mentality a fundamental division between social classes. The two arenas in which *parakara* most marked and made real these divisions were in articles concerning marriage and violence.

Parakara dealing with marriage focused particularly on the need to know and preserve blood lines, especially in the case of divorce, since early modern Makassarese increasingly viewed blood as the guarantor of rank in society. Recall, for example, Figure 7, which ordered Makassarese social hierarchy according to the mixture of red and white blood each person possessed. As an introduction to the social legislation concerning marriage, consider these two *parakara*.

If there is a person who says to a husband, "Your wife is adulterous," though the person who spoke those words is indeed trustworthy, the husband cannot take action because it is merely a story. If caught sleeping together, he is allowed to kill them. But if they go to the ruler or to their patron, it is not permitted to kill them. The truth is just investigated. Up until the death of the man and the woman, money is paid by the man who committed adultery.[70]

If a man desires another's wife, and that wife returns his love, though nothing [sexual] takes places, if it is clear in the eyes of the husband, then the two, woman and man, have wronged the husband of the woman. The fine is divided in two up until the two are dead.[71]

At first glance these *parakara* seem simple confirmation of the sexual jealousy so often remarked upon as typical among Makassarese. Catching people engaged in the act of adultery legitimized their murder, and even the appearance of an improper sexual liaison was criminal. By the seventeenth century, Makassarese were famous for this jealousy. Francois Valentijn wrote that they could not "let the least slight or insult go unchallenged," especially when it came to their women. Paulus de Bok, for instance, was stabbed to death by a Makassarese slave in 1678 for such an offense.[72] Two other *parakara* at first glance seemed to make the same point. One declared that if a man joked sexually with another's wife and she became angry and reported him, he was fined. Another said that if a man made sexual advances toward another's wife and she objected or cried and this became known, he was fined and the money given to her husband.[73]

But this easy conclusion that we are simply dealing with a culture in which sexual jealousy was common and often led to violence, while not untrue, stops short of the full significance of this preoccupation with marital fidelity. The creation of a social order based on blood rank required careful proscriptions on sexual liaisons to ensure the true progenitors and thus the rank of offspring. Any uncertainty about descent muddied and undermined the social hierarchy. Certainly significant too is that the husband was considered the aggrieved party in these *parakara;* to him went the fines. Never is there mention of aggrieved wives receiving compensation, or of their husbands being punished for adultery. Another *parakara* stressing the disproportionate burden laid on Makassarese women made this point even more clearly.

If there is a man staying in a house, and there is a woman of the household inside, and they desire each other, and he sleeps with the woman not by going up the ladder,[74] *and the owner of the house is angered, the man is fined one real of eight. The woman is fined two reals of sixteen. If the woman approached the man, those punishments are just the same.*[75]

In this article the woman was held twice as accountable as the man committing adultery. Moreover, it matters not who initiated the liaison: in either case both were wrong, but the woman was doubly wrong.

Recall too the *rapang* stating that a noblewoman who married a male slave was guilty of unnatural and improper sexual behavior, and that whereas a male *karaeng* could take female slaves as wives, a female *karaeng* could not take male slaves as husbands. As one *parakara* further emphasized,

If there are people who want to marry and they go to a religious official and request to be married, their freedom first is investigated well by the religious official. If there is no proof they are slaves, and also no one claims "That is my slave," then they can be married. Even after they already have grandchildren, if a person claims one as "my slave," the person who claimed one as a slave does not get any share [of the offspring]. If it is indeed known by the religious official that the man is a slave and the woman free, the religious official is fined. The father then gets a share of the children.[76]

Here is what we might consider the legal foundation for the cultural "rule" that men could marry women of any status, but that women could only marry men of their own or higher rank. Moreover, it was not the existence of these texts alone that was vital: texts are not simple reflections of the predominant cultural values of the era that produced them, but active agents in the production of those values. The enforcement of these *parakara*, whether through clemency following what Makassarese considered a just murder, the payment of fines, or sanctioned violence, helped establish the boundaries by which actions would be judged, and in the process defined this portion of Makassarese culture.

A further area in which *parakara* established firm cultural boundaries concerned offspring. The *parakara* cited above stated that part of the children of an improper marriage went to the slave father and part to the free mother. Implicit in the *parakara* was that the marriage was dissolved. The following *parakara* are similar.

If a man runs off with a woman who has a husband, and they go to another community, and there in their time together children are born, and then they are found by her husband and taken before a ruler, the man [she ran off with] does not get a share of the children; also the man and woman are fined. The fine the man and woman are charged is given to the husband of the woman. So too the children are given to the husband of the woman.[77]

If there is a [Makassarese] ally of the Company who lives with a Boné woman, whether he pays brideprice or does not pay brideprice, whether lawfully married or not lawfully married, and there are children and the woman says, "He is the father of my children," [if they separate] the children are divided. This was an agreement between the Company and Boné.[78]

Though different in substance, these *parakara* were united in their goal of clarifying descent. Legitimacy and the need to establish progeniture definitively were vital. Both aimed at resolving ambiguities that might preclude determining clearly the rank and with it the proper social position of offspring. Also entangled in these *parakara* was the recognition that Makassarese wanted possession of their children. As Gervaise remarked, "The love of Women, and the desire of Children, is the Prevailing Passion of the Country; insomuch that they Sacrifice every thing for the sake of it, and frequently make Vows to *Mahomet*, that they may have a Numerous Posterity."[79] But the ability to claim progeny as one's own was more than the desire to keep children after a separation. According to Makassarese cultural logic, one's status as a revered ancestor and the likelihood of being included in written genealogies, and thus of being remembered, depended on links through children. Not gaining possession of offspring meant that it was unlikely the true father would be so recalled and that also the opportunity to influence how children positioned themselves in society—within a strategically chosen network of relatives, patrons, and allies—would be lost.

While *parakara* dealing with marriage focused on establishing the guidelines for marriage and the determination of blood rank, *parakara* dealing with violence focused on establishing the boundaries between classes in this new social hierarchy. A necessary prerequisite was establishing that the administration of justice was the preserve of noble rulers who dispensed decisions based on written texts. Numerous *parakara* themselves reinforced the position of rulers as authorities with the right to impose the dictates of these written laws on others. For example, one declares that if a slave performing the duty his *karaeng* gave him is beaten up, the attacker is fined one real, or two reals if the slave bleeds.[80] More than simply treating the slave as property whose damage must be compensated, this *parakara* emphasized the aura of inviolability that surrounded the *karaeng* and his governing. Other *parakara* established rulers as the lawful arbitrators of disputes.

If there are free people who quarrel and knife-fight, and one person is killed and the other caught by the dead man's family, he is treated the same. Now if he runs to the house of the ruler, it is not permitted to treat him the same, he is only warned. Then if it is a male [victim he is fined] thirty, and if a female [victim he is fined] forty; punished too is the person who killed him. According to VOC regulations, he is just fined and not punished.[81]

If an anaq karaeng *commits a crime and is killed by a commoner and he is caught, he is treated the same. Now if he runs to the ruler or to another community, he is not treated the same but is just fined 1 katti and 1 tai. If the murderer cannot pay the fine, then it falls on his children and wives because it was a person of higher rank that he killed* (lanrinna tau irateanra nabuno).[82]

If someone kills and runs to an official, the killer is guilty and the person who was killed is compensated; it is given to the family of the person killed. He too committed a crime. This is the law of the Company: the debt of a life is paid with a life, a debt of blood is paid with blood, a debt of money is paid with money. Slaves and free people are treated just the same by the Company.[83]

Three commonalities in these *parakara* are noteworthy. First, the decision to punish and the fines imposed became standardized in early modern Makassar; regardless of the particularities of the individual event and the personalities involved, written norms were being created and referred to that transcended context. Second, Makassarese culture in the eighteenth century in particular was in part defined in terms of VOC-promulgated laws; as is so often the case, identity lay in difference. Third, these *parakara* entrusted rulers (by the texts they themselves produced, it is true) with a pivotal social role. To rulers fell the task and right to consult written manuscripts and ensure that the cultural rules within them were properly applied.

Other *parakara* further defined aspects of what Makassarese increasingly conceived of as their culture. For example, "If there is an insane person who burns down a house and is killed too by someone said to have run amok, [the person who rank amok] is not treated the same."[84] How often could this have occurred? Regarding a more common but more complicated case, one *parakara* stated that if a person killed someone, then ran to a family member in another community, then was later encountered by a relative of the murdered person and himself killed, this relative was set free because the murder was an act of *siriq*. On the other hand, if this relative was in turn murdered for revenge by a family member of the first killer, that family member was punished.[85] Like some of the *rapang* described earlier, these *parakara* were probably made in response to certain incidents. These *parakara* spelled out increasingly specific and detailed aspects of Makassarese culture. More than the details about how Makassarese culture would treat such events, what is significant for our purposes is that these details were being spelled out. Making *parakara* was making culture.

No aspect of the culture *parakara* made is more evident than the focus on boundaries between social classes. Consider again the article cited above in which punishment fell on the family of a murderer because he killed someone of higher rank, and the following *parakara* as well:

If an anaq karaeng *kills a slave, the fine is halved. For a male victim twenty, for a female victim thirty. Now though the one who killed the slave is caught he cannot be treated the same way because it was a person of lower rank he killed* (katau irawangana nabuno) *This is the VOC regulation: he is only fined not punished.*[86]

If there is an anaq karaeng *or* karaeng *who kills someone who has not done wrong, the killer is wrong. The fine for the killer is one-half.*[87]

Another *parakara* seemed to take the opposite viewpoint: fines were indeed graduated according to social class, but those of higher rank paid proportionally more. A *karaeng* was fined five tai, *anaq karaeng* close to the ruler two tai and ten, *anaq karaeng* distant from the ruler one tai and ten, *gallarrang* in office five tai, local chiefs one tai, *gallarrang* no longer in office one tai and ten, distinguished officials two tai and ten, common officials one tai and ten, lesser officials one tai, commoner males one-half, commoner females one tai; no fine was imposed on slaves, the *parakara* notes, because that is just what one should expect from slaves.[88] In fact, though seemingly at odds, all three of these *parakara* achieved the same end: reinforcing a social hierarchy demarcating the lines between classes. By presuming they existed and then punishing transgressions against them, *parakara* made these boundaries real To use Bourdieu's famous term, the assumption that society was naturally divided into different and defined classes became part of the early modern Makassarese habitus, principles that "generate and organize practices and representations that can be objectively adapted to their outcomes without presupposing a conscious aiming at ends or an express mastery of the operations necessary in order to attain them."[89] That is, they ceased to be constructed rules and became ingrained as natural reflections of the way the world fundamentally was, not values but *beliefs*.

There is an important point to make here about how scholars have viewed premodern Southeast Asia. A widespread pattern in this period is the progression, as in Makassar, from custom and punishment as a matter of consensus, context, and the opinions of elders to the evolution of abstract and absolute legal codes promulgated by increasingly powerful rulers. A surprisingly resilient interpretation is that this progression marks the establishment of what Marx first called Oriental Despotism. Should we, looking from the decks of European ships with Gervaise, Jourdain, and Navarrete, see a Makassarese society that had become increasingly despotic, driven by the exercise of brute power? Was there a passage from societies characterized by tolerance to ones characterized by centralized control? Does a pattern of diffused, small-scale trading networks giving way to economies authorized and dominated by rulers of powerful states signify this passage? Were Makassarese rulers truly absolutist? Does positing the rise and then the greed-driven implosion of absolutist states adequately explain early modern Southeast Asian history and the assumption of power by colonial regimes?

What is missing in this view is the social and cultural context that gave the punishments and the exercise of authority that Europeans witnessed meaning. The rulers of Gowa were not merely powerful despots imposing their will on others, but participants in more sweeping and fundamental social, political, and cultural changes transforming early modern Makassar. Consider the explanation Greg Dening gave of the violence and death in the Marquesas that similarly shocked Europeans: "Violent death sustained their tribal divisions: violent death sustained the social divisions between *kikino* and *tapu*: violent death of the *heana* sustained the lines of descent and the position of the *haka'iki*: violent death sustained the male as *toa*. Violent death had its functions in the creation of order, status and identity."[90] Violence was not culturally meaningless, not simply cruel or despotic; it inscribed and made visible the Marquesan sense of the boundaries and values that defined their world. Could not the way Makassarese imposed punishments and carried out sentences in this new manner be interpreted as acts that established and gave meaning to a new social and cultural order?

The discriminate use of violence is one of the most effective tools humans have developed to make social boundaries public and significant. Spectacle gives substance to cultural values, both in forming them and in making what is intangible tangible. *Parakara* played an important role in the creation of a defined social hierarchy based on blood descent in early modern Makassar. They did so because of the social presence *parakara* manuscripts enjoyed. More than many other genres, *parakara* were written, consulted, and used with regularity; these practices inscribed on Makassarese society the dictates, norms, and rules the *parakara* contained. Behind the public executions Europeans witnessed lay a wave of changes producing a new social order. Punishment made that manifest. In place of the shifting and malleable customs of Makassarese oral societies, an articulated Makassarese culture centered at Gowa and located in manuscripts was coalescing. At the heart of cultural change was the idea of culture itself.

"Culture" and Cultural Change

One of the most important realizations that has emerged in recent anthropology is that culture is not an invariant or autonomous pattern removed from its historical context. Cultures must be historicized and the links between culture, political power, and social change brought into the light. Makassar is no exception. The core cultural values taking shape during this period were not divorced from the political and social formations being created. The social hierarchicalization and political instead of expanding the list of transforming factors as Lieberman did, Wyatt suggested an altogether different agenda for scholarly attention. He argued that an excessive focus on the visible dimensions of political and economic change on mainland Southeast Asia limits our understanding of the region. The formation of large states was not the simple result of political and economic developments, but of deeper intellectual and cultural shifts that undergirded these surface manifestations. Wyatt called for a renewed focus on cultural and intellectual histories that aim at "examining (or at least thinking about) what was happening inside people's heads."[3] Wyatt, in short, believes that intellectual and cultural transformations are of greater weight in shaping the world than political and economic factors are. This perception, however, is at odds with the predominant trend within Southeast Asian history.

The predilection to focus on the effects of rising commerce as the key agent structuring and transforming the region stems from the kind of arguments modern Western historians are most comfortable making: arguments privileging economic forces and concomitant social and political change. Local historical texts are read for the referential information they contain about the past. Once texts are excerpted in this manner, and placed alongside other similar sources, an argument is made that the production of these texts is a symptom of a deeper historical force, in this case commerce. Commercial activity, its waxing and waning, caused the changes and drove the developments in all spheres of Southeast Asian life, including rising literacy. Not only political trends—always a close ally of economic forces for Western historians—but also the social and religious changes that marked early modern Southeast Asia are traced back to commerce.[4] I believe that there are further possibilities. In this work I have been most concerned to read surviving Makassarese historical manuscripts as more than sources from which information can be lifted to construct a narrative account. I have instead tried to envision these same manuscripts within their social and cultural context in the sixteenth and seventeenth centuries and have argued that what have been construed as sources were in fact of tremendous significance as a historical force in their own right. What might be the result if we look at "evidence" not as the visually apparent, surface manifestations of some other force at work, but as a historical agent itself? What if local historical writings are not construed as sources from which information can be mined, but as objects and practices that themselves may have the potential to shape the world around them? Turning from what is most familiar, visible, and amenable to analysis to making histories in the grayer spaces of what is not easily seen and argued for is never easy. But I believe it will repay our efforts by contributing to an understanding of early modern Southeast Asia that is richer, more complex, and more cognizant of the diverse possibilities and patterns of influence that both past and present hold. We should ask, then, what a history of history in Southeast Asia might look like.

Toward a History of History in Southeast Asia

Scholars have only begun to sketch an outline of historical sensibilities and the transformations they have undergone in the divergent societies of the Indonesian archipelago, to say nothing of broader Southeast Asia. The first sustained efforts to grasp Southeast Asians' historical consciousness took place within a debate over whether these sensibilities were "really" historical at all.[5] Although the debate over the historicity of local texts has not been resolved to anyone's satisfaction, today few would insist that Southeast Asian perceptions of the past were or are simply politically motivated or religiously inspired myths. We have recognized that the modern, Western historical consciousness that seemed so natural, inevitable, and right is in fact merely one way of apprehending, organizing, and making use of the past. Understanding the variety of ways that this was done across Southeast Asia was the focus of the aptly titled volume *Perceptions of the Past*.[6] Within its pages insightful studies of diverse historiographical practices competed for the reader's attention. While much work has been done by individuals, no similar comparative work has appeared in the last twenty years.

Members of local societies have perceived their pasts in a congeries of forms. In the structure of their relationships between past and present, in the nature of their links to diverse historiographical traditions, and in narrative structure, social place, cultural intent, and political significance, they show impressive variety across Southeast Asia. The prophetic *Babad Jaka Tingkir* manuscript Nancy Florida explores, the stories of head-hunting and travel Ilongot tell, and the *phongsawadan* chronicles of Thai kings vary widely in these respects. Similarly, the Tagalog adoption of the Catholic narrative of Christ's crucifixion, the Malay encounter with British colonial historiography, and the centuries-long Vietnamese incorporation of Chinese dynastic record keeping all suggest that the traditions of history-making have diverse paths.

A better understanding of the history of history in Southeast Asia must be woven from many strands. Paramount among these are inves-

∞ *Conclusion* ∞

tigations into how the past is perceived, how it is manifested in the present, what meanings are attached to these manifestations, and what effects they have in terms of both conscious manipulations and unplanned consequences. So too it must encompass how forms or genres of history-making interact and affect each other and what the role of historical traditions and transformations in social change has been—that is, evaluating their significance as historical forces in their own right.[7] It is the two final strands about which the most can now be said, and as examples I review briefly history-making in two other Indonesian societies.[8]

In terms of how history-making practices or genres interact, John Bowen's work on the Gayo of northern Sumatra is illuminating. He describes how incorporation into the Indonesian state and the spread of modernist Islam both prompted reexaminations of the past. Existing histories and practices of history-making (what Bowen terms "Gayo historical poetics") in some instances were reworked in accordance with the narrative frameworks and assumptions of a modernist national history and a universal religious tradition. With few exceptions, the result was histories that sought to mediate local historical sensibilities with these externally derived standards for history-making and to reconcile local traditions of Gayo origins and pasts within the context of these newly introduced narratives.[9] As with all historical transformations, this one has been debated and contested in ways that reflect existing social, political, and cultural dynamics, and it promises to transform them. This transformation is not the first among the Gayo, whose earlier histories had been reformed in response to histories from Aceh, their powerful neighbor, and also reflected exposure to Malay historical traditions, but the scope, intensity, and potential to transform Gayo history-making is probably unprecedented. It is certain that the perceptions, meanings, and uses of the past will continue to play a vital role in shaping Gayo life.

As the Gayo and Makassarese cases demonstrate, the advent and spread of literacy had enormous potential to fuel reformations in history-making in part because of the way in which Islam was received. Across Southeast Asia the spread of literacy often took place within the context of expanding universal scripturalist religions including Buddhism, Christianity, and Islam. Each provided frameworks and narratives that transcended or encompassed local perceptions of the past and helped give birth to a profusion of history-making forms. These new frameworks, practices, and genres could be employed in diverse ways, and although the tenor of the exchange between local and foreign is inevitably conditioned by local contexts, we always witness an ongoing and dynamic interplay between existing and novel that spans centuries and unleashes formidable forces for change. Histories are always in play, and always at work.

Nevertheless, despite what these developments engender, we should be wary of describing what has taken place in terms of "shifts" or "transitions." The smallest and seemingly most vulnerable communities have demonstrated ways of apprehending the past that are both firmly grounded in the immediate social context and supremely durable. Written histories have not supplanted oral histories; nationalist narratives have not erased local narratives; modern linear plots have not replaced existing patterns of history-making. Coexisting in ways too diverse and changing to fix in any chart or typography are rich and often-unpredictable mélanges of styles of making the past mean. But although categories elude us, we may yet discern patterns and commonalities that resonate across Southeast Asia. One such pattern might be found in the way new forms of history-making are adapted to existing forms. Another might appear in the way that Southeast Asian societies have been shaped by their historical practices.

In terms of the role of history-making as a shaping social force, Kenneth George's account of mock head-hunting raids in upland Sulawesi evidences a social order profoundly shaped by its conception and use of the past. Head-hunting raids in which coconuts are taken rather than heads are journeys into the past that attempt to carry power and moral order from the remembered past into the present. Living in the upstream highland of central Sulawesi, the *mappurondo* are a marginalized group in the modern Indonesian state. Their head-hunting rites recall and in their commemoration implement (albeit temporarily) a historical (albeit idealized) social order in which the *mappurondo* were at least the equals of their neighbors. These rites are extraordinary acts of public history-making, and by wedding past to present they also renew the authority of men of high standing. "Remembering and mimetic enactments long have been central to the reproduction of the mappurondo social order."[10]

The force of the remembered, chanted, enacted, or written past is a ubiquitous presence. The *mappurondo* case is exemplary here too. Engaging in the act of head-hunting and its concomitant rituals is a way of articulating and responding to labor and trade exchanges, as well as regional and national political relationships in which the *mappurondo* are clearly subordinate and disadvantaged. So too the reversion to a more palatable past that head-hunting journeys enact cannot be disentangled from the local politics of status rivalry, the formation of gender relations, and the emotional context of mourning. Finally, the way the past is made present and its significance asserted among these latter-day headhunters conflicts with the historical interpretations and social visions of the "modern" Christians and Muslims who share the *mappurondo pangngae* heritage. "That Muslims and Christians," George observed, "are busy remembering or forgetting pangngae places them in direct contest with the mappurondo communities for ideological control of the past."[11] More than that, it places these groups in direct contest for authority in shaping the present and giving form to the future. Here as elsewhere, the perception and deployment of situated histories of the past infect all aspects of social life; the past grips the present in innumerable ways. Mapping the main routes by which histories allow the past entry into the present—and the harvest of social turmoil, contestation, and change they yield—is a task we are only beginning, but one well worth undertaking and one that prompts reflection on how the histories we write link past and present.

History-Making, Making History

Any history worth its salt speaks to the present as much as it speaks of the past. Spending years engaged with Makassarese histories, language, and the work of producing this work has accentuated my sense of this doubleness. Indeed, if I am ever going to have a strong sense of how historians understand the relationship between past and present and what "doing history" ultimately amounts to, it is now. This writing also comes at a time when the historical profession, it seems to me, is making important decisions about how perceptions of the past can be evaluated as well as about its own role in American society. Much of this searching stems from the tumultuous appearance of an assortment of intellectual cannonades, relativist assertions, and political stances collectively known as postmodernism.

In a review of recent historiographical trends, Perez Zagorin wrote that the questions, problems, and challenges postmodernism posed to historians are neither damning, convincing, nor even all that new. Good historians have never been credulous about objectivity, unaware of the effects of language, or purveyors of simplistic metanarratives. As Terry Eagleton wryly commented, there is no need to worry about confronting historians who believe that history unfolds in a progressive, unilinear, and deterministic fashion regardless of what we write about it because there aren't any. "Unless they are hiding in caves somewhere, too shamefaced to come out, such people disappeared from the face of the earth a long time ago."[12] Zagorin concluded his review by writing,

> Whatever contributions may be attributed to postmodernism, it is not a tenable set of theories. Founded on a mistaken conception of the nature and function of language, [postmodernism] fails to accord with some of the strongest intuitions and convictions that historians bring to their work, and does not illuminate the nature of history as a discipline dedicated in principle to a true depiction and understanding of the human past. It is probable that its influence will increasingly fade, as seems to be already apparent. Any useful purposes it has served in compelling historians to think afresh about the nature of their inquiry, or in showing them new ways to read texts, or in helping to broaden the horizons of historiography through the inclusion of subjects and forms of life either neglected or ignored by earlier generations of scholars, are to its credit; but such purposes have no dependence on any particular postmodernist doctrines and may be pursued from other and quite different philosophical standpoints. As Kant once said of skepticism, it is not a dwelling place for the human mind; I believe that the same is equally true of postmodernism.[13]

Zagorin's own position is clear, and his critique itself can be accused of portraying postmodernism in its most extreme, inflexible, and unnuanced guises. Nevertheless, it is true that historians have been less receptive to the issues postmodernism raised than have their colleagues in many other disciplines. In large measure this is due to postmodern claims about the elusiveness of knowledge and its privileging of the constructed, arbitrary properties of language over its property as a medium capable of reliably communicating meaning. Historians' faith in the linearity of time and the ability of narrative to describe it is not easily shaken. So too the common postmodern assertion that the past cannot be known raises the ire of historians. To assert that any history we write is but a reflection of the present whose links to the past are illusory flies in the face of what to historians seems the obvious and obviously knowable series of events whose consequences have produced the world in which we live.

Scholarship, however, is not an election, and individual historians do not face a stark choice between only two parties. Histories do not contain simple truths or infinite possibilities, irreproachable facts or irredeemable fictions. Narrative representations are not neutral, reliable transcriptions of the past, but translations, and a historian who pays little heed to the variety of ideological, rhetorical, and cultural ways these translations become convincing robs the past of vitality. Yet agreeing with the strong (and strongly utopian) versions of postmodernism that all is ultimately merely the ironic play of language, that the past is a colorful, fortuitous collage or bricolage, is a theft of equal weight. This is an easy but foolish abrogation of the need to explore the social consequences of history-making. The layers and dimensions of the past are many but not infinite and are tied to particular contexts rather than free-floating. The challenge is acknowledging the multiple facets of the knowledge historians seek about the past. These knowledges are both constructed and found. There is causation in the past (because events do take place that inescapably have repercussions) and in the histories written about it (because rhetorical properties of language inescapably affect meaning). There are narratives and then there are narratives, as it were. There is content and there is form, even if we are hard-pressed to sift the one from the other.

Take the history you now hold as an example. It has had many aims: to construct reasoned arguments about developments in early modern Makassar and their implications for that world, to highlight what I feel are the extraordinary intricacy and complexity of historical change, to explore the relevance of histories and especially of history-making in both past and present. Achieving these aims has involved presenting "facts," examining causation, and defending interpretations. It has also involved crafting narratives, choosing language, and employing the arts of writing to gain its effects. It is an ideological, rhetorical, and cultural artifact of a particular sort. So too readers come to *Making Blood White* with many expectations: to gauge and learn from my historical skills, to reflect upon their own understanding of past and present, perhaps to be convinced that a history of early modern Makassar holds something of interest to them, and certainly to be told if not the unassailable truth about Makassar's past, then at least to read well-reasoned arguments about what was happening, how, why, and to what effect.

Histories are about the past, but not about the past alone. Indeed, history is far more than the interpretation of the past. It involves interpreting the present as well, and careful reflection on how the past is made present, used, and has concrete social, political, and cultural effects. Histories such as this one are referential—meaning they are descriptive accounts of the past—but they are also statements about how we go about creating and manipulating our social world today. We have no need to be content with either "traditional" or "postmodern" varieties of history-making, and much incentive to be attentive to both.

For many the great challenge that postmodernism poses for historians is the specter of being unable to produce referential accounts of the past that are more than creative fictions. The short answer is that, of course, certainty is unattainable; we will always dwell somewhere between truths and tales. But is this really a problem? Perhaps the answer raised by the fact that we can never be sure epistemologically of our ability to wade through the elusive sources and shifting sands of memory to the bedrock of the past itself is to step back and ask whether it is our desire to reach closure and surety that bears closer examination. Our desire for authenticity and true statements is strong indeed. Is the inescapable conclusion to our inability to fulfill these desires a fall into a relativist abyss where fact and falsehood collapse, where all statements are equally valid? I think the answer must be no. The epistemological impossibility of making confident, conclusive, final statements about the past neither implies nor necessitates doubting the ontological existence of people, places, and events in the past and the presence of relationships between them. The meanings, motives, effects, causes, contexts, and what have you of the Holocaust (to take the most politically charged of possible past events) will never reach closure and surety, but that does not mean we must doubt the existence of the Holocaust itself (whatever the arguments of Holocaust negationists).

Doing history means we should think, talk, and write about our past because it is so entangled with and significant to the present. History is present tense, not past perfect. Doing history means trying to grasp the effects of the past on what followed. Making a history is working through the past in order to return to the present enriched. Doing history means seeing history-making as a vital and consequential activity, as part of an ongoing struggle for meaning and understanding that never achieves completion. Instead of praising the faithfulness or condemning the faithlessness of representations of the past, we should acknowledge societies' need for such narratives and the way they are circulated in the present. History-making is like breathing: remembering and forgetting are the inhalations and exhalations of thought, as omnipresent and unreflected upon—and as vital—as the breathing we do throughout our lives. As James Young noted, histories do not resolve the significance of the past, but encourage us to examine and reexamine the complexity and weight of the past on the present.[14] What we seek is not finished bricks in a century-old wall of knowledge removed from the present, but productive engagement with the past because it means so much to us today. Understanding these truths, exploring their complex consequences, and appreciating both the possibilities and responsibilities that history-making entails—these all are surely the tasks of historians.

APPENDIX
EARLY MODERN RULERS OF GOWA AND TALLOQ

Names in brackets are alternate names by which a ruler was known. G and T indicate Gowa and Talloq; the number following the letter indicates the ruler's place on the list.

Rulers of Gowa to 1753

1. Tumanurung — mid-fourteenth century
2. Tumassalangga Barayang (son)
3. Puang Loe Lembang (son)
4. Tuniatabanri (son)
5. Karampang ri Gowa (son)
6. Tunatangkalopi (son) — mid-fifteenth century
7. Batara Gowa (son) [Tumamenang ri Parallakkenna] — mid- to late fifteenth century
8. Tunijalloq ri Passukkiq (son) — late fifteenth century to late 1510 or early 1511
9. Tumapaqrisiq Kallonna (son) [Karaeng Manngutungi, Gallarrang Loaya] — ruled late 1510 or early 1511 to late 1546
10. Tunipalangga (son) [Karaeng Lakiung] — ruled late 1546 to early 1565; lived 1511 to 1565
11. Tunibatta (brother) [Karaeng Dataq] — ruled forty days in 1565; lived 1517 to 1565
12. Tunijalloq (son) [Karaeng Bontolangkasaq] — ruled 1565 to 1590; lived 1545 to late 1590

13. Tunipasuluq (son) (deposed) [Karaeng Bontolangkasaq] — ruled late 1590 to early 1593; lived 1575 to 5 July 1617

14. Tumamenang ri Gaukanna (brother) [Sultan Ala'uddin] — ruled 1593 to 15 June 1639; lived 1586 to 15 June 1639

15. Tumamenang ri Papambatuna (son) [Sultan Malikussaid/ Muhammad Said; Karaeng Ujung; Karaeng Lakiung] — ruled 1639[1] to 5 November 1653; lived 11 December 1607[2] to 5 November 1653

16. Tumamenang ri Ballaq Pangkana (son) (abdicated) [Sultan Hasanuddin; Karaeng Bontomangape] — ruled 1653 to 17 June 1669; lived 12 January 1631 to 12 June 1670

17. Tumammaliang ri Alluq (son) [Sultan Amir Hamzah] — ruled 29 June 1669 to 7 May 1674; lived 31 March 1656 to 7 May 1674

18. Tumatea ri Jakattaraq (brother) (deposed) [Sultan Muhammad Ali; Karaeng Bisei] — ruled 3 October 1674 to 27 July 1677; lived 29 November 1654 to 15 March 1681

19. Tumamenang ri Lakiung (brother) [Sultan Abdul Jalil; Karaeng Sanrabone] — ruled 27 July 1677 to 17 September 1709; lived 18 August 1652 to 17 September 1709

20. Tumamenang ri Sombaopu (grandson)[3] (deposed) [Sultan Ismail; Karaeng Anaq Moncong] — ruled 21 September 1709 to 24 August 1712; lived 18 January 1690 to 1 April 1724[4]

21. Tumamenang ri Pasi (son of T11)[5] (abdicated) [Karaeng Kanjilo; Sultan Sirajuddin; Tumammaliang ri Talloq] — ruled 31 August 1712 to 5 November 1735; lived 17 November 1687 to 22 January 1739

---

1. There are two possible dates. The *lontaraq bilang* report both that he received the royal umbrella on 3 July 1639 and was installed on 19 December 1639. Usually, ceremonially receiving the royal umbrella signified being installed as ruler.

2. This is the *lontaraq bilang* date. According to the *Gowa Chronicle* he was born in 1606.

3. Son of La Patau by a daughter of Abdul Jalil. Thus his claim to the throne came through his mother's side.

4. He ruled Bone from 22 January 1720 to 8 January 1724, when he was deposed.

5. Also grandson of Karaeng Bisei (G18), through which his claim to the throne derived.

22. Tumamenang ri Gowa (grandson of G21, son of T14) [Sultan Abdul Khair Almansyur; I Mallawanggau]   ruled 5 November 1735[6] to 28 July 1742[7]; lived 12 February 1727[8] to 28 July 1742

23. Karaeng Bontolangkasaq   ruled 10 April 1739 to 8 September 1739[9]; lived 14 March 1694 to 8 September 1739

24. Tumamenang ri Kalaqbiranna (brother of G22) [Sultan Abdul Kudus]   ruled 28 July 1742 to 1753[10]; lived December 1733[11] to 1753

Rulers of Talloq to 1760

1. Karaeng Loe ri Sero (son of G6)   mid- to late fifteenth century

2. Tunilabu ri Suriwa (son)   late 15th century to 1500s

3. Tunipasuruq [Karaeng ri Pasi] (son)   1500s to 1540 or 1543

4. Tumenanga ri Makkoayang (son) [Karaeng Pattingalloang]   ruled 1540 or 1543 to 1576; lived 1520 to 1576

5. Karaeng Bainea (daughter) [Karaeng Pattingalloang]   late 1576 to 1590

6. Tunipasuluq (son)   late 1590 to early 1593

7. Karaeng Matoaya (brother) [Sultan Abdullah; Tumamenang ri Agamana; Karaeng Kanjilo; Karaeng Segeri]   ruled 1593 to 1623 (advised son to 1636); lived 1573 to 1636

---

6. On this date all the regalia were brought to him, making him ruler. On 9 November 1735 he received the title *patimatarang*, given to designate a successor.

7. For a period he was ousted by Karaeng Bontolangkasaq. He fled to Talloq on 9 April 1739 and returned to Gowa on 11 October 1740.

8. Based on backdating that he died at age fifteen years, five months, and sixteen days. Not recorded in the *lontaraq bilang*.

9. Not recorded in the *lontaraq bilang*. This date comes from Abdurrazak, *Sejarah Gowa*, 76.

10. This date comes from Abdurrazak, *Sejarah Gowa*, 77.

11. Exact date not given; 20 Rajab 1146 is the Islamic date.

8. Karaeng Kanjilo (son) [Sultan Mudhaffar; Tumammaliang ri Timoroq] — ruled 1623 to 18 May 1641; lived 1598 to 18 May 1641

9. Karaeng Pattingalloang (brother) [Sultan Mahmud; Tumamenang ri Bontobiraeng] — ruled 1641 to 15 September 1654; lived August 1600 to 15 September 1654

10. Tumamenang ri Lampana (son) [Sultan Harrunarasyid] — ruled 1654[12] to 16 June 1673; lived 3 November 1640 to 16 June 1673

11. Tumamenang ri Passiringanna (son) [Sultan Abdul Kadir] — ruled 1673 to 8 January 1709; lived 7 January 1666 to 8 January 1709

12. Tumamenang ri Pasi (son) [Karaeng Kanjilo; Sultan Sirajuddin; Tumammaliang ri Talloq] — ruled 12 August 1709 to 1714[13]; ruled 25 April 1729 to 1739[14]; lived 17 November 1687 to 22 January 1739

13. Tumamenang ri Jawaya (son) [Sultan Najamuddin] — ruled 1714[15] to 24 April 1729; lived 23 December 1708 to 24 April 1729

14. Karaeng Lempangang (brother) [Safiyuddin] — ruled 1739 to 1760[16]; lived 7 December 1709 to 1760

---

12. According to a small collection of *lontaraq bilang* found in NBG 17, pages 135–136, he was installed in early 1655, which is quite possible.

13. Exact date unknown. See note 15.

14. This date comes from A. Ligtvoet, "Geschiedenis van de afdeeling Tallo (Gouvernement van Celebes)," *TBG* 18 (1872): 54.

15. Exact date unknown. Sirajuddin's intention to make him ruler of Talloq was first announced 18 November 1713, while on 19 May 1714 the Dutch were informed he had been installed as ruler of Talloq.

16. These dates come from Ligtvoet, "Geschiedenis van de afdeeling Tallo," 54.

NOTES

A Note on Makassarese Language and Translation

1. Cf. Benedict Anderson's reading of Pramoedya Ananta Toer in *Imagined Communities: Reflections on the Origins and Spread of Nationalism* (London: Verso, 1991 [1983]), 147–148.

2. Cf. Nancy Florida's discussion of Benjamin in her reading of a Javanese text in *Writing the Past, Inscribing the Future: History as Prophecy in Colonial Java* (Durham, N.C.: Duke University Press, 1995), 4–8, 85–37.

3. The closest to an "authority" on Makassarese transcription and spelling is A. A. Cense and Abdurrahim's *Makassaars-Nederlands Woordenboek* ('s-Gravenhage: Martinus Nijhoff, 1979).

4. In this I follow the sensible guidelines proposed by Martin Rössler in his "Note on Orthography and Pronunciation" in H. Th. Chabot, *Kinship, Status, and Gender in South Celebes* (Leiden: KITLV, 1996 [1950]), 55–57.

Introduction

1. Louis A. Montrose, "Professing the Renaissance: The Poetics and Politics of Culture," in *The New Historicism*, ed. H. Aram Veeser (New York: Routledge, 1989), 20.

2. Hendrik M. K. Maier, *In the Center of Authority: The Malay Hikayat Merong Mahawangsa* (Ithaca, N.Y.: Cornell University Southeast Asia Program, 1988). The opposite approach to the historicity of Malay texts is found in C. Skinner's introduction to the *Sja'ir Perang Mengkasar*. C. Skinner. ed. and trans., *Sja'ir Perang Mengkasar* ('s-Gravenhage: Martinus Nijhoff, 1963), 6–18.

3. Keith Windschuttle, *The Killing of History: How a Discipline is Being Murdered by Literary Critics and Social Theorists* (Paddington, Australia: Macleay Press, 1996), 249, 220–221.

4. Stanley Fish, "Commentary: The Young and the Restless," in *The New Historicism*, ed. H. Aram Veeser (New York: Routledge, 1989), 312.

5. John Pemberton, *On the Subject of "Java"* (Ithaca, N Y.: Cornell University Press, 1994).

6. Though perhaps awkwardly lumped together, in addition to Pemberton's *On the Subject of "Java,"* see the following works: Benedict R. O'G Anderson, *Language and Power: Exploring Political Cultures in Indonesia* (Ithaca, N.Y.: Cornell University Press, 1990); Florida, *Writing the Past;* James Siegel, *Solo in the New Order: Language and Hierarchy in an Indonesian City* (Princeton, N.J.: Princeton University Press, 1993); Anna Tsing, *In the Realm of the Diamond Queen: Marginality in an Out-of-the-Way Place* (Princeton, N.J.: Princeton University Press, 1993). Another way to approach this discourse would be to examine Cornell's journal *Indonesia,* particularly its articles on popular culture and the writer Pramoedya Ananta Toer.

7. Greg Dening, *History's Anthropology: The Death of William Gooch* (Washington, D.C.: University Press of America, 1988), 3, 100.

8. No more precise definition of "history" will be offered in this work. Tales, accounts, stories, narratives, histories—all are statements about the past in the present. To circumscribe the meaning of the term "history" typically involves according it a privileged status based on rules of evidence, purpose, and narration peculiar to the Western historical tradition. No such move is made or necessary here.

9. David Lowenthal, *The Past Is a Foreign Country* (Cambridge: Cambridge University Press, 1985), xv.

10. Compare this with Hoskins' identification of three such mediums on Sumba: oral narratives, objects, and actions. Janet Hoskins, *The Play of Time: Kodi Perspectives on Calendars, History, and Exchange* (Berkeley: University of California Press, 1993), chapters 3–5. See also her recent *Biographical Objects: How Things Tell the Stories of People's Lives* (New York: Routledge, 1998).

11. Keith H. Basso, *Western Apache Language and Culture: Essays in Linguistic Anthropology* (Tucson: University of Arizona Press, 1990), 170.

12. Renato Rosaldo, *Ilongot Headhunting 1883–1974: A Study in Society and History* (Stanford, Calif.: Stanford University Press, 1980), 56.

13. See Mona Ozouf, *Festivals and the French Revolution,* trans. Alan Sheridan (Harvard: Harvard University Press, 1988 [1976]), 126–157.

14. Sigmund Freud, *Civilization and Its Discontents,* ed. and trans. James Strachey (New York: Norton, 1961 [1930]), 18.

15. Richard E. Strassberg, *Inscribed Landscapes: Travel Writing from Imperial China* (Berkeley: University of California Press, 1994), 6–7.

16. See David I. Kertzer, *Ritual, Politics, and Power* (New Haven, Conn.: Yale University Press, 1988).

17. Hoskins, *The Play of Time,* chapter 5.

18. Toby Alice Volkman, *Feasts of Honor: Ritual and Change in the Toraja Highlands* (Urbana: University of Illinois Press, 1985), 21.

19. Paul Connerton, *How Societies Remember* (Cambridge: Cambridge University Press, 1989), 70, 102.

20. Hoskins, *The Play of Time,* 166.

21. Ibid., 137–138.

22. For introductions to and commentaries on this tradition see Nicholas Thomas, *Entangled Objects: Exchange, Material Culture, and Colonialism in the Pacific* (Cambridge: Harvard University Press, 1991), and Annette B. Weiner, *Inalienable Possessions: The Paradox of Keeping-While-Giving* (Berkeley: University of California Press, 1992).

23. See Annette B. Weiner and Jane Schneider, eds., *Cloth and Human Experience* (Washington, D.C.: Smithsonian Institution Press, 1991).

24. Skinner, *Sja'ir Perang Mengkasar*, 122–123, 126–127.

25. Greg Dening, *Islands and Beaches: Discourse on a Silent Land: Marquesas 1774–1880* (Chicago: Dorsey Press, 1980), 21.

26. R. Blok, "Beknopte geschiedenis van het Makasaarsche Celebes en Onderhoorigheden," *TNI* 10 (1848): 4.

27. Interestingly, it seems that after 1669 chronicle writing in South Sulawesi shifted away from the Makassarese to the victorious Bugis, whose *Boné Chronicle* in particular was modeled on the *Gowa Chronicle* and written in the late seventeenth century.

Chapter 1. Early Modern Makassar and Its Contexts

1. The designation "early modern" is ambiguous. Originally the term was used as a convenient label for the period in between the decline of Southeast Asia's "classical" polities at the end of the thirteenth century and the colonial period beginning in the late eighteenth century. This periodization poorly fits Makassar, however, because there was no extensive state prior to the rise of Gowa in the sixteenth century and the area was subject to Dutch colonial rule in the late seventeenth century. There is simply no good alternative, and "early modern" should be considered as a topic for debate rather than an established category.

2. J. D. Legge, "The Writing of Southeast Asian History," in *The Cambridge History of Southeast Asia*, Volume 1: *From Early Times to c. 1800*, ed. Nicholas Tarling (Cambridge: Cambridge University Press, 1992), 46–47. See also C. C. Berg, "Javanese Historiography—A Synopsis of Its Evolution," in *Historians of Southeast East Asia*, ed. D. G. E. Hall (London: Oxford University Press, 1961); H. J. de Graaf, "Later Javanese Sources and Historiography," in *An Introduction to Indonesian Historiography*, ed. Soedjatmoko et al. (Ithaca, N.Y.: Cornell University Press, 1965); and M. C. Ricklefs, "Javanese Sources in the Writing of Modern Javanese History," in *Southeast Asian History and Historiography*, ed. C. D. Cowan and O. W. Wolters (Ithaca, N.Y.: Cornell University Press, 1976), 333–337.

3. Adrian Vickers, "Balinese Texts and Historiography," *History and Theory* 29, 2 (1990): 160, 161.

4. J. Noorduyn, "Origins of South Celebes Historical Writing," in *An Introduction to Indonesian Historiography*, ed. Soedjatmoko et al. (Ithaca, N.Y.: Cornell University Press, 1965), 140. See also J. Noorduyn, "Some Aspects of Macassar-

Buginese Historiography," in *Historians of Southeast East Asia*, ed. D. G. E. Hall (London: Oxford University Press, 1961).

5. Relevant works by Helen Creese include "Balinese *Babad* as Historical Sources: A Reinterpretation of the Fall of Gelgel," *BKI* 147 (1991); "The Balinese *Kakawin* Traditions: A Preliminary Description and Inventory," *BKI* 155, 1 (1999); and *Parthayana—The Journeying of Partha; An Eighteenth-century Balinese Kakawin* (Leiden: KITLV, 1998). See also Raechelle Rubinstein's invaluable work *Beyond the Realm of the Senses: The Balinese Ritual of Kakawin Composition* (Leiden: KITLV, 2000).

6. Anthony Reid, *Southeast Asia in the Age of Commerce 1450–1680*, 2 vols. (New Haven, Conn.: Yale University Press, 1988, 1993).

7. Indonesian nationalist historiography and practice are discussed in Anthony Reid, "The Nationalist Quest for an Indonesian Past," in *Perceptions of the Past in Southeast Asia*, ed. Anthony Reid and David Marr (Singapore: Asian Studies Association of Australia, 1979), and Janet Hoskins, *The Play of Time*, chapter 11.

8. Together these two themes structure the history of early modern Indonesia written by that nation's foremost historian. See Sartono Kartodirdjo, *Pengantar Sejarah Indonesia Baru: 1500–1900. Dari Emporium Sampai Imperium* (Jakarta: Gramedia, 1992 [1987]).

9. Important secondary sources recounting some portion of this story include Dg. Patunru Abdurrazak, *Sedjarah Gowa* (Ujung Pandang: Jajasan Kebudajaan Sulawesi Selatan dan Tenggara, 1969); Leonard Andaya, *The Heritage of Arung Palakka: A History of South Sulawesi (Celebes) in the Seventeenth Century* (The Hague: Martinus Nijhoff, 1981); F. D. Bulbeck, "A Tale of Two Kingdoms: The Historical Archaeology of Gowa and Tallok, South Sulawesi, Indonesia" (Ph.D. diss., Australia National University, 1992); Mattulada, *Menyusuri Jejak Kehadiran Makassar dalam Sejarah (1510–1700)* (Ujung Pandang: Hasanuddin University Press, 1991); Christian Pelras, *The Bugis* (Oxford: Blackwell, 1996); Anthony Reid, "A Great Seventeenth-Century Indonesian Family: Matoaya and Pattingalloang of Makassar," *Masyarakat Indonesia* 8, 1 (1981), and "The Rise of Makassar," *Review of Indonesian and Malaysian Affairs* 17 (1983).

10. These events, and the wider historical context of early Indonesian history, are discussed and the relevant literature reviewed in Peter Bellwood, *Prehistory of the Indo-Malaysian Archipelago*, revised edition (Honolulu: University of Hawai'i Press, 1997).

11. Roger Frederick Mills, "Proto South Sulawesi and Proto Austronesian Phonology" (Ph.D. diss., University of Michigan, 1975), 503–504.

12. This evidence is discussed in Pelras, *The Bugis*, 25–26, 66–67.

13. See in particular the evaluation of early European sources in Christian Pelras, "Les premières données occidentales concernant Célèbes-sud," *BKI* 133, 2 and 3 (1977).

14. Campbell Macknight, *The Voyage to Marege': Macassan Trepangers in Northern Australia* (Carlton, Australia: Melbourne University Press, 1976).
15. Bulbeck, "A Tale of Two Kingdoms."
16. The rulers of Gowa and Talloq are listed in the appendix.
17. Reid, "Rise of Makassar," 117.
18. Tomé Pires, *The Suma Oriental: An Account of the East, from the Red Sea to Japan,* trans. Armando Cortesão (London: Hakluyt Society, 1944), 326–327.
19. Cited in Francois Valentijn, *Oud en Nieuw Oost-Indien,* vol. 3 (Amsterdam: J. C. van Kesteren, 1862), 154–155.

Chapter 2. Culture and History-Making

1. The issue of "visibility" and seeing past what European archival sources depict is an important theme in much recent work on the archipelago. In terms of economic activity, see Heather Sutherland, "Believing Is Seeing: Perspectives on Political Power and Economic Activity in the Malay World 1700–1940," *JSEAS* 26, 1 (1995). Juxtaposing what is visible and significant in Western and Balinese culture is the theme of Margaret J. Wiener, *Visible and Invisible Realms: Power, Magic, and Colonial Conquest in Bali* (Chicago: University of Chicago Press, 1995).
2. The writer used the *lontaraq beru* script to transcribe Arabic. The script is poorly suited to the task because the sounds do not correspond to any commonly encountered Islamic statement. Literally transliterated, the sounds are separated into two words: "a/u ta u/a pa la la ta" and 'ra ja sa ha ma ra da." The museum catalog number for the roll is A4561.
3. A similar example is a sash that the queen of Tanete gave B. F. Matthes. Inscribed with a short Bugis text and Arabic declaration, the sash so inscribed became a talisman capable of warding off disaster and other magical tasks. B. F. Matthes, "Over een' Boegineeschen Krisband of Sjerp," in *Feestbundel van Taal-, Letter-, Geschied- en Aardrijkskundige Bijdragen ter Gelegenheid van zijn Tachtigsten Geboortedag aan Dr. P. J. Veth* (Leiden: E. J. Brill, 1894).
4. Anderson, *Language and Power,* 127. Similarly, "For others, however, Hebrew was all the more sacred and efficacious for remaining incomprehensible. The less it was penetrable, the brighter its aura of 'mana' shone, and the more its dictates escaped human intelligences, the more they became clear and ineluctable to supernatural agents." Umberto Eco, *The Search for the Perfect Language* (Oxford: Blackwell, 1995), 123.
5. Jane Drakard, *A Kingdom of Words: Language and Power in Sumatra* (Oxford: Oxford University Press, 1999). Further examples of the use of Arabic and its ability to transform mundane objects into powerful protective amulets could consume many pages. For a particularly intriguing discussion of a belt buckle and the mystical interpretation of Arabic letters it depicted, see Paul Michael Taylor and Lorraine V. Aragon, *Beyond the Java Sea: Art of Indonesia's Outer Islands*

(Washington, D.C.: National Museum of Natural History, Smithsonian Institution, 1991), 301.

6. Barbara Watson Andaya, *To Live as Brothers: Southeast Sumatra in the Seventeenth and Eighteenth Centuries* (Honolulu: University of Hawai'i Press, 1993), 90, 146.

7. Vicente Rafael, *Contracting Colonialism: Translation and Christian Conversion in Tagalog Society under Early Spanish Rule* (Ithaca, N.Y.: Cornell University Press, 1988), 117.

8. Mattulada, "Islam di Sulawesi Selatan," in *Agama dan Perubahan Sosial,* ed. Taufik Abdullah (Jakarta: Yayasan Ilmu-Ilmu Sosial, 1983), 221. A more elaborate version of this legend is found in Russell Jones, "Ten Conversion Myths from Indonesia," in *Conversion to Islam,* ed. Nehemia Levtzion (New York: Holmes and Meier, 1979), 149–150.

9. Mattulada, "Islam di Sulawesi Selatan," 222.

10. Rubinstein, *Beyond the Realm of the Senses.*

11. Though many works could be cited, see Jane Monnig Atkinson, *The Art and Politics of Wana Shamanship* (Berkeley: University of California Press, 1989); Joel Kuipers, *Power in Performance: The Creation of Textual Authority in Weyewa Ritual Speech* (Philadelphia: University of Pennsylvania Press, 1990); and Robert W. Hefner, *Hindu Javanese: Tengger Tradition and Islam* (Princeton, N.J.: Princeton University Press, 1985).

12. And beyond. Umberto Eco described kabbalistic perceptions in Europe that "words in Hebrew appeared as forces, as sounds which, as soon as they are unleashed, are able to influence the course of events . . . a language whose utterances set supernatural forces in motion." Eco, *Search,* 122–123.

13. C. C. Berg, "The Javanese Picture of the Past," in *An Introduction to Indonesian Historiography,* ed. Soedjatmoko et al. (Ithaca, N.Y.: Cornell University Press, 1965), 89. See also Amin Sweeney, *A Full Hearing: Orality and Literacy in the Malay World* (Berkeley: University of California Press, 1987), 108–110.

14. Leonard Andaya, "Treaty Conceptions and Misconceptions: A Case Study from South Sulawesi," *BKI* 134, 2 and 3 (1978).

15. Ahmad Rahman et al., *Sastra Lisan Makassar: Laporan Penelitian* (Jakarta: Departemen Pendidikan dan Kebudayaan, 1976), 43–44.

16. Lorraine M. Gesick, *In the Land of Lady White Blood: Southern Thailand and the Meaning of History* (Ithaca, N.Y.: Cornell University Southeast Asia Program, 1995), chapter 3.

17. Drs. G. J. Wolhoff and Abdurrahim, *Sedjarah Goa* (Ujung Pandang: Jajasan Kebudajaan Sulawesi Selatan dan Tenggara, 1959), 18. Much cited, this brief sentence is often taken to mean that Daeng Pamatteq designed the Makassarese alphabet *(lontaraq beru)* or perhaps the now rare and archaic old Makassarese script *(jangang-jangang).* In fact, Daeng Pamatteq was the first to record historical information on palm leaves, thereby creating the first Makassarese *documents (lontaraq).* Fachruddin reached the same conclusion in his work. Fachruddin

Ambo Enre, "Ritumpanna Welenrennge: Telaah Filologis Sebuah Episoda Sastera Bugis Klasik Galigo" (Ph.D. diss., Universitas Indonesia, 1983), 35–40.

18. Wolhoff and Abdurrahim, *Sedjarah Goa*, 18.

19. Rahim and Ridwan, *Sejarah Kerajaan Tallo' (Suatu Transkripsi Lontara')* (Ujung Pandang: Lembaga Sejarah dan Antropologi, 1975), 9.

20. See his comments in *Makassaarsche Spraakkunst* (Amsterdam: Nederlandsch Bijbelgenootschap, 1858), xi.

21. See his article "Medeedeelingen over Makassaarsche Taal- en Letterkunde," *BKI* 6 (1863).

22. See, for example, Parawansa et al., *Sastra Sinrilik Makassar* (Jakarta: Departemen Pendidikan dan Kebudayaan, 1992).

23. An overview is found in Rahman et al., *Sastra Lisan Makassar*.

24. It is always hazardous to argue that such an absence points to a particular conclusion. Yet we should recognize that literacy is often restricted to particular domains, rather than being a generally applied practice. Among Tengger priests and premodern rural Islamic scholars, to cite only one possible example, writing was applied to religious matters but not to secular ones. Hefner, *Hindu Javanese*, 205–206.

25. Two surveys of issues surrounding Makassarese scripts are Abdul Kadir Manyambeang, "Lontaraq Riwayaqna Tuanta Salamaka ri Gowa: Suatu Analisis Linguistik Filologis" (Ph.D. diss., Hasanuddin University, 1996), 26–31; and J. Noorduyn, "Variation in the Bugis/Makasarese Script," *BKI* 149, 3 (1993).

26. Rubinstein, *Beyond the Realm of the Senses*, 26, 38.

27. Mills noted in his discussion of South Sulawesi languages that there were no Sanskrit words that are not also found in Malay or Javanese. His comments on the origins of the Makassarese script are found in Mills, "Proto South Sulawesi," 600–603. See also Matthes, *Makassaarsche Spraakkunst*, ix.

28. Noorduyn, "Origins," 144, 154.

29. Rahim and Ridwan, *Sejarah Kerajaan Tallo'*, 11.

30. ANRI 26/22, page 37.

31. Cf. Pierre-Yves Manguin, "Shipshape Societies: Boat Symbolism and Political Systems in Insular Southeast Asia," in *Southeast Asia in the Ninth to Fourteenth Centuries*, ed. David G. Marr and A. C. Milner (Singapore Institute of Southeast Asian Studies, 1986).

32. Rahim and Ridwan, *Sejarah Kerajaan Tallo'*, 11.

33. Though also found in Matthes' *Makassaarsche Chrestomathie* on page 250, this slightly more explicit wording is taken from ANRI 26/21, page 1. Matthes' work is the best-known and most important collection of Makassarese texts. The second edition is B. F. Matthes, *Makassaarsche Chrestomathie: Oorspronkelijke Makassaarsche geschriften in proza en poëzij uitgegeven* ('s-Gravenhage: Martinus Nijhoff, 1883).

34. The term "diary" is misleading because of the connotations it carries in English. The idea of a private record of the internal thoughts of an individual is

inappropriate in early modern South Sulawesi. See A. A. Cense, "Old Buginese and Macassarese Diaries," *BKI* 122, 4 (1966).

35. H. D. Kamaruddin et al., *Lontarak Bilang Raja Gowa dan Tallok (Naskah Makassar),* vol. 1 (Ujung Pandang: Proyek Penelitian dan Pengkajian Kebudayaan Sulawesi Selatan La Galigo, 1969), 26–27. The Dutch version contains only four of these entries for the entire year. A. Ligtvoet, "Transcriptie van het Dagboek der Vorsten van Gowa en Tello," *BKI* 28 (1880): 18.

36. N10, page 6.

37. M. C. Ricklefs has reached similar conclusions about the perceived need to transmit sacred manuscripts unchanged in early-eighteenth-century Java. M. C. Ricklefs, *The Seen and Unseen Worlds in Java 1726–1749* (St. Leonards, Australia: Asian Studies Association of Australia; Honolulu: University of Hawai'i Press, 1998), 34. At the same time, contrast this with the *Babad Tanah Jawi,* which underwent extensive textual manipulations over the course of its history to meet changing needs for political legitimation. An entry point for the substantial work done on this history is found in E. P. Wieringa, "An Old Text Brought to Life Again: A Reconsideration of the 'Final Version' of the *Babad Tanah Jawi" BKI* 155, 2 (1999).

38. Cornelis Speelman, "Notitie dienende voor eenen Korte Tijd en tot nader last van de Hoge Regering op Batavia" (typed manuscript at KITLV based on a 1670 original), 342–343; Blok, "Beknopte geschiedenis," 4–24; "Makassaarsche Historiën," *TBG* 4 (1855), 111–118; Matthes, *Makassaarsche Chrestomathie* [1883], 146–184.

39. N11, pages 10, 26, 32.

40. ANRI 8/16, page 17.

41. Ibid., page 74.

42. Raechelle Rubinstein, "Colophons as a Tool for Mapping the Literary History of Bali: Ida Pedanda Made Sidemen—Poet, Author and Scribe," *Archipel* 52 (1996), 190.

43. John R. Bowen, *Muslims through Discourse: Religion and Ritual in Gayo Society* (Princeton, N.J.: Princeton University Press, 1993); Gesick, *Lady White Blood.*

44. This is a feature of other Austronesian languages as well, such as Hawaiian and Maori.

45. For parallel discussions of Balinese conceptions of history and its social context, see Putu Davies, "The Historian in Bali," *Meanjin* 50, 1 (1991), and Henk Schulte Nordholt, "Origin, Descent and Destruction: Text and Context in Balinese Representations of the Past," *Indonesia* 54 (1992).

46. Manyambeang, "Lontaraq Riwayaqna Tuanta Salamaka," 190.

47. Rubinstein, *Beyond the Realm of the Senses,* 63.

48. For example, the smearing of the banners *(bate)* of Gowa is specifically mentioned in the Gowa *lontaraq bilang* entry for 15 November 1634. Ligtvoet, "Dagboek der Vorsten van Gowa en Tello," 6, 95.

49. Cense and Abdoerrahim, *Makassaars-Nederlands Woordenboek,* 836–837.

50. Manyambeang, "Lontaraq Riwayaqna Tuanta Salamaka," 187.

51. Nicholas Gervaise, *An Historical Description of the Kingdom of Macasar* (London: N.p., 1701 [1685]), 140–141.

52. Leonard Y. Andaya, "The Nature of Kingship in Bone," in *Pre-Colonial State Systems in Southeast Asia*, ed. Anthony Reid and Lance Castles (Kuala Lumpur: Malayan Branch of the Royal Asiatic Society, 1975).

53. Chabot, *Kinship, Status and Gender*, 83–84; Martin Rössler, "Cultural Models and Socio-Religious Change: An Example from South Sulawesi," *Antropologi Indonesia* 49 (1991): 68–69.

54. Local scholars in South Sulawesi place particular importance on *siriq* as the basis for this. See, for example, Mohamad Laica Marzuki, *Siri': Bagian Kesadaran Hukum Rakyat Bugis-Makassar (Sebuah Telaah Filsafat Hukum)* (Ujung Pandang: Hasanuddin University Press, 1995).

55. N9, page 4.

Chapter 3. Transformations in Makassarese Perceptions of the Past

1. Two exemplary Dutch representatives are M. J. Friedericy, "De Gowa-Federatie (1926)," Adatrechtbundels 31: *Selebes* ('s-Gravenhage: Martinus Nijhoff, 1929); B. F. Matthes, "Boegineesche en Makassaarsche Legenden," *Dr. Benjamin Frederik Matthes: Zijn Leven en Arbeid*, ed. H. van den Brink (Amsterdam: Nederlandsch Bijbelgenootschap, 1943).

2. Significant attention has been paid to the manipulation of the past in modern Indonesia. Three illuminating analyses are found in Hoskins, *The Play of Time*; Pemberton, *On the Subject of "Java"*; and Margaret Wiener, "Making Local History in New Order Bali: Public Culture and the Politics of the Past," in *Staying Local in the Global Village: Bali in the Twentieth Century*, ed. Raechele Rubinstein and Linda H. Connor (Honolulu: University of Hawai'i Press, 1999), 51–89.

3. See Amin Sweeney, *Authors and Audiences in Traditional Malay Literature* (Berkeley: University of California Center for South and Southeast Asia Studies, 1980).

4. Sweeney, *A Full Hearing*, 65.

5. On the more general Austronesian tendency to link origins and identity see James J. Fox, "Austronesian Societies and Their Transformations," in *The Austronesians: Historical and Comparative Perspectives*, ed. Peter Bellwood, James J. Fox, and Darrell Tryon (Canberra: Research School of Pacific and Asian Studies, Australia National University, 1995). On the cultural importance Austronesians placed on origins and the foundations of communities, see Peter Bellwood, "Hierarchy, Founder Ideology and Austronesian Expansion," in *Origins, Ancestry, and Alliance: Explorations in Austronesian Ethnography*, ed. James J. Fox and Clifford Sather (Canberra: Australia National University, 1996).

6. Connerton, *How Societies Remember*, 102.

7. Cf. Daniel L. Schacter, *Searching for Memory: The Brain, the Mind, and the Past* (New York: Basic Books, 1996), chapters 9–10.

8. This text (N9 in the bibliography), recording a previously orally trans-

mitted account of the past, comes from a recently collected manuscript. A copy was made for me in 1997 from an existing written text owned by Haja Sadariah Daeng Asseng of Sungguminasa. The date of this original is not known. The oral stories Friedericy collected and recorded in the 1920s correspond surprisingly closely with the text presented here. Friedericy, "De Gowa-Federatie," 398–402.

9. "Cinde" in Makassarese means a piece of cotton cloth or silk, usually South Asian, woven in a distinctive and colorful pattern different from South Sulawesi weaving traditions. As in other places in the archipelago, many Makassarese saw such cloths as valuable heirlooms.

10. A kind of Makassarese flute.

11. A kind of tropical magnolia.

12. A kind of large, tall, and straight tree.

13. Friedericy, "De Gowa-Federatie," 403.

14. Speculatively, it is possible the information about the recent past his Pattalassang informants remembered was included at Friedericy's urging, since a continuous account from past to present was certainly what Friedericy believed comprised a proper history.

15. Annette B. Weiner, "Inalienable Wealth," *American Ethnologist* 12, 2 (1985), 210.

16. Wolhoff and Abdurrahim, *Sedjarah Goa*, 23–24.

17. N8, pages 1–3.

18. ANRI 60/80, page 33.

19. Ibid., pages 40–41.

20. Helen Creese, *In Search of Majapahit: The Transformation of Balinese Identities* (Clayton, Australia: Monash University Centre of Southeast Asian Studies, 1997), 12.

21. This very modest Islamization of the past is a common feature of Indonesian oral histories and stems from the importance of Islam in the period the story was told. Cf. Bowen, *Muslims through Discourse*, chapter 9.

22. The position of Makassarese women on this is hard to divine from the sources. Interestingly, the verb *lariang* does not distinguish between elopement and kidnapping. That is, the acquiescence or resistance of the woman involved is not a factor Makassarese men consider when reacting to *lariang*.

23. Friedericy, "De Gowa-Federatie," 397.

24. Andaya, *Arung Palakka*, 168–169.

25. Chabot, *Kinship, Status and Gender*, 236–246.

26. ANRI 18/23, page 13.

27. Chabot, *Kinship, Status and Gender*, 104–105. My translation differs from the English translation provided in the book.

28. Unfortunately, we still await a detailed study of Makassarese oral composition and traditions.

29. James J. Fox, "A Rotinese Dynastic Genealogy: Structure and Event," in

The Translation of Culture: Essays to E. E. Evans-Pritchard, ed. T. O. Beidelman (London: Tavistock, 1971), 44.

30. Wolhoff and Abdurrahim, *Sedjarah Goa*, 53–56.

31. A "half banner" was a type of royal umbrella with a top shaped like a half circle.

32. Makassarese used "Javanese" as an umbrella term to refer to peoples from the western archipelago; most often they are referring to Malays.

33. See A. A. Cense, "Enige aantekeningen over Makassaars-Boeginese geschiedschrijving," *BKI* 107 (1951).

34. Cf. Noorduyn, "Origins."

35. Marshall Sahlins, *Islands of History* (Chicago: University of Chicago Press, 1985), 41.

36. The first mention of a date in which Makassarese conceptions of time and history intersect with imported calendrical systems is found in Wolhoff and Abdurrahim, *Sedjarah Goa*, 55.

37. Chabot, *Kinship, Status and Gender*, 90. Oral genealogical memory also allows more flexibility than detailed written accounts permit. For example, on page 86 Chabot notes that if for three generations no marriages are contracted between the descendants of two siblings, they are considered strangers or only vaguely related. "In such cases people are not certain any more about the exact relationship. Statements contradict each other, and in such cases of uncertainty there is a tendency to settle on that kin relationship which one regards as proper and normal for a marriage between kin."

38. Bugis genealogies are discussed at length in Shelly Errington, *Meaning and Power in a Southeast Asian Realm* (Princeton, N.J.: Princeton University Press, 1989), 217–226.

39. Rahim and Ridwan, *Sejarah Kerajaan Tallo'*, 21–23

40. This refers to a custom in which two sets of parents agree to have their infants nursed by the same woman, thereby creating a special bond between the two infants that will persist into adulthood. A poignant example of the emotional depth of this bond was illustrated by the husband of the Bugis lord Arung Palakka's milk-mother, who sacrificed his life to allow Arung Palakka time to reach safety from pursuing Makassarese troops. Andaya, *Arung Palakka*, 57.

41. Errington, *Meaning and Power*, 223, 258–259.

42. Christian Pelras, "L'Oral et l'écrit dans la tradition Bugis," *Asie du Sud-East et Monde Insulindien* 10 (1979).

43. The delicate relationship between writing and speaking, between written texts and oral performance, as conditioned by a particular social context elsewhere in Sulawesi is addressed in Kenneth M. George, *Showing Signs of Violence: The Cultural Politics of a Twentieth-Century Headhunting Ritual* (Berkeley: University of California Press, 1996), chapter 7.

44. Sweeney, *Authors and Audiences;* Shelly Errington, "Some Comments on Style in the Meanings of the Past," *JAS* 38, 2 (1979); James J. Fox, ed., *To Speak*

in *Pairs: Essays on the Ritual Languages of Eastern Indonesia* (Cambridge: Cambridge University Press, 1988).

45. Wolhoff and Abdurrahim, *Sedjarah Goa*, 9.

46. This was also true of Malay historical writing. Errington, "Some Comments on Style," 237.

47. Ian Caldwell, "South Sulawesi A.D. 1300–1600: Ten Bugis Texts" (Ph.D. diss., Australia National University, 1988), 167.

48. *Tumassalangga barayang* means "the one with shoulders like a barayang tree." A barayang tree has branches that reach up and branches that reach down. Cense and Abdurrahim, *Makassaars-Nederlands Woordenboek*, 78.

49. Wolhoff and Abdurrahim, *Sedjarah Goa*, 9–12. The translation is mine, except the passage spoken by Tumassalangga Barayang's mother. Here I rely on J. Noorduyn's painstaking work in "The Manuscripts of the Makasarese Chronicle of Goa and Talloq: An Evaluation," *BKI* 147, 4 (1991).

50. Wolhoff and Abdurrahim, *Sedjarah Goa*, 12.

51. Rahim and Ridwan, *Sejarah Kerajaan Tallo'*, 5–6.

52. This portion in roman type is not found in the 1975 Rahim and Ridwan edition. It can be consulted in the 1979 text, page 28. This longer version is the correct one; it is found, for example, in ANRI 62/2. Furthermore, Matthes 1883, page 186, has this as well, but instead of the father of Kanre Suwaya being implied, says that it was Gallarrang ri Lekoqbodong, perhaps another name for Kasuianga ri Lampasaile *(tu Unti nanibaineammo ri Gallarranga ri Lekoqbodong naanaqmo Kanre Suwaya)*.

53. Not simply "killed," but the victim of someone who ran amok.

54. Rahim and Ridwan, *Sejarah Kerajaan Tallo'*, 6–7.

55. William Cummings, "Reading the Histories of a Maros Chronicle," *BKI* 156, 1 (2000); Campbell Macknight and Mukhlis Paeni, "The Chronicle of Bone" (manuscript).

56. A. C. Milner, *Kerajaan: Malay Political Culture on the Eve of Colonial Rule* (Tucson: University of Arizona Press, 1982), 82; Helen Creese, "Balinese *Babad*," 241.

57. Wolhoff and Abdurrahim, *Sedjarah Goa*, 40. What I have translated as "cut down" is *nijalloq*, meaning "killed by a person who had gone berserk or run amok." His name could be as I have written, or what I have interpreted as the action he took (spoke not, *tamakana*) could possibly be part of his name. If so the last passage would read simply, "A man from Majannang named I Lolo Tamakana cut him down." It is impossible to know which reading was intended.

58. Gervaise himself never visited South Sulawesi, relying on informants for his information. Christian Pelras, "La première description de Célèbes-sud en français et la destinée remarquable de deux jeunes princes makassar dans la France de Louis XIV," *Archipel* 54 (1997), 70.

59. Gervaise, *The Kingdom of Macasar*, 2–3.

60. Wolhoff and Abdurrahim, *Sedjarah Goa*, 73.

61. This account is in NBG 18, pages 1–18.

62. Ian Caldwell, "Power, State and Society Among the Pre-Islamic Bugis," *BKI* 151, 3 (1995): 413–414.

63. Wolhoff and Abdurrahim, *Sedjarah Goa*, 21–22.

64. Though not common, at least two copies of this story are available. Matthes collected one in the codex NBG 17, pages 75–80. A second copy collected later for the Matthes Stichting is found in codex MS 193, pages 3–5.

65. Wolhoff and Abdurrahim, *Sedjarah Goa*, 30–31.

66. These two episodes in the early relations between Gowa and Talloq are explored in detail in William Cummings, "'Only One Ruler but Two Peoples:' Re-Making the Past in Seventeenth-Century Makassarese Chronicles," *BKI* 155, 1 (1999).

Chapter 4. Historical Literacy and Social Hierarchicalization

1. Robert Blust, "Linguistic Evidence for Some Early Austronesian Taboos," *American Anthropologist* 83, 2 (1981): 307.

2. See in particular Chabot, *Kinship, Status and Gender;* Susan Bolyard Millar, *Bugis Weddings: Rituals of Social Location in Modern Indonesia* (Berkeley: University of California, Center for South and Southeast Asia Studies, 1989).

3. A. J. A. E. Eerdmans, *Het Landschap Gowa* (Batavia Albrecht; 's-Gravenhage: Martinus Nijhoff, 1987), 34. Similarly, Ian Caldwell notes an eighteenth-century Bugis manuscript from Luwuq that refers to a child's afterbirth stored in a jar. Caldwell, "Ten Bugis Texts," 43.

4. Eerdmans, *Het Landschap Gowa*, 35.

5. Gervaise, *The Kingdom of Macasar*, 133–135.

6. Contemporary circumcisions are also held at about this age, though in the nineteenth century Eerdmans wrote that only high-ranking children were circumcised at this age; commoners were circumcised sometime between ages ten and fifteen. Eerdmans, *Het Landschap Gowa*, 35.

7. Gervaise, *The Kingdom of Macasar*, 135–139.

8. Errington, *Meaning and Power*, 113.

9. For these three examples see Creese, *Parthayana;* Sirtjo Koolhof, "The 'La Galigo': A Bugis Encyclopedia and Its Growth," *BKI* 155, 3 (1999): 374–378; and Pemberton, *On the Subject of "Java."*

10. Gervaise, *The Kingdom of Macasar*, 141–147.

11. J. S. Cummins, ed., *The Travels and Controversies of Friar Domingo Navarrete, 1618–1686* (Cambridge: Hakluyt Society, 1962), 118.

12. Eerdmans, *Het Landschap Gowa*, 42.

13. See in particular the detailed discussion of clothing and bodily decorations such as dyed red nails and filed and dyed black or red teeth in Gervaise, *The Kingdom of Macasar*, 76–81.

14. Aburaerah Arief and Zainuddin Hakim, eds., *Sinrilikna Kappalak Tallumbatua* (Jakarta: Yayasan Obor, 1993).

15. See, for example, the *tumanurung* story from Borisallo in Friedericy, "De Gowa-Federatie," 405.

16. Gervaise, *The Kingdom of Macasar*, 77, 93.

17. Eerdmans, *Het Landschap Gowa*, 54.

18. H. J. Friedericy, "De Standen bij de Boegineezen en Makassaren," *BKI* 90 (1933): 572–573.

19. C. R. Boxer, *Francisco Vieira de Figueiredo: A Portuguese Merchant-Adventurer in South East Asia, 1624–1667* ('s-Gravenhage: Martinus Nijhoff, 1967), 24. It is interesting that both Portuguese and Makassarese were concerned that Francisco Mendes (the Portuguese secretary of Sultan Hasanuddin) receive a knighthood in the Order of Christ, and not in a lesser order. This knighthood was eventually awarded, but when a ship from the viceroy at Goa promising it arrived in Gowa without bringing the requisite insignia, the rulers of Gowa and Talloq were disappointed and indicated their disappointment in their replies to the viceroy. Ibid., 16–17, 22, 102.

20. Eerdmans, *Het Landschap Gowa*, 24; Gervaise, *The Kingdom of Macasar*, 59.

21. Cf. B. F. Matthes, "Over de Bîssoe's of Heidensche Priesters en Priesteressen der Boegineezen," in *Dr. Benjamin Frederik Matthes: Zijn Leven en Arbeid*, ed. H. van den Brink, (Amsterdam: Nederlandsch Bijbelgenootschap, 1943), 508.

22. Eerdmans, *Het Landschap Gowa*, 55.

23. Friedericy, "De Gowa-Federatie," 396–397, 403.

24. By "ideology" I mean the signifying practices and attending perceptions that naturalize, legitimate, and promote the interests of a certain social group. See Terry Eagleton, *Ideology: An Introduction* (New York: Verso, 1991).

25. In this work "rank" is used to denote the ascribed position within the Makassarese social hierarchy that a person was born with based on the rank of his or her parents. "Status" denotes the achieved position a person gains (or loses) as achievements, abilities, and character modify birth rank. Status is thus fluid and based on the judgment of others.

26. "Makassaarsche Historiën," 113–114.

27. Cf. Gesick, *Lady White Blood*. Similarly, a story of beings magically appearing upon a hill who are believed to have descended from the heavens and are installed as rulers appears in the *Sejarah Melayu*. See O. W. Wolters, *The Fall of Srivijaya in Malay History* (Ithaca, N.Y.: Cornell University Press, 1970), 128–129.

28. Sahlins, *Islands of History*. Nor is this simply mythical. The *orang laut* or "sea people" in the Strait of Melaka played a crucial role in the rise of Melaka, a role perhaps played by the Bajo (also translated as "sea people") in the rise of Gowa. See the overview in Leonard Andaya, "Historical Links between the Aquatic Populations and the Coastal Peoples of the Malay World and Celebes," in *Historia: Essays in Commemoration of the Twenty-fifth Anniversary of the Depart-*

ment of History University of Malaya, ed. Muhammad Abu Bakar et al. (Kuala Lumpur: Malaysian Historical Society, 1984).

29. Martin Rössler, "Striving for Modesty: Fundamentals of the Religion and Social Organization of the Makassarese Patuntung," *BKI* 146, 2 and 3 (1990): 321–323.

30. "Spotted horn."

31. To commit a crime is literally "to be disliked by the land."

32. N10, pages 3–11.

33. Leonard Andaya, pers. comm.

34. ANRI 18/23, pages 2–3.

35. Bulbeck, "A Tale of Two Kingdoms," 97–101.

36. Cf. Hawai'i, another Austronesian society. Jocelyn Linnekin, *Sacred Queens and Women of Consequence: Rank, Gender, and Colonialism in the Hawaiian Islands* (Ann Arbor: University of Michigan Press, 1990).

37. An insightful if dehistoricized analysis of Makassarese social relations emphasizing marriage is F. D. Bulbeck, "The Politics of Marriage and the Marriage of Polities in Gowa, South Sulawesi, During the 16th and 17th Centuries," in *Origins, Ancestry and Alliance: Explorations in Austronesian Ethnography*, ed. James J. Fox and Clifford Sather (Canberra: Australia National University, 1996), 280–315.

38. Christian Pelras, "Patron-Client Ties among the Bugis and Makassarese of South Sulawesi," in *Authority and Enterprise among the Peoples of South Sulawesi*, ed. Roger Tol, Kees van Dijk, and Greg Acciaioli (Leiden: KITLV, 2000), 51.

39. MS 200a, pages 29–32.

40. Birgitt Röttger-Rössler, "Shared Responsibility: Some Aspects of Gender and Authority in Makassar Society," in *Authority and Enterprise among the Peoples of South Sulawesi*, ed. Roger Tol, Kees van Dijk, and Greg Acciaioli (Leiden: KITLV, 2000), 145–146.

41. When exactly they divorced is uncertain; either date could be correct. They did remarry sometime after 3 February 1663, as on 30 January 1665 the pair divorced a second time.

42. Rahim and Ridwan, *Sejarah Kerajaan Tallo'*, 7.

43. Wolhoff and Abdurrahim, *Sedjarah Goa*, 29–31, 34, 38.

44. Florida, *Writing the Past*.

45. Bulbeck, "A Tale of Two Kingdoms," 103–109.

46. Rahim and Ridwan, *Sejarah Kerajaan Tallo'*, 11.

47. On the closeness of this relationship and the accomplishments of these rulers see Reid, "A Great Seventeenth-Century Indonesian Family."

48. Wolhoff and Abdurrahim, *Sedjarah Goa*, 52.

49. Bulbeck, "A Tale of Two Kingdoms," 107.

50. Friedericy, "De Gowa-Federatie," 418–419.

51. N8, page 4.

52. N9, page 1. The parallel significance of titles in the Malay world is explored in Milner, *Kerajaan*, chapter 9.
53. ANRI 18/23, page 26.
54. Wolhoff and Abdurrahim, *Sedjarah Goa*, 65, 73.
55. ANRI 62/1, pages 12–13.
56. Roger Chartier, *The Order of Books* (Stanford, Calif.: Stanford University Press, 1994), 23.
57. John R. Bowen, *Sumatran Politics and Poetics: Gayo History, 1900–1989* (New Haven, Conn.: Yale University Press, 1991), 139.
58. Andaya, *Arung Palakka*, 11–16; idem, "Kingship in Bone."
59. Campbell Macknight, *The Early History of South Sulawesi: Some Recent Advances* (Clayton, Victoria: Monash University Centre of Southeast Asian Studies, 1993), 41.
60. Martin Rössler, "From Divine Descent to Administration: Sacred Heirlooms and Political Change in Highland Gowa," in *Authority and Enterprise among the Peoples of South Sulawesi*, ed. Roger Tol, Kees van Dijk, and Greg Acciaioli (Leiden: KITLV, 2000).
61. Alfred Russel Wallace, *The Malay Archipelago* (New York: Dover, 1962 [1869]), 166.
62. The fascinating allure Makassarese *kalompoang* and their attendant rituals had for at least one high-ranking Kodi man is described in Hoskins, *Biographical Objects*, 100–109.
63. A general analysis of the cultural significance placed on distant origins is Mary Helms, *Ulysses' Sail: An Ethnographic Odyssey of Power, Knowledge, and Geographical Distance* (Princeton, N.J.: Princeton University Press, 1988).
64. Rössler, "Striving for Modesty," 309.
65. Cf. Eerdmans, *Het Landschap Gowa;* Friedericy, "De Gowa-Federatie"; and C. Nooteboom, "Naar Aanleiding van de Rijkssieraden van Zuid-Celebes," *Koloniaal Tijdschrift* 26 (1937).
66. See in particular Drakard, *A Kingdom of Words*, 192–196, and Hoskins, *Biographical Objects*.
67. Wiener, *Visible and Invisible Realms*, 64.
68. NBG 18, pages 1–18.
69. See for example Friedericy, "De Gowa-Federatie;" "Makassaarsche Historiën," 134–136; J. Tideman, *Catalogus van voorwerpen van Makassaarschen oorsprong* (Den Haag: N.p., 1909), unpaginated.
70. Drakard, *A Kingdom of Words*, 184.
71. E. D. Lewis traced a similar process among the people of Sikka Natar on the island of Flores. There too manuscripts incarnated the past and became "ownable knowledge" conferring prestige and influence on their possessors. E. D. Lewis, "The Tyranny of the Text: Oral Tradition and the Power of Writing in Sikka and Tana ?Ai, Flores," *BKI* 154, 3 (1998).
72. Tribute demanded of conquered polities, typically paid in gold.

73. Wolhoff and Abdurrahim, *Sedjarah Goa,* 23–24.

74. N8, pages 2–3. Dating the war is difficult, but it probably took place in the 1640s or 1650s. The text mentions that this ruler of Gowa was named Karaeng ri Popoq, which was actually the title of a son of Karaeng Matoaya of Talloq (r. 1593–1623). As far as I have been able to determine, no ruler of Gowa bore this *karaeng* title. Karaeng ri Popoq may very well have been the commander of the campaign to subdue Bontonompo, for his son was the first to bear the title Karaeng Bontonompo. Rahim and Ridwan, *Sejarah Kerajaan Tallo',* 21.

75. Most famously, see Benedict Anderson, "The Idea of Power in Javanese Culture," in *Culture and Politics in Indonesia,* ed. Clare Holt, Benedict Anderson, and James Seigel (Ithaca, N.Y.: Cornell University Press, 1972).

76. Alternatively, the degree to which Makassarese viewed rulers as the foremost of the regalia akin to the founding *tumanurung* declined.

77. "Makassaarsche Historiën," 126–128.

78. See Mukhlis, "Batara Gowa: Mesianisme Dalam Gerakan Sosial di Tanah Makassar," in *Dari Babad dan Hikayat sampai Sejarah Kritis,* ed. T. Ibrahim Alfian et al. (Yogyakarta: Gadjah Mada University Press, 1992).

79. Drakard, *A Kingdom of Words,* chapter 9.

80. Wiener, *Visible and Invisible Realms,* 101.

81. Wolters, *The Fall of Srivijaya.*

Chapter 5. Historical Literacy and Gowa as the Center of Makassar

1. See in particular Reid, *The Age of Commerce,* 2 vols.

2. "Classical" is a term laden with connotations. Outside scholars most commonly use the term to designate polities that rose before the end of the thirteenth century, but Southeast Asians use the term more broadly to encompass the past kingdoms from whom their heritage derives.

3. Most notably, see Clifford Geertz, *Negara: The Theater State in Nineteenth-Century Bali* (Princeton, N.J.: Princeton University Press, 1980).

4. Richard J. Parmentier, *The Sacred Remains: Myth, History, and Polity in Belau* (Chicago: University of Chicago, 1987), 14, 37.

5. See also the similiar oral history recorded almost a century ago in J. Tideman, "De Toe Badjeng en de Legende omtrent Hun Oorsprong," *BKI* 60 (1908).

6. N13, pages 8–32.

7. "The snake hanging over Mamampang."

8. One of the most ancient sites within Gowa.

9. N16, pages 2–14.

10. Friedericy, "De Gowa-Federatie," 413.

11. Wiener, *Visible and Invisible Realms,* 66–67; I Wayan Rekan is cited in Schulte Nordholt, "Origin, Descent, and Destruction," 38n.

12. Dipesh Chakrabarty, "Postcoloniality and the Artifice of History: Who Speaks for 'Indian' Pasts?" *Representations* 37 (1992): 1. Such a process does not

require written texts, however. The changing nature of the social force and use of the words of the ancestors among the Weyewa is the focus of Kuipers, *Power in Performance*.

13. The uneven presence of genres of writing in South Sulawesi should be emphasized more than it has been in studies of the region. It is surely of immense significance, for example, that nearly all Bugis diaries come from the Boné court. Roger Tol, "A Royal Collection of Bugis Manuscripts," *BKI* 149, 3 (1993): 619.

14. The Sanrabone, Maros, and Binamuq chronicles are common texts found in Makassarese codices, and many copies exist. I have used Matthes' published versions, supplementing them with readings from other manuscripts. Matthes, *Makassaarsche Chrestomathie* [1883], 203–207.

15. This Karaeng Bambang should not be confused with his grandfather Tunibatta, who also bore the title Karaeng Bambang.

16. In David Bulbeck's terminology, the *karaeng*-ship of Sanrabone was "captured" by Gowa. See his analysis of title transmission and genealogically based political maneuvering in "The Politics of Marriage."

17. The name of the Maros palace. *"Patanna Langkana"* means "the owner of Langkana."

18. The Makassarese verb *akkatuo* does not mean adopting an orphan, but taking and caring for the child of another as a means of forming a special tie between the parents.

19. Wolhoff and Abdurrahim, *Sedjarah Goa*, 63.

20. The effort to walk this fine line is a major theme in Bulbeck, "A Tale of Two Kingdoms."

21. Caldwell, "Power, State and Society," 397–401. On upland-lowland rivalry in South Sulawesi see Kenneth M. George, "Headhunting, History, and Exchange in Upland Sulawesi," *JAS* 50, 3 (1991), and Albert Schrauwers, "Houses, Hierarchy, Headhunting and Exchange: Rethinking Political Relations in the Southeast Asian Realm of Luwu'," *BKI* 153, 3 (1997).

22. Pelras, "Patron-Client Ties," 26.

23. Based on NBG 16, pages 142–144, supplemented by a second text in MS 193, pages 6–7, a third text in KITLV Or. 6266, pages 1–4, and a fourth text in ANRI 62/1, pages 10–11. Minor discrepancies and errors in the different versions have been corrected without notation; only substantial variations are noted.

24. Based on NBG 16, pages 139–141, supplemented by a second text in MS 193, page 6, and a third text in ANRI 62/1, page 10. As with the *Bangkalaq Chronicle* text, minor discrepancies and errors in the different versions have been corrected without notation; only substantial variations are noted.

25. Schulte Nordholt, "Origin, Descent and Destruction." See also Creese, *In Search of Majapahit*.

26. Sweeney, *Authors and Audiences*, 71.

27. Pierre Bourdieu, *Language and Symbolic Power* (Cambridge: Harvard University Press, 1991), 116.

28. N14, pages 19–22.

29. Matthes, *Makassaarsche Chrestomathie* [1883], 221–270.

30. See in particular Reid, "A Great Seventeenth Century Indonesian Family."

31. In general this may be the roots of the association among Makassarese of literacy with the lowlands and orality with the highlands; the Makassarese highlands even today are considered an area of unpredictable, dangerous magic, while the lowlands are seen as the repository for ancient traditions and centers of learning.

32. See chapter 3, "The Stranger King; or, Dumézil among the Fijians," in Sahlins, *Islands of History*.

33. A. H. Johns, "The Turning Image: Myth and Reality in Malay Perceptions of the Past," in *Perceptions of the Past in Southeast Asia*, ed. Anthony Reid and David Marr (Singapore: Asian Studies Association of Australia, 1979), 52.

34. Rössler, "Striving for Modesty," 321–323.

35. Friedericy reached the same conclusion that the title *karaeng* originated in and spread outward from Gowa. See his example about the community of Limbung in Friedericy, "De Standen," 564–565.

36. But see the story from Kajang below.

37. Rössler, "Striving for Modesty," 323.

38. Bourdieu, *Language and Symbolic Power*.

39. Andi Halilintar Lathief, ed., *Cerita Rakyat Daerah Sulawesi Selatan* (Yogyakarta: Institut Press, 1984), 41–42.

40. Stories about princesses appearing from water or bamboo are a common motif in much of the archipelago. See J. J. Ras, *Hikayat Banjar: A Study in Malay Historiography* (The Hague: Martinus Nijhoff, 1968), chapter 4.

41. Bambang Suwondo, ed., *Cerita Rakyat (Mite dan Legenda) Daerah Sulawesi Selatan* (Jakarta: Departemen Pendidikan dan Kebudayaan, 1980–81), 38–42.

42. The conception that misshapen individuals possessed spiritual potency is found in much of Southeast Asia. For example, Javanese believed that unusual or misshapen beings, including dwarves, albinos, and deformed individuals, possessed special supernatural abilities. Claire Holt, *Art in Indonesia: Continuities and Change* (Ithaca, N.Y.: Cornell University Press, 1967), 83.

43. Ian Caldwell, "Ten Bugis Texts," 166.

44. Matthes, "Boegineesche en Makassaarsche Legenden," 405–406.

45. N13, pages 6–7.

46. Wolhoff and Abdurrahim, *Sedjarah Goa*, 20.

47. A fascinating account of how siblingship idioms and their moral authority have been transformed in upland Sulawesi is found in George, *Showing Signs of Violence*.

48. This unpaginated manuscript is one in an uncatalogued bundle of Makassarese manuscripts found in KITLV Or. 365.

49. J. Noorduyn, "De Islamisering van Makasar," *BKI* 112, 3 (1956).

50. See the various perspectives on this issue in Leonard Andaya, "Kingship-Adat Rivalry and the Role of Islam in South Sulawesi," *JSEAS* 15, 1 (1984); Noorduyn, "De Islamisering van Makasar"; Christian Pelras, "Religion, Tradition and the Dynamics of Islamization in South Sulawesi," *Indonesia* 57 (1994); Reid, *The Age of Commerce*, vol. 2.

51. Mattulada, "Islam di Sulawesi Selatan," 221. Al-Fatihah is the first sura of the Qur'an and implores Allah to guide believers on the correct path.

52. George, *Showing Signs of Violence*, 34.

53. Friedericy, "De Gowa-Federatie," 390–391.

54. This religious hierarchy is discussed in Gervaise, *The Kingdom of Macasar*, 153–159.

55. Cense and Abdoerrahim, *Makassaars-Nederlands Woordenboek*, 460; J. Noorduyn, "Makasar and the Islamization of Bima," *BKI* 142, 2 and 3 (1987): 322.

56. This translation is based on one made by Noorduyn in "Makasar and the Islamization of Bima," 318. On *mokkeng* see also the notes by A. A. Cense in KITLV Or. 545/75E.

57. Mark R. Woodward, *Islam in Java: Normative Piety and Mysticism in the Sultanate of Yogyakarta* (Tucson: University of Arizona Press, 1989), 147.

58. Gervaise, *The Kingdom of Macasar*, 63–64.

59. *Syaraf* is the morphology of Arabic roots; *nahwu*, Arabic grammar; *tafsir*, Qur'anic exegesis; *mantiq*, logical reasoning; and *minhaj*, which refers to the *Minhaj al-taliben*, a widely studied work of jurisprudence by the Shafii legal scholar Al Nawawi. Manyambeang, "Lontaraq Riwayaqna Tuanta Salamaka," 208.

60. There is far too vast a literature on Syekh Yusuf to cite comprehensively. The following sources are a good introduction to Syekh Yusuf's life, teachings, and historical context: Azyumardi Azra, *Jaringan Ulama: Timur Tengah dan Kepulauan Nusantara Abad XVII dan XVIII* (Bandung: Penerbit Mizan, 1994); Martin van Bruinessen, "The Origins and Development of the Naqshabandi Order in Indonesia," *Der Islam* 67 (1990); Martin van Bruinessen, "The Tariqa Khalwatiyya in South Celebes," in *Excursies in Celebes*, ed. Harry A. Poeze and Pim Schoorl (Leiden: KITLV, 1991); Abu Hamid, *Syekh Yusuf: Seorang Ulama, Sufi dan Pejuang* (Jakarta: Yayasan Obor Indonesia, 1994); Manyambeang, "Lontaraq Riwayaqna Tuanta Salamaka." An Indonesian description of Syekh Yusuf's Islamic writings is found in Tudjimah, *Syekh Jusuf Makasar: Riwayat Hidup, Karya, dan Ajarannya* (Jakarta: Departemen Pendidikan dan Kebudayaan, 1987).

61. William Cummings, "The Melaka Malay Diaspora in Makassar, c. 1500–1669," *JMBRAS* 71, 1 (1998).

62. Manyambeang, "Lontaraq Riwayaqna Tuanta Salamaka," 216.

63. Boxer, *Francisco Vieira de Figueiredo*, 8–9.

64. Isaac Commelin, ed., *Begin ende Voortgangh van de Vereenighde Neederlandtsche Geoctroyeerde Oost-Indische Compagnie,* vol. 4 (Amsterdam: N.p., 1646 [reprinted 1974]), 38.

65. See Reid, "A Great Seventeenth-Century Indonesian Family"; Boxer, *Francisco Vieira de Figueiredo,* 4–5, 23.

66. Rahim and Ridwan, *Sejarah Kerajaan Tallo',* 16.

67. Cf. the seventeenth-century commentary about Makassarese religious practices: "Because they believe them too be practis'd at *Mecca,* which they look upon as the Center of their Religion, and the Pattern which they ought to follow." Gervaise, *The Kingdom of Macasar,* 133. Similarly, the *Story of Syekh Yusuf* describes Mekka as the land where the most complete mystical religious knowledge is found. Manyambeang, "Lontaraq Riwayaqna Tuanta Salamaka," 216, 222.

68. Wolhoff and Abdurrahim, *Sedjarah Goa,* 56–57.

69. Rahim and Ridwan, *Sejarah Kerajaan Tallo',* 19. This translation is based on one made by Noorduyn after he consulted several versions of the chronicle. Noorduyn, "Makasar and the Islamization of Bima," 315.

70. Mattulada, "Islam di Sulawesi Selatan," 222.

71. N7, page 4.

72. Friedericy, "De Standen," 529.

73. Cf. the descriptions of the obligations of Gowa's vassals in Blok, "Beknopte geschiedenis," 27–77.

74. Rössler, "From Divine Descent," 165.

75. Michael Lambek, "Certain Knowledge, Contestable Authority: Power and Practice on the Islamic Periphery," *American Ethnologist* 17 (1990): 25.

76. Nostalgia for a lost past is common in peripheral communities in modern Indonesia. For a Sumatran example, see Bowen, *Sumatran Politics and Poetics,* 208–209.

77. Wiener, *Visible and Invisible Realms;* Drakard, *A Kingdom of Words.*

Chapter 6. Historical Literacy and Makassarese Culture

1. Mukhlis, "Landasan Kultural dalam Pranata Sosial Bugis-Makassar," in *Dinamika Bugis-Makassar* (N.p.: Pusat Latihan Penelitian Ilmu-Ilmu Sosial, 1986), 1–41; Mattulada, *Latoa,* 339–87.

2. Cf. Talal Asad, "Toward a Genealogy of the Concept of Ritual," in *Vernacular Christianity: Essays in the Social Anthropology of Religion Presented to Godfrey Lienhardt,* ed. W. James and D. H. Johnson (Oxford: Journal of the Anthropological Society of Oxford, 1988). This list of mental constructs could be multiplied. For example, Terry Eagleton remarks in his *Ideology: An Introduction,* "Nobody has ever clapped eyes on an ideological formation, any more than on the Freudian unconscious or a mode of production" (page 193). It is through such essential but essentially heuristic conceptualizations that we order and make sense of the world.

3. Walter Ong, *Orality and Literacy: The Technologizing of the Word* (New York: Routledge, 1982), 12.

4. See his chapter "Some Psychodynamics of Orality" in *Orality and Literacy*, 31–57.

5. Andaya, *To Live as Brothers*, 7, 8.

6. Sweeney makes a similar point about Malay oral traditions in *A Full Hearing*, 197–198.

7. Ibid., 306.

8. Jack Goody, *Literacy in Traditional Societies* (Cambridge: Cambridge University Press, 1968), 28.

9. See Schacter, *Searching for Memory*.

10. Maier, *In the Center of Authority*, 84.

11. The two excerpts are from Manyambeang, "Riwayaqna Tuanta Salamaka," 212, 228.

12. Chartier, *The Order of Books*, 90–91.

13. N14, pages 1–2.

14. The broader context of how upland-lowland relations as the Mandar highlands became enmeshed in Makassarese political relations is sketched in George, *Showing Signs of Violence*, chapter 3.

15. N14, pages 33–37.

16. See his chapter of the same name in Ong, *Orality and Literacy*, 78–116.

17. Jack Goody, *The Interface between the Written and the Oral* (Cambridge; New York:Cambridge University Press, 1987), chapters 10 and 11.

18. Compare Liaw Yock Fang, *Undang-Undang Melaka: The Laws of Melaka* (The Hague: Martinus Nijhoff, 1976), and Ph. O. L. Tobing, *Hukum Pelayaran dan Perdagangang Amanna Gappa* (Makassar: Jajasan Kebudajaan Sulawesi Selatan dan Tenggara, 1961).

19. Matthes, *Makassaarsche Chrestomathie* [1883], 254.

20. ANRI 8/16, page 13.

21. N11, page 14.

22. Ibid., page 30.

23. Ibid., pages 8, 17.

24. Drakard, *A Kingdom of Words*, 153.

25. Cf. Matthes, *Makassaarsche Chrestomathie* [1883], 260.

26. N11, page 26.

27. ANRI 62/1, page 52.

28. ANRI 26/22, page 31.

29. ANRI 8/16, page 32. *Rapang* texts also contain numerous commandments to obey hadith. See in particular ANRI 26/21, which has a higher than average proportion of *rapang* from famed *ulama*.

30. Matthes, *Makassaarsche Chrestomathie* [1883], 240.

31. Goody, *Interface*, 137.

32. ANRI 62/1, page 88.
33. Ibid., pages 52–53.
34. ANRI 8/16, page 9.
35. Drakard, *A Kingdom of Words*, 171–172. See also Sweeney, *A Full Hearing*, 109, for a similar evaluation of the impression written texts had on nonliterate Malays.
36. Ibid., page 6, 17.
37. N11, page 32.
38. ANRI 62/1, page 112.
39. Matthes, *Makassaarsche Chrestomathie* [1883], 250–251.
40. ANRI 8/16, page 34.
41. A *rapang* decrying the damaging actions of earlier rulers before the coming of these guidelines is found in Matthes, *Makassaarsche Chrestomathie* [1883], 252–253. Several other *rapang* exhorting rulers to behave with fairness and honesty can be consulted ibid., 248–249.
42. N11, page 15.
43. ANRI 8/16, page 81.
44. Matthes, *Makassaarsche Chrestomathie* [1883], 255–256.
45. ANRI 26/22, pages 65–66.
46. ANRI 62/1, page 62.
47. ANRI 8/16, page 17.
48. ANRI 62/1, page 92.
49. ANRI 8/16, pages 11–12.
50. Ibid., page 35.
51. ANRI 62/1, page 88.
52. ANRI 8/16, page 36.
53. ANRI 62/1, page 59.
54. Ibid., page 96. Cf. one *parakara* that declared that if a feast is held in which a water buffalo is slaughtered, one leg must be given to the *gallarrang;* if a *gallarrang* holds a feast and slaughters a water buffalo, one leg must to given to the *karaeng*. Matthes, *Makassaarsche Chrestomathie* [1883], 247.
55. ANRI 62/1, page 125.
56. Matthes, *Makassaarsche Chrestomathie* [1883], 265. *Gaduq* was a kind of tunic worn, Makassarese today report, before conversion to Islam. It was often rolled up around the waist to leave the chest bare. *Limagaduq* were strips of material that hung down on the front of the *gaduq* but that could easily be tucked in.
57. Kertzer, *Ritual, Politics, and Power*, 95.
58. ANRI 8/16, page 14. Note, however, that in one case I have discovered a *rapang*, precisely dated November 13, 1631, that annulled an earlier *rapang* concerning the division of children between separating parents. Ibid., page 21.
59. ANRI 26/11, page 4.

60. ANRI 8/16, page 33. This does not refer to the later Bungaya treaty signed with the Dutch, but to an earlier agreement also made there but whose contents we do not know.

61. Woodward, *Islam in Java*, 50.

62. Matthes, *Makassaarsche Chrestomathie* [1883], 266.

63. Dagh-Register Gehouden int Casteel Batavia, 1637, 286–287.

64. Ibid., 1640–1641, 383–384.

65. Gervaise, *The Kingdom of Macasar*, 3, 99.

66. William Foster, ed., *The Journal of John Jourdain, 1608–1617* (Cambridge: Hakluyt Society, 1905), 295.

67. Cummins, *Friar Domingo Navarrete*, 121–122.

68. Gervaise, *The Kingdom of Macasar*, 97–98.

69. ANRI 23/34.

70. Matthes, *Makassaarsche Chrestomathie* [1883], 233–234.

71. Ibid., 234–235.

72. Valentijn, *Oud en Nieuw Oost-Indien*, vol. 3, 117. See also the additional references in the discussion of sexual rivalry in chapter 5.

73. Matthes, *Makassaarsche Chrestomathie* [1883], 235.

74. That is, by doing so illicitly.

75. Matthes, *Makassaarsche Chrestomathie* [1883], 235–236.

76. Ibid., 236.

77. Ibid., 234.

78. Ibid., 237.

79. Gervaise, *The Kingdom of Macasar*, 68.

80. Matthes, *Makassaarsche Chrestomathie* [1883], 226.

81. Ibid., 223.

82. Ibid., 223–224.

83. Ibid., 224–225.

84. Ibid., 233.

85. Ibid., 224.

86. Ibid., 224.

87. Ibid., 224.

88. Ibid., 222–223.

89. Pierre Bourdieu, *The Logic of Practice* (Stanford, Calif.: Stanford University Press, 1990), 53.

90. Dening, *Islands and Beaches*, 247.

91. ANRI 26/22, page 37.

Conclusion: The Force of History

1. O. W. Wolters, *History, Culture, and Region in Southeast Asian Perspectives*, revised edition (Ithaca, N.Y.: Cornell University Southeast Asia Program, 1999).

2. Victor Lieberman, "Local Integration and Eurasian Analogies: Structur-

ing Southeast Asian History, c. 1350–c. 1830," *Modern Asian Studies* 27, 3 (1993): 511.

3. David Wyatt, "Southeast Asia 'Inside Out,' 1300–1800: A Perspective from the Interior," *Modern Asian Studies* 31, 3 (1997): 689.

4. See also Anthony Reid, "Islamization and Christianization in Southeast Asia: The Critical Phase, 1550–1650," in *Southeast Asia in the Early Modern Era: Trade, Power, and Belief,* ed. Anthony Reid (Ithaca, N.Y.: Cornell University Press, 1993).

5. Cf. D. G. E. Hall, ed., *Historians of South East Asia* (London: Oxford University Press, 1961), and Soedjatmoko et al., eds., *An Introduction to Indonesian Historiography* (Ithaca, N.Y.: Cornell University Press, 1965).

6. Anthony Reid and David Marr, eds., *Perceptions of the Past in Southeast Asia* (Singapore: Asian Studies Association of Australia, 1979).

7. This agenda expands on Michael Lambek's description of "a sociology or political economy of knowledge: how textual knowledge is reproduced and circulated; what the social factors are that mediate access to texts; who is able to read, and in what manner; who has the authority to represent what is written; and how challenges to such authority are mediated." Lambek, "Certain Knowledge," 24.

8. Naturally far more could be said here, and there are many more examples worth citing. I have said little, for example, about the interplay between history-making and forces such as tourism, modernity, and nationalism. Each is profoundly influenced by and seeks to influence interpretations of the past, and in this dialectic each has dramatically affected local societies in places as obvious as Bali and as obscure as southern Kalimantan. My hope is that the questions posed and issues raised here will encourage further research in these and other areas.

9. Bowen, *Sumatran Politics and Poetics*. On modernist Islamic histories in particular see Bowen, *Muslims through Discourse*.

10. George, *Showing Signs of Violence,* 187. See also Connerton, *How Societies Remember,* for an influential generalized discussion of ritual practice, history, and communal identity.

11. George, *Showing Signs of Violence,* 238.

12. Terry Eagleton, *The Illusions of Postmodernism* (Oxford: Blackwell, 1996), 45.

13. Perez Zagorin, "History, the Referent, and Narrative: Reflections on Postmodernism Now," *History and Theory* 38, 1 (1999): 24

14. James E. Young, *The Texture of Memory: Holocaust Memorials and Meaning* (New Haven, Conn.: Yale University Press, 1993), 11.

GLOSSARY

aru	An oath of loyalty, chanted while dancing, sworn before battle or at the installation of a new ruler. Its aggressive tone and presentation convey martial ferocity.
Bajo	"Sea people." Collective term referring to those groups that lived along the littorals of Sulawesi, many of whom swore oaths of loyalty to Gowa's rulers.
Bate Salapang	The Nine Banners; the advisory council of Gowa composed of rulers of the nine original polities who first formed the core of Gowa.
daeng	A title distinguishing nobles from commoners, usually chosen to reflect a physical or mental characteristic of the person named.
gallarrang	A title of local rulers beneath the level of *karaeng*.
gaukang	Sacred stones that are the ritual focus and locus of identity in Makassarese *paqrasangang*.
jangang-jangang	The oldest Makassarese script.
kalompoang	"Greatness"; denotes sacred objects or regalia possessed by many Makassarese *paqrasangang*.
karaeng	A title granted to high-ranking nobles, usually but not always based on the toponym of a *paqrasangang* that became the appanage of the title holder.
kelong	A genre of Makassarese literature, originally oral but now often recorded in writing. Four-line rhyming poems similar to Malay *pantun*.
lontaraq	Used in several different senses; in this work usually refers to a physical manuscript (because *lontaraq* were originally written on lontar palm leaves).
lontaraq beru	"New lontaraq"; refers to the most common Makassarese script.

lontaraq bilang	A genre of Makassarese writing. A diary or court record of important events, dated and in chronological order.
mokkeng	Title given to those the ruler of Gowa appointed to attend Friday prayer services, to ensure that the minimum forty people required by *shafi'ite* doctrine for services to be valid were present.
pacce	Emotional sense of belonging and unity shared by members of a family or *paqrasangang*.
paqrasangang	Settlement, village, community, polity, kampung.
parakara	A genre of Makassarese writing. Legal articles that most commonly concern inheritance rights, property protection, and criminal penalties.
patturioloang	A genre of Makassarese writing. Literally, "that which is about the ancestors"; usually translated as "chronicle."
raga	An athletic competition in which participants keep a rattan ball airborne. Still popular today, skill in *raga* was believed to evidence the personal or supernatural power of the competitors.
rapang	A genre of Makassarese writing. Guidelines or advice from renowned and revered ancestors.
sabannaraq	Harbormaster of Gowa.
saukang	Sacrificial altars or miniature houses placed at the sacred center of a community and often the ritual focus of annual harvest ceremonies.
serang	Makassarese written in Arabic script.
sinriliq	A genre of Makassarese literature. A story, often based on historical events, chanted to the accompaniment of a Makassarese violin, or *keso-keso*.
siriq	Means both "self-worth" and "shame." A core part of Makassarese cultural values.
Somba	A title meaning "august overlord"; generally reserved for the ruler of Gowa.
Sudanga	The sacred regalia-sword of Lakipadada given to the rulers of Gowa.
Tanisamaang	The sacred golden chain the *tumanurung* gave to her son and later rulers of Gowa.
tumabicarabutta	"The speaker of the land"; chief adviser and minister of Gowa.
tumailalang	Trio of ministers that acted as intermediaries within Gowa.
tumanurung	Literally, "the person who descended"; refers to a heavenly ancestor of pure white blood who was recognized and installed as the first ruler of a new kingdom by the people of the land.

BIBLIOGRAPHY

Archival Sources and Unpublished Manuscripts

Arsip Nasional Republic Indonesia, Wilayah Sulawesi Selatan (ANRI). A collection of more than a thousand manuscripts containing Makassarese texts are kept on microfilm here. Manuscripts are listed by the roll and item number used in the collection's unpublished catalog. For example, "AN 8/16" means the sixteenth manuscript on roll 8.

British Library, Department of Oriental Manuscripts, London (BL). Referred to in the notes as, for example, "BL 12351."

Koninklijk Instituut voor Taal-, Land- en Volkenkunde, Leiden (KITLV). Makassarese manuscripts are in the Historical Documentation Department, generally as part of the collected papers of Dutch scholars and former colonial officials. They are referred to in the notes as, for example, "KITLV Or. 545/76." In the case of the typed manuscript of Cornelis Speelman's 1670 crucial work "Notitie dienende voor eenen Korte Tijd en tot nader last van de Hoge Regering op Batavia," the full title is cited.

Koninklijk Instituut voor de Tropen, Amsterdam. Referred to in the notes as, for example, "KIT 668/216."

Privately-Owned South Sulawesi Manuscripts. Manuscripts are listed here and cited by a simple list of N1 through N18. Except for the first three, these manuscripts were acquired by Djohan during the course of my research. In almost all cases where manuscripts came via Djohan, the manuscript was recopied by hand for me, making dating the originals impossible and increasing the chance of copyist errors.

N1	Genealogy of rulers of Gowa and Talloq; Ballaq Lompoa, Sungguminasa.	N2	Book of Islamic prayers and instruction; M. Guntur, Ujung Pandang.

N3 Chronicles, *parakara, rapang,* and other historical texts; Darmawan, Ujung Pandang.

N4 Genealogy of rulers of Maros.

N5 King list from Sanrabone.

N6 History of Sanrabone.

N7 Treaty between Sanrabone and Gowa.

N8 History of Bontonompo and Jipang.

N9 History of Pattallassang; in-law relations; and Ballaq Lompoa etiquette.

N10 Bate Salapang agreement with the first Karaeng Gowa.

N11 Collection of *rapang*.

N12 Two stories about Karaenga ri Mangkasaraq.

N13 Story about history of Bajeng.

N14 Story about history of Balanipa in Mandar.

N15 Collection of *parakara*.

N16 Story about history of Tunisomba ri Baku.

N17 Accounts of the arrival of Islam in Sanrabone, the building of the first mosque in Sanrabone, and the first appearance of garuda in Sanrabone (*serang* script).

N18 History of Siang (Indonesian).

Staatsbibliotheek Preuszischer Kulturbesitz, Berlin (SBPK). Referred to in the notes as, for example, "SBPK Or. 386."

Universiteits Bibliotheek, Rijks Universiteit, Leiden (UB). The majority of these come from the eighty-seven Makassarese manuscripts B. F. Matthes had made by Makassarese scribes while working for the Nederlandsch Bijbel Genootschap (NBG); they are on permanent loan to the university and found in the Oosterse Letteren en Geschiedenis (OLG) department. They are referred to in the notes as, for example, "NBG 17." Additional manuscripts collected in subsequent years are uncataloged and merely listed in a handwritten catalog available in the OLG. These are referred to in the notes as, for example, "UB Cod. Or. 6266."

Yayasan Kebudayaan Sulawesi Selatan (former Matthes Stichting [MS]). This collection is rapidly dwindling in size as manuscripts decay or are lost. Parts of the original collection, however, have been either copied or microfilmed. Therefore, missing manuscripts, especially the typed transcriptions of A. Cense, could perhaps be in KITLV or in one of four microfilm collections: the Perpustakaan Pusat Pembinaan dan Pengembangan Bahasa, Jakarta; the Universiteits Bibliotheek, Rijks Universiteit, Leiden; the Arsip Nasional Republic Indonesia, Wilayah Sulawesi Selatan, Ujung Pandang; or the collection of twenty-four reels of microfilm made by Campbell Macknight in 1974. However, the collection in its entirety was never systematically microfilmed, and some manuscripts are irretrievably lost. The remaining manuscripts have been renumbered several times, but the original Matthes *stichting* cataloging numbers are used here. They are referred to in the notes as, for example, "MS 193."

Published Sources

Abdurrazak, Dg. Patunru. *Sedjarah Gowa*. Ujung Pandang: Jajasan Kebudajaan Sulawesi Selatan dan Tenggara, 1969.

Andaya, Barbara Watson. *To Live as Brothers: Southeast Sumatra in the Seventeenth and Eighteenth Centuries*. Honolulu: University of Hawai'i Press, 1993.

Andaya, Leonard Y. *The Heritage of Arung Palakka: A History of South Sulawesi (Celebes) in the Seventeenth Century*. The Hague: Martinus Nijhoff, 1981.

———. "Historical Links between the Aquatic Populations and the Coastal Peoples of the Malay World and Celebes." In *Historia: Essays in Commemoration of the 25th Anniversary of the Department of History University of Malaya*, ed. Muhammad Abu Bakar et al., 34–51. Kuala Lumpur: Malaysian Historical Society, 1984.

———. "Kingship-*Adat* Rivalry and the Role of Islam in South Sulawesi." *JSEAS* 15, 1 (1984): 22–42.

———. "The Nature of Kingship in Bone." In *Pre-Colonial State Systems in Southeast Asia*, ed. Anthony Reid and Lance Castles, 115–125. Kuala Lumpur: Malayan Branch of the Royal Asiatic Society, 1975.

———. "Treaty Conceptions and Misconceptions: A Case Study from South Sulawesi." *BKI* 134, 2 and 3 (1978): 275–295.

Anderson, Benedict R. O'G. "The Idea of Power in Javanese Culture." In *Culture and Politics in Indonesia*, ed. Clare Holt, Benedict Anderson, and James Seigel, 1–69. Ithaca, N.Y.: Cornell University Press, 1972.

———. *Imagined Communities: Reflections on the Origins and Spread of Nationalism*. London: Verso, 1991 [1983].

———. *Language and Power: Exploring Political Cultures in Indonesia*. Ithaca, N.Y.: Cornell University Press, 1990.

Arief, Aburaerah, and Zainuddin Hakim, eds. *Sinrilikna Kappalak Tallumbatua*. Jakarta: Yayasan Obor Indonesia, 1993.

Asad, Talal. "Toward a Genealogy of the Concept of Ritual." In *Vernacular Christianity: Essays in the Social Anthropology of Religion Presented to Godfrey Lienhardt*, ed. W. James and D. H. Johnson, 73–87. Oxford: Journal of the Anthropological Society of Oxford, 1988.

Atkinson, Jane Monnig. *The Art and Politics of Wana Shamanship*. Berkeley: University of California Press, 1989.

Azra, Azyumardi. *Jaringan Ulama: Timur Tengah dan kepulauan Nusantara Abad XVII dan XVIII*. Bandung: Penerbit Mizan, 1994.

Basso, Keith H. *Western Apache Language and Culture: Essays in Linguistic Anthropology.* Tucson: University of Arizona Press, 1990.

Bellwood, Peter. *Prehistory of the Indo-Malaysian Archipelago.* Revised edition. Honolulu: University of Hawai'i Press, 1997.

———. "Hierarchy, Founder Ideology and Austronesian Expansion." In *Origins, Ancestry, and Alliance: Explorations in Austronesian Ethnography,* ed. James J. Fox and Clifford Sather, 18–40. Canberra: Australia National University, 1996.

Berg, C. C. "Javanese Historiography—A Synopsis of Its Evolution." In *Historians of Southeast East Asia,* ed. D. G. E. Hall, 13–23. London: Oxford University Press, 1961.

———. "The Javanese Picture of the Past." In *An Introduction to Indonesian Historiography,* ed. Soedjatmoko et al., 87–117. Ithaca, N.Y.: Cornell University Press, 1965.

Blok, R. "Beknopte geschiedenis van het Makasaarsche Celebes en Onderhoorigheden." *TNI* 10 (1848): 3–77.

Blust, Robert. "Linguistic Evidence for Some Early Austronesian Taboos." *American Anthropologist* 83, 2 (1981): 285–319.

Bourdieu, Pierre. *Language and Symbolic Power.* Cambridge: Harvard University Press, 1991.

———. *The Logic of Practice.* Stanford, Calif.: Stanford University Press, 1990.

Bowen, John R. *Muslims through Discourse: Religion and Ritual in Gayo Society.* Princeton, N.J.: Princeton University Press, 1993.

———. *Sumatran Politics and Poetics: Gayo History, 1900–1989.* New Haven, Conn.: Yale University Press, 1991.

Boxer, C. R. *Francisco Vieira de Figueiredo: A Portuguese Merchant-Adventurer in South East Asia, 1624–1667.* 's-Gravenhage: Martinus Nijhoff, 1967.

van Bruinessen, Martin. "The Origins and Development of the Naqshabandi Order in Indonesia." *Der Islam* 67 (1990): 150–179.

———. "The Tariqa Khalwatiyya in South Celebes." In *Excursies in Celebes,* ed. Harry A. Poeze and Pim Schoorl, 251–269. Leiden: KITLV, 1991.

Bulbeck, F. D. "The Politics of Marriage and the Marriage of Polities in Gowa, South Sulawesi, during the 16th and 17th Centuries." In *Origins, Ancestry and Alliance: Explorations in Austronesian Ethnography,* ed. James J. Fox and Clifford Sather, 280–315. Canberra: Australia National University, 1996.

———. "A Tale of Two Kingdoms: The Historical Archaeology of Gowa and Tallok, South Sulawesi, Indonesia." Ph.D. diss., Australia National University, 1992.

Caldwell, Ian. "Power, State and Society among the Pre-Islamic Bugis." *BKI* 151, 3 (1995): 394–421.

———. "South Sulawesi A.D. 1300–1600: Ten Bugis Texts." Ph.D. diss., Australia National University, 1988.

Cense, A. A. "Enige aantekeningen over Makassaars-Boeginese geschiedschrijving." *BKI* 107 (1951): 42–60.

———. "Old Buginese and Macassarese Diaries." *BKI* 122, 4 (1966): 416–428.

Cense, A. A., and Abdoerrahim. *Makassaars-Nederlands Woordenboek*. 's-Gravenhage: Martinus Nijhoff, 1979.

Chabot, H. Th. *Kinship, Status and Gender in South Celebes*. Leiden: KITLV, 1996 [1950].

Chakrabarty, Dipesh. "Postcoloniality and the Artifice of History: Who Speaks for 'Indian' Pasts?" *Representations* 37 (1992): 1–26.

Chartier, Roger. *The Order of Books*. Stanford, Calif.: Stanford University Press, 1994.

Commelin, Isaac, ed. *Begin ende Voortgangh van de Vereenighde Neederlandtsche Geoctroyeerde Oost-Indische Compagnie*. 4 vols. Amsterdam: N.p., 1646 [reprinted 1974].

Connerton, Paul. *How Societies Remember*. Cambridge Cambridge University Press, 1989.

Creese, Helen. "Balinese *Babad* as Historical Sources: A Reinterpretation of the Fall of Gelgel." *BKI* 147 (1991): 236–260.

———. "The Balinese *Kakawin* Traditions: A Preliminary Description and Inventory." *BKI* 155, 1 (1999): 45–96.

———. *Parthayana—The Journeying of Partha, An Eighteenth-century Balinese Kakawin*. Leiden: KITLV, 1998.

———. *In Search of Majapahit: The Transformation of Balinese Identities*. Working paper 101. Clayton, Australia: Monash University Centre of Southeast Asian Studies, 1997.

Cummins, J. S., ed. *The Travels and Controversies of Friar Domingo Navarrete, 1618–1686*. Vol. 1. Cambridge: Hakluyt Society, 1962.

Cummings, William. "Reading the Histories of a Marcs Chronicle." *BKI* 156, 1 (2000): 1–31.

———. "The Melaka Malay Diaspora in Makassar, c. 1500–1669." *JMBRAS* 71, 1 (1998): 106–121.

———. "'Only one Ruler but Two Peoples:' Re-Making the Past in Seventeenth-Century Makassarese Chronicles." *BKI* 155, 1 (1999): 97–120.

Davies, Putu. "The Historian in Bali." *Meanjin* 50, 1 (1991): 63–80.

Dening, Greg. *History's Anthropology: The Death of William Gooch*. ASAO Special Publications, no. 2, Washington, D.C.: University Press of America, 1988.

———. *Islands and Beaches: Discourse on a Silent Land: Marquesas 1774–1880.* Chicago: Dorsey Press, 1980.

Drakard, Jane. *A Kingdom of Words: Language and Power in Sumatra.* Oxford: Oxford University Press, 1999.

Eagleton, Terry. *Ideology: An Introduction.* New York: Verso, 1991.

———. *The Illusions of Postmodernism.* Oxford: Blackwell, 1996.

Eco, Umberto. *The Search for the Perfect Language.* Oxford: Blackwell, 1995.

Eerdmans, A. J. A. E. *Het Landschap Gowa.* Verhandelingen van het Bataviaasch Genootschap van Kunsten en Wetenschappen. Batavia: Albrecht; 's-Gravenhage: M. Nijhoff, 1897.

Errington, Shelly. *Meaning and Power in a Southeast Asian Realm.* Princeton, N.J.: Princeton University Press, 1989.

———. "Some Comments on Style in the Meanings of the Past." *JAS* 38, 2 (1979): 231–244.

Fachruddin Ambo Enre. "Ritumpanna Welenrennge: Telaah Filologis Sebuah Episoda Sastera Bugis Klasik Galigo." Ph.D. diss., Universitas Indonesia, 1983.

Fish, Stanley. "Commentary: The Young and the Restless." In *The New Historicism,* ed. H. Aram Veeser, 303–316. New York: Routledge, 1989.

Florida, Nancy. *Writing the Past, Inscribing the Future: History as Prophecy in Colonial Java.* Durham, N.C.: Duke University Press, 1995.

Foster, William, ed. *The Journal of John Jourdain, 1608–1617.* Cambridge: Hakluyt Society, 1905.

Fox, James J. "Austronesian Societies and Their Transformations." In *The Austronesians: Historical and Comparative Perspectives,* ed. Peter Bellwood, James J. Fox, and Darrell Tryon, 214–228. Canberra: Research School of Pacific and Asian Studies, Australia National University, 1995.

———. "A Rotinese Dynastic Genealogy: Structure and Event." In *The Translation of Culture: Essays to E. E. Evans-Pritchard,* ed. T. O. Beidelman, 37–77. London: Tavistock, 1971.

Fox, James J., ed. *To Speak in Pairs: Essays on the Ritual Languages of Eastern Indonesia.* Cambridge: Cambridge University Press, 1988.

Freud, Sigmund. *Civilization and Its Discontents.* Ed. and trans. James Strachey. New York: Norton, 1961 [1930].

Friedericy, M. J. "De Gowa-Federatie (1926)." *Adatrechtbundels.* Vol. 31: Selebes, 364–427. 's-Gravenhage: Martinus Nijhoff, 1929.

———. "De Standen bij de Boegineezen en Makassaren." *BKI* 90 (1933): 447–602.

Geertz, Clifford. *Negara: The Theater State in Nineteenth-Century Bali.* Princeton, N.J.: Princeton University Press, 1980.

George, Kenneth M. "Headhunting, History, and Exchange in Upland Sulawesi." *JAS* 50, 3 (1991): 536–564.

———. *Showing Signs of Violence: The Cultural Politics of a Twentieth-Century Headhunting Ritual*. Berkeley: University of California Press, 1996.

Gervaise, Nicholas. *An Historical Description of the Kingdom of Macasar*. London: N.p., 1701 [1685].

Gesick, Lorraine M. *In the Land of Lady White Blood: Southern Thailand and the Meaning of History*. Ithaca, N.Y.: Cornell University Southeast Asia Program, 1995.

Goody, Jack. *The Interface between the Written and the Oral*. Cambridge; New York: Cambridge University Press, 1987.

———, ed. *Literacy in Traditional Societies*. Cambridge: Cambridge University Press, 1968.

Graaf, H. J. de. "Later Javanese Sources and Historiography." In *An Introduction to Indonesian Historiography*, ed. Soedjatmoko et al., 119–136. Ithaca, N.Y.: Cornell University Press, 1965.

Hall, D. G. E., ed. *Historians of South East Asia*. London: Oxford University Press, 1961.

Hamid, Abu. *Syekh Yusuf: Seorang Ulama, Sufi dan Pejuang*. Jakarta: Yayasan Obor Indonesia, 1994.

Hefner, Robert W. *Hindu Javanese: Tengger Tradition and Islam*. Princeton, N.J.: Princeton University Press, 1985.

Helms, Mary. *Ulysses' Sail: An Ethnographic Odyssey of Power, Knowledge, and Geographical Distance*. Princeton, N.J.: Princeton University Press, 1988.

Holt, Claire. *Art in Indonesia: Continuities and Change*. Ithaca, N.Y.: Cornell University Press, 1967.

Hoskins, Janet. *Biographical Objects: How Things Tell the Stories of People's Lives*. New York: Routledge, 1998.

———. *The Play of Time: Kodi Perspectives on Calendars, History, and Exchange*. Berkeley: University of California Press, 1993.

Johns, A. H. "The Turning Image: Myth and Reality in Malay Perceptions of the Past." In *Perceptions of the Past in Southeast Asia*, ed. Anthony Reid and David Marr, 43–67. Singapore: Asian Studies Association of Australia, 1979.

Jones, Russell. "Ten Conversion Myths from Indonesia." In *Conversion to Islam*, ed. Nehemia Levtzion, 129–158. New York: Holmes and Meier, 1979.

Kamaruddin, H. D., et al. *Lontarak Bilang Raja Gowa dan Tallok (Naskah Makassar)*. 2 vols. Ujung Pandang: Proyek Penelitian dan Pengkajian Kebudayaan Sulawesi Selatan La Galigo, 1969, 1986.

Kartodirdjo, Sartono. *Pengantar Sejarah Indonesia Baru: 1500–1900. Dari Emporium Sampai Imperium*. Jakarta: Gramedia, 1992 [1987].

Kertzer, David I. *Ritual, Politics, and Power.* New Haven, Conn.: Yale University Press, 1988.

Koolhof, Sirtjo. "The 'La Galigo': A Bugis Encyclopedia and Its Growth." *BKI* 155, 3 (1999): 362–387.

Kuipers, Joel. *Power in Performance: The Creation of Textual Authority in Weyewa Ritual Speech.* Philadelphia: University of Pennsylvania Press, 1990.

Lambek, Michael. "Certain Knowledge, Contestable Authority: Power and Practice on the Islamic Periphery." *American Ethnologist* 17 (1990): 23–40.

Lathief, Andi Halilintar, ed. *Cerita Rakyat Daerah Sulawesi Selatan.* Yogyakarta: Institut Press, 1984.

Legge, J. D. "The Writing of Southeast Asian History." In *The Cambridge History of Southeast Asia.* Volume 1: *From Early Times to c. 1800,* ed. Nicholas Tarling, 1–50. Cambridge: Cambridge University Press, 1992.

Lewis, E. D. "The Tyranny of the Text: Oral Tradition and the Power of Writing in Sikka and Tana ?Ai, Flores." *BKI* 154, 3 (1998): 457–477.

Liaw Yock Fang. *Undang-Undang Melaka: The Laws of Melaka.* The Hague: Martinus Nijhoff, 1976.

Lieberman, Victor. "Local Integration and Eurasian Analogies: Structuring Southeast Asian History, c. 1350–c. 1830." *Modern Asian Studies* 27, 3 (1993): 475–572.

Ligtvoet, A. "Geschiedenis van de afdeeling Tallo (Gouvernement van Celebes)," *TBG* 18 (1872): 54.

———. "Transcriptie van het Dagboek der Vorsten van Gowa en Tello." *BKI* 28 (1880): 1–259.

Linnekin, Jocelyn. *Sacred Queens and Women of Consequence: Rank, Gender, and Colonialism in the Hawaiian Islands.* Ann Arbor: University of Michigan Press, 1990.

Lowenthal, David. *The Past Is a Foreign Country.* Cambridge: Cambridge University Press, 1985.

Macknight, Campbell. *The Early History of South Sulawesi: Some Recent Advances.* Working Paper 81. Clayton, Victoria: Monash University Centre of Southeast Asian Studies, 1993.

———. *The Voyage to Marege': Macassan Trepangers in Northern Australia.* Carlton, Australia: Melbourne University Press, 1976.

Macknight, Campbell, and Mukhlis Paeni. "The Chronicle of Bone." Manuscript.

Maier, Hendrik M. K. *In the Center of Authority: The Malay Hikayat Merong Mahawangsa.* Ithaca, N.Y.: Cornell University Southeast Asia Program, 1988.

"Makassaarsche Historiën." *TBG* 4 (1855): 111–145.

Manguin, Pierre-Yves. "Shipshape Societies: Boat Symbolism and Political Systems in Insular Southeast Asia." In *Southeast Asia in the 9th to 14th Centuries,* ed. David G. Marr and A. C. Milner, 187–213. Singapore: Institute of Southeast Asian Studies, 1986.

Manyambeang, Abdul Kadir. "Lontaraq Riwayaqna Tuanta Salamaka ri Gowa: Suatu Analisis Linguistik Filologis." Ph.D. diss., Hasanuddin University, 1996.

Marzuki, Mohamad Laica. *Siri': Bagian Kesadaran Hukum Rakyat Bugis-Makassar (Sebuah Telaah Filsafat Hukum).* Ujung Pandang: Hasanuddin University Press, 1995.

Matthes, B. F. "Boegineesche en Makassaarsche Legenden." In *Dr. Benjamin Frederik Matthes: Zijn Leven en Arbeid in Dienst van het Nederlandsch Bijbelgenootschap,* ed. H. van den Brink, 377–425. Amsterdam: Nederlandsch Bijbelgenootschap, 1943.

———. *Makassaarsche Chrestomathie: Oorspronkelijke Makassaarsche geschriften in proza en poëzij uitgegeven.* 's-Gravenhage: Martinus Nijhoff, 1883.

———. *Makassaarsche Spraakkunst.* Amsterdam: Nederlandsch Bijbelgenootschap, 1858.

———. "Over de Bîssoe's of Heidensche Priesters en Priesteressen der Boegineezen." In *Dr. Benjamin Frederik Matthes: Zijn Leven en Arbeid in Dienst van het Nederlandsch Bijbelgenootschap,* ed. H. van den Brink, 497–530. Amsterdam: Nederlandsch Bijbelgenootschap, 1943.

———. "Over een' Boegineeschen Krisband of Sjerp." In *Feestbundel van Taal-, Letter-, Geschied- en Aardrijkskundige Bijdragen ter Gelegenheid van zijn Tachtigsten Geboortedag aan Dr. P. J. Veth,* 121–122. Leiden: E. J. Brill, 1894.

Mattulada. "Islam di Sulawesi Selatan." In *Agama dan Perubahan Sosial,* ed. Taufik Abdullah, 211–321. Jakarta: Yayasan Ilmu-Ilmu Sosial, 1983.

———. *Latoa: Satu Lukisan Analitis terhadap Antropologi Politik Orang Bugis.* Ujung Pandang: Hasanuddin University Press, 1995 [1985]

———. *Menyusuri Jejak Kehadiran Makassar dalam Sejarah (1510–1700).* Ujung Pandang: Hasanuddin University Press, 1991.

Millar, Susan Bolyard. *Bugis Weddings: Rituals of Social Location in Modern Indonesia.* Center for South and Southeast Asia Monograph Series, no. 29. Berkeley: University of California, Center for South and Southeast Asia Studies, 1989.

Mills, Roger Frederick. "Proto South Sulawesi and Proto Austronesian Phonology." Ph.D. diss., University of Michigan, 1975.

Milner, A. C. *Kerajaan: Malay Political Culture on the Eve of Colonial Rule.* Tucson: University of Arizona Press, 1982.

Montrose, Louis A. "Professing the Renaissance: The Poetics and Politics of Culture." In *The New Historicism,* ed. H. Aram Veeser, 15–36 New York: Routledge, 1989.

Mukhlis. "Batara Gowa: Mesianisme Dalam Gerakan Sosial di Tanah Makassar." In *Dari Babad dan Hikayat sampai Sejarah Kritis,* ed. T. Ibrahim Alfian et al., 65–101. Yogyakarta: Gadjah Mada University Press, 1992.

———. "Landasan Kultural dalam Pranata Sosial Bugis-Makassar." In *Dinamika Bugis-Makassar,* ed. Mukhlis, 1–41. N.p.: Pusat Latihan Penelitian Ilmu-Ilmu Sosial, 1986.

Niemann, G. K. "Mededeelingen over Makassaarsche Taal- en Letterkunde." *BKI* 6 (1863): 58–88.

Noorduyn, J. "De Islamisering van Makasar." *BKI* 112, 3 (1956): 247–266.

———. "Makasar and the Islamization of Bima." *BKI* 142, 2 and 3 (1987): 312–342.

———. "The Manuscripts of the Makasarese Chronicle of Goa and Talloq: An Evaluation." *BKI* 147, 4 (1991): 454–484.

———. "Origins of South Celebes Historical Writing." In *An Introduction to Indonesian Historiography,* ed. Soedjatmoko et al., 137–155. Ithaca, N.Y.: Cornell University Press, 1965.

———. "Some Aspects of Macassar-Buginese Historiography." In *Historians of South East Asia,* ed. D. G. E. Hall, 29–36. London: Oxford University Press, 1961.

———. "Variation in the Bugis/Makasarese Script." *BKI* 149, 3 (1993): 533–570.

Nooteboom, C. "Naar Aanleiding van de Rijkssieraden van Zuid-Celebes." *Koloniaal Tijdschrift* 26 (1937): 167–176.

Ong, Walter. *Orality and Literacy: The Technologizing of the Word.* New York: Routledge, 1982.

Ozouf, Mona. *Festivals and the French Revolution.* Trans. Alan Sheridan. Cambridge: Harvard University Press, 1988 [1976].

Parawansa et al. *Sastra Sinrilik Makassar.* Jakarta: Departemen Pendidikan dan Kebudayaan, 1992.

Parmentier, Richard J. *The Sacred Remains: Myth, History, and Polity in Belau.* Chicago: University of Chicago Press, 1987.

Pelras, Christian. *The Bugis.* Oxford: Blackwell, 1996.

———. "L'Oral et l'écrit dans la tradition Bugis." *Asie du Sud-East et Monde Insulindien* 10 (1979): 271–297.

———. "Patron-Client Ties among the Bugis and Makassarese of South Sulawesi." In *Authority and Enterprise among the Peoples of South Sulawesi,* ed. Roger Tol, Kees van Dijk, and Greg Acciaioli, 15–54. Leiden: KITLV, 2000.

———. "La première description de Célèbes-sud en français et la destinée remarquable de deux jeunes princes makassar dans la France de Louis XIV." *Archipel* 54 (1997): 63–80.

———. "Les premières données occidentales concernant Célèbes-sud." *BKI* 133, 2 and 3 (1977): 227–260.

———. "Religion, Tradition and the Dynamics of Islamization in South Sulawesi." *Indonesia* 57 (1994): 133–154. Originally published in *Archipel* 29 (1985): 107–135.

Pemberton, John. *On the Subject of "Java."* Ithaca, N.Y.: Cornell University Press, 1994.

Pires, Tomé. *The Suma Oriental: An Account of the East, from the Red Sea to Japan.* Trans. Armando Cortesão. London: Hakluyt Society, 1944.

Rafael, Vicente. *Contracting Colonialism: Translation and Christian Conversion in Tagalog Society under Early Spanish Rule.* Ithaca, N Y.: Cornell University Press, 1988.

Rahim and Ridwan. *Sejarah Kerajaan Tallo' (Suatu Transkripsi Lontara').* Ujung Pandang: Lembaga Sejarah dan Antropologi, 1975.

Rahman, Ahmad, et al. *Sastra Lisan Makassar: Laporan Penelitian.* Jakarta: Departemen Pendidikan dan Kebudayaan, 1976.

Ras, J. J. *Hikayat Banjar: A Study in Malay Historiography* The Hague: Martinus Nijhoff, 1968.

Reid, Anthony. "A Great Seventeenth-Century Indonesian Family: Matoaya and Pattingalloang of Makassar." *Masyarakat Indonesia* 8, 1 (1981): 1–28.

———. "Islamization and Christianization in Southeast Asia: The Critical Phase, 1550–1650." In *Southeast Asia in the Early Modern Era: Trade, Power, and Belief,* ed. Anthony Reid, 151–179. Ithaca, N.Y.: Cornell University Press, 1993.

———. "The Nationalist Quest for an Indonesian Past." In *Perceptions of the Past in Southeast Asia,* ed. Anthony Reid and David Marr, 281–298. Singapore: Asian Studies Association of Australia, 1979.

———. "The Rise of Makassar." *Review of Indonesian and Malaysian Affairs* 17 (1983): 117–160.

———. *Southeast Asia in the Age of Commerce 1450–1680.* 2 vols. New Haven, Conn.: Yale University Press, 1988, 1993.

Reid, Anthony, and David Marr, eds. *Perceptions of the Past in Southeast Asia.* Singapore: Asian Studies Association of Australia, 1979.

Ricklefs, M. C. "Javanese Sources in the Writing of Modern Javanese History." In *Southeast Asian History and Historiography,* ed. C. D. Cowan and O. W. Wolters, 332–344. Ithaca, N.Y.: Cornell University Press 1976.

———. *The Seen and Unseen Worlds in Java 1726–1749.* St. Leonards, Australia: Asian Studies Association of Australia; Honolulu: University of Hawai'i Press, 1998.

Rosaldo, Renato. *Ilongot Headhunting 1883–1974: A Study in Society and History.* Stanford, Calif.: Stanford University Press, 1980.

Rössler, Martin. "Cultural Models and Socio-Religious Change: An Example from South Sulawesi." *Antropologi Indonesia* 49 (1991): 66–78.

———. "From Divine Descent to Administration: Sacred Heirlooms and Political Change in Highland Gowa." In *Authority and Enterprise among the Peoples of South Sulawesi,* ed. Roger Tol, Kees van Dijk, and Greg Acciaioli, 161–182. Leiden: KITLV, 2000.

———. "Striving for Modesty: Fundamentals of the Religion and Social Organization of the Makassarese Patuntung." *BKI* 146, 2 and 3 (1990): 289–324.

Röttger-Rössler, Birgitt. "Shared Responsibility: Some Aspects of Gender and Authority in Makassar Society." In *Authority and Enterprise among the Peoples of South Sulawesi,* ed. Roger Tol, Kees van Dijk, and Greg Acciaioli, 143–160. Leiden: KITLV, 2000.

Rubinstein, Raechelle. *Beyond the Realm of the Senses: The Balinese Ritual of Kakawin Composition.* Leiden: KITLV, 2000.

———. "Colophons as a Tool for Mapping the Literary History of Bali: Ida Pedanda Made Sidemen—Poet, Author and Scribe." *Archipel* 52 (1996): 173–191.

Sahlins, Marshall. *Islands of History.* Chicago: University of Chicago Press, 1985.

Schacter, Daniel L. *Searching for Memory: The Brain, the Mind, and the Past.* New York: Basic Books, 1996.

Schrauwers, Albert. "Houses, Hierarchy, Headhunting and Exchange: Rethinking Political Relations in the Southeast Asian Realm of Luwu'." *BKI* 153, 3 (1997): 356–380.

Schulte Nordholt, Henk. "Origin, Descent and Destruction: Text and Context in Balinese Representations of the Past." *Indonesia* 54 (1992): 27–58.

Siegel, James. *Solo in the New Order: Language and Hierarchy in an Indonesian City.* Princeton, N.J.: Princeton University Press, 1993.

Skinner, C., ed. and trans. *Sja'ir Perang Mengkasar.* 's-Gravenhage: Martinus Nijhoff, 1963.

Soedjatmoko et al., eds. *An Introduction to Indonesian Historiography.* Ithaca, N.Y.: Cornell University Press, 1965.

Strassberg, Richard E. *Inscribed Landscapes: Travel Writing from Imperial China.* Berkeley: University of California Press, 1994.

Sutherland, Heather. "Believing Is Seeing: Perspectives on Political Power and Economic Activity in the Malay World 1700–1940." *JSEAS* 26, 1 (1995): 133–146.

Suwondo, Bambang, ed. *Cerita Rakyat (Mite dan Legenda) Daerah Sulawesi Selatan*. Jakarta: Departemen Pendidikan dan Kebudayaan, 1980–1981.

Sweeney, Amin. *Authors and Audiences in Traditional Malay Literature*. Center for South and Southeast Asia Studies Monograph Series, no. 20. Berkeley: University of California, Center for South and Southeast Asia Studies, 1980.

———. *A Full Hearing: Orality and Literacy in the Malay World*. Berkeley: University of California Press, 1987.

Taylor, Paul Michael, and Lorraine V. Aragon. *Beyond the Java Sea: Art of Indonesia's Outer Islands*. Washington, D.C.: National Museum of Natural History, Smithsonian Institution, 1991.

Thomas, Nicholas. *Entangled Objects: Exchange, Material Culture, and Colonialism in the Pacific*. Cambridge: Harvard University Press, 1991.

Tideman, J. *Catalogus van voorwerpen van Makassaarschen oorsprong*. Den Haag: N.p., 1909.

———. "De Toe Badjeng en de Legende omtrent Hun Oorsprong." *BKI* 60 (1908): 488–500.

Tobing, Ph. O. L. *Hukum Pelayaran dan Perdagangang Amanna Gappa*. Makassar: Jajasan Kebudajaan Sulawesi Selatan dan Tenggara, 1961.

Tol, Roger. "A Royal Collection of Bugis Manuscripts." *BKI* 149, 3 (1993): 612–629.

Tsing, Anna. *In the Realm of the Diamond Queen: Marginality in an Out-of-the-Way Place*. Princeton, N.J.: Princeton University Press, 1993.

Tudjimah. *Syekh Jusuf Makasar: Riwayat Hidup, Karya, dan Ajarannya*. Jakarta: Departemen Pendidikan dan Kebudayaan, 1987.

Valentijn, Francois. *Oud en Nieuw Oost-Indien*. Vol. 3. Amsterdam: J. C. van Kesteren, 1862.

Vickers, Adrian. "Balinese Texts and Historiography." *History and Theory* 29, 2 (1990): 158–178.

Volkman, Toby Alice. *Feasts of Honor: Ritual and Change in the Toraja Highlands*. Urbana: University of Illinois Press, 1985.

Wallace, Alfred Russel. *The Malay Archipelago*. New York: Dover, 1962 [1869].

Weiner, Annette B. *Inalienable Possessions: The Paradox of Keeping-While-Giving*. Berkeley: University of California Press, 1992.

———. "Inalienable Wealth." *American Ethnologist* 12, 2 (1985): 210–227.

Weiner, Annette B., and Jane Schneider, eds. *Cloth and Human Experience*. Washington, D.C.: Smithsonian Institution Press, 1991.

Wiener, Margaret J. "Making Local History in New Order Bali: Public Culture and the Politics of the Past." In *Staying Local in the Global Village: Bali in the*

Twentieth Century, ed. Raechelle Rubinstein and Linda H. Connor, 51–89. Honolulu: University of Hawai'i Press, 1999.

———. *Visible and Invisible Realms: Power, Magic, and Colonial Conquest in Bali.* Chicago: University of Chicago Press, 1995.

Wieringa, E. P. "An Old Text Brought to Life Again: A Reconsideration of the 'Final Version' of the *Babad Tanah Jawi.*" *BKI* 155, 2 (1999): 244–263.

Windschuttle, Keith. *The Killing of History: How a Discipline Is Being Murdered by Literary Critics and Social Theorists.* Paddington, Australia: Macleay Press, 1996.

Wolhoff, Drs. G. J. and Abdurrahim. *Sedjarah Goa.* Ujung Pandang: Jajasan Kebudajaan Sulawesi Selatan dan Tenggara, 1959.

Wolters, O. W. *The Fall of Srivijaya in Malay History.* Ithaca, N.Y.: Cornell University Press, 1970.

———. *History, Culture, and Region in Southeast Asian Perspectives.* Revised edition. Ithaca, N.Y.: Cornell University Southeast Asia Program, 1999.

Woodward, Mark R. *Islam in Java: Normative Piety and Mysticism in the Sultanate of Yogyakarta.* Tucson: University of Arizona Press, 1989.

Wyatt, David. "Southeast Asia 'Inside Out,' 1300–1800: A Perspective from the Interior." *Modern Asian Studies* 31, 3 (1997): 689–709.

Young, James E. *The Texture of Memory: Holocaust Memorials and Meaning.* New Haven, Conn.: Yale University Press, 1993.

Zagorin, Perez. "History, the Referent, and Narrative: Reflections on Postmodernism Now." *History and Theory* 38, 1 (1999): 1–24.

INDEX

Abdul Jalil, Sultan. *See* Lakiung, Tumamenang ri
Abdurrahim, xiii
Ala'uddin, Sultan, 30, 32, 33, 160, 208. *See also* Gaukanna, Tumamenang ri
Andaya, Barbara Watson, 38, 166
Andaya, Leonard, 55, 119
Arabic, 37–38, 39, 42, 44, 154–163, 173
aru, 40. *See also* oaths
Arung Palakka, 33, 70, 106

Bajeng, 131–133, 135, 137, 153
Bajo, 224n. 28
Baku, 131, 133–135, 167
Bali, 20, 39, 49, 68, 83, 93, 96, 121, 127, 135–136, 138, 145, 163, 235n. 8
Ballaq Lompoa, 12, 136, 159, 161, 162, 178
Ballaq Pangkana, Tumamenang ri. *See* Hasanuddin, Sultan
Banda, 82
Bandang, Datoq of, 38
Bangkalaq, 137, 143–145, 150
Bangkalaq Chronicle, 143–144
Bantaeng, 23, 35, 80, 137, 151, 152
Barombong, 134, 162
Batara Gowa, 81, 86, 122, 207
Bate Salapang, 25, 29, 65, 70, 98, 100–102, 105, 114, 126, 134, 151
Bayo, Karaeng, 25, 29, 79, 85, 93–108, 121–122, 134, 152
Belau, 130
Berg, C. C., 18, 19, 39

Bima, 32, 109–110, 116, 157
Binamuq, 137
Binamuq Chronicle, 138, 141–142, 145
Bisampole, 151
Blok, Roelof, 13, 49
Blust, Robert, 93
Boné, 26, 27, 42, 65, 73, 111, 114, 124, 188, 228n. 13
Boné Chronicle, 82, 213n. 27
Bontoalaq, 48, 156
Bontobiraeng, Tumamenang ri, 47, 76, 115, 148, 175, 177, 210. *See also* Pattingalloang, Karaeng
Bontolangkasaq, Karaeng, 111, 115, 124, 209
Bontomangape, Karaeng. *See* Hasanuddin, Sultan
Bontonompo, 68, 113, 123, 132, 135
Bontoramba, 71–72
Bontosunggu, Karaeng, 180
Borisallo, 176, 224n. 15
Bourdieu, Pierre, 146, 150, 153, 191
Bowen, John, 117, 199
Bugis, 12–13, 19, 22, 26–27, 32, 34, 40, 42, 44, 75, 77, 106, 114, 124, 129, 143, 149, 152, 164, 173, 228n. 13
Bulbeck, David, 25, 107, 111, 112, 228n. 16
Buton, 28, 31, 73

Caldwell, Ian, 79, 86, 152, 223n. 3
Camba, 137, 153
Cenrana, 137, 143–145, 150

Cenrana Chronicle, 144–145
Cense, A. A., xiii, 240
Chabot, Hendrik Th., 55, 70, 71, 75
Chartier, Roger, 117, 169
chronicle. See *patturioloang*
Cikoang, 158
community. See *paqrasangang*
Connerton, Paul, 9, 62
Creese, Helen, 20, 68

Datoq ri Bandang, 160
Dening, Greg, 4, 5, 10, 60, 192
Djajadiningrat, Husein, 18
Djohan, xi–xiii, 52–53, 239
Drakard, Jane, 122, 163, 177
Dutch East India Company. See VOC

Eagleton, Terry, 201–202, 231n. 2
Eerdmans, A. J. A. E., 95, 97
Errington, Shelly, 75, 76

Fish, Stanley, 3
Flores, 193, 226n. 71
Florida, Nancy, 111, 198
Fox, James J., 72
Freud, Sigmund, 7
Friedericy, M. J., 65–66, 155, 229n. 35

Galesong, 131–132, 137
Garassiq, 82
gaukang, 55, 56, 119
Gaukanna, Tumamenang ri, 76, 112, 114, 116, 138, 140, 160, 193, 208. See also Ala'uddin, Sultan
Gayo, 49, 117, 199
Geertz, Clifford, 129
genealogy, 66, 71, 72, 74–77, 103–111, 114–118, 122, 126, 139, 141, 167, 188, 221nn. 37, 40, 228n. 16
George, Kenneth, 200–201
Gervaise, Nicholas, 54, 85, 95, 96–97, 156, 183–184, 188, 191, 222n. 58
Gesick, Lorraine, 41
Goody, Jack, 168, 173, 177
Gowa, 11–12, 17, 22–34, 39, 40, 46, 47, 48, 52–53, 63–65, 68–73, 76–83, 86–88, 94, 97, 98, 100–116, 119–126, 128–153, 154, 156–163, 167, 168–171, 173, 174–176, 179, 182, 183, 192–194, 195, 207–209
Gowa Chronicle, 13, 25, 26, 27, 28, 34, 42, 44, 49, 53, 67, 72–88, 98, 100, 106–107, 112, 113, 123, 136, 137–146, 149, 152–153, 160, 162, 213n. 27

Harunarasyid, Sultan, 110, 210
Hasanuddin, Sultan, 10, 22, 34, 52–53, 80, 83, 85, 109–110, 114–115, 125, 139, 208
Hikayat Aceh, 149
history: ethnographic, 4, 35, 49–52, 119, 201–205; making of, 4–12, 198–205; oral, 58–72 (*see also* orality); written, 59–60 (*see also* literacy; manuscripts)
history, conceptions of: Makassarese, 6, 8, 10–12, 49–51, 61–63, 73–89, 129, 217n. 34; modern Indonesian, 22, 214nn. 7, 8, 219n. 2; Western, 1–5, 49–51, 69, 73–74, 84, 88–89, 103, 191–192, 196–198, 201–205, 212n. 8
Hoskins, Janet, 9

Islam: conversion to, 32, 38–39, 63, 69, 73, 154–155, 160–161, 163, 164, 233n. 56; institutional hierarchy, 156–162; perceptions of, 38–39, 53, 154–156, 159–160, 163; rituals, 12, 54, 95, 125, 130, 155–162, 176, 177
Islamization, wars of, 32, 154, 193

jangang-jangang, 43–44, 46–47, 122. See also script, Makassarese
Jipang, 176
Jourdain, John, 184, 191

Kajang, 150–152
kalompoang, 11, 12, 53–57, 64–71, 74, 77, 85, 86, 88, 119–125, 130–137, 139, 142, 150–151, 154, 155–156, 159, 162, 163, 167, 171–172, 209, 226n. 62, 227n. 76
Karunrung, Karaeng, 109–110, 148
Kasepekang, 150
Kasiang Salapang. See Bate Salapang
Kertzer, David, 182
Krom, N. J., 18, 19

La Galigo, 42, 96
Lakipadada, 79, 85, 101, 121, 238
Lakiung, Tumamenang ri, 76, 110, 113, 139, 141, 148, 175, 180, 182, 208
Lambek, Michael, 161–162, 235n. 7
Lamuru, 123, 135
Lengkeseq, 153
Lieberman, Victor, 196–197
literacy, 77–89, 93, 102–104, 115–117, 118, 157–158, 159, 165–174, 195, 196, 199, 200, 229n. 31
Loe ri Sero, Karaeng, 81–82, 86, 122, 209
lontaraq beru, 43–44, 122. *See also* script, Makassarese
lontaraq bilang, 29, 41, 46, 47–48, 50, 53, 108–110, 114, 118, 122, 124, 156, 173, 208–210
Lowenthal, David, 6
Luwuq, 9, 26, 68, 73, 106, 129, 140, 149, 152

Macknight, Campbell, 119, 240
Maier, Hendrik M. K., 2, 18, 168
Makassarese language, xii–xiii. *See also* literacy; manuscripts; orality; script, Makassarese
Makkoayang, Tumamenang ri, 46, 112, 139, 140, 180, 209
Malay language, 31, 42, 44–45, 83, 157–158, 168
Malays, 23, 27–29, 30–31, 32, 44, 74, 108, 157–158, 164, 169, 173
Malikussaid, Sultan, 30, 34, 85, 109, 114, 158
Mandar, 26, 146–149, 170–172, 232n. 14
Manngasa, Gallarrang, 148, 169, 175, 179, 180
manuscripts: composition of, 41–49, 52–54, 72–88, 122, 137–149, 152, 158–159, 215n. 2, 216n. 17; as historical force, 12–14, 21, 35–37, 93–94, 125–127, 163, 187–188, 194, 195–201; perceptions of, 37–41, 52–57, 84–89, 103, 104, 115, 117–118, 122, 129, 142, 195; possession of, 37–38, 40, 52–54, 57, 59, 63, 84–85, 88–89, 104, 115–126, 129–137, 154–163, 176–178, 189–190, 192, 193; spread of, 116–118, 130, 137–153, 156–159, 161–162. *See also* genealogy; *parakara; patturioloang; rapang*
Maros, 23, 28, 31. 42, 73, 85, 86, 100, 106, 112, 114, 123, 137, 140, 141, 152
Maros Chronicle, 70, 82, 106, 114, 138, 139–141, 145–146, 152
marriage, politics of, 107–118, 126, 134, 140, 141–145, 150–151, 162, 193, 225n. 37, 228n. 16
Marx, Karl, 191
Matoaya, Karaeng, 30, 31, 32, 38–39, 46, 47, 73, 75, 112, 148, 154, 157, 159–160, 175, 176, 177, 179, 193, 209–210, 227n. 74
Matthes, B. F., 42, 49, 148, 185, 240
Mekka, 157, 159
Melaka, 26, 82, 127, 128, 224n. 28
Melaka Maritime Laws, 173
Millar, Susan B., 96
Mills, Roger, 23
Minangkabau, 38, 126, 160, 163, 175, 177
mokkeng, 156–157, 230n. 56
Montrose, Louis, 2

Navarrete, Friar Domingo, 184, 191
Niemann, G. K., 42
Noorduyn, Jacobus, 19, 45, 53
Nordholt, Henk Schulte, 145

oaths, 40–41, 46
Ong, Walter, 166, 173
orality, 77–89, 102–104, 115–117, 118, 149–153, 159, 160, 165–174, 200, 229n. 31

pacce, 56, 135, 164
Paceqlang, 68
Panakkukang, 33
Papambatuna, Tumamenang ri, 112, 116, 208
paqrasangang, 55–56, 61, 65, 67, 71
parakara, 46, 147–148, 181, 183–192, 193, 233n. 54
Parigi, 113, 135
Parmentier, Richard, 130

Pattallassang, 63–72, 74, 77, 80, 98, 113, 135
Pattingalloang, Karaeng, 30, 31, 112, 158, 210. *See also* Bontobiraeng, Tumamenang ri
patturioloang, 41, 42, 44, 46, 48, 50, 56, 66, 100, 103, 104, 111, 115, 118, 122, 126, 136, 137–146, 149, 153, 167
Pelras, Christian, 77, 107
Pemberton, John, 4, 96
Pires, Tomé, 28
Polombangkeng, 25, 28, 42, 82, 86, 153

Qur'an, 54, 154–155, 157–159

Rafael, Vicente, 38
rapang, 42, 46, 47, 49, 118, 122, 147–149, 164, 173, 174–183, 190, 193, 232n. 29
Reed, Lou, xi
regalia. *See kalompoang*
Reid, Anthony, 21, 28, 34, 35–37, 196
Rosaldo, Renato, 7
Rössler, Martin, 100, 119, 121, 150–151, 161, 211n. 4
Roti, 72, 75
royal palace of Gowa. *See* Ballaq Lompoa
Rubinstein, Raechelle, 20, 49, 53

sabannaraq, 29, 111–112
Sahlins, Marshall, 74, 100, 149
Salakowa, 12
Sangkilang, 125
Sanrabone, 25, 52–53, 100, 108, 137–139, 141, 153, 154–155, 157, 161, 169, 176
Sanrabone Chronicle, 138–139, 140–141, 145–146
saukang, 55, 56
script, Makassarese, xii–xiii, 41, 43–44, 46–47, 122, 215n. 2, 216n. 17, 222n. 57
Segeri, 139
Selayar, 23, 80
serang, 44, 122. *See also* script, Makassarese
sexual rivalry, 70, 85–86, 142–143, 186–187, 234n. 72
Siang, 23, 25, 82, 137

Sidenreng, 26
sinriliq, 42
Sinriliq Kappalaq Tallumbatua, 8, 97
Sirajuddin, Sultan, 111, 115, 208–209, 210. *See also* Talloq, Tumammaliang ri
siriq, 56, 70, 135, 164, 190
Sja'ir Perang Mengkasar, 10, 44
Skinner, C., 211n. 2
Somba Opu, 31, 120, 180
Soppeng, 27
Speelman, Cornelis, 49
status-rivalry, 56, 93–98, 106–108
Story of Syekh Yusuf, 52, 54, 157, 158, 168–169
Sudanga, 12, 79, 85, 101, 121–122, 124–125, 159
Sudiang, 70, 98, 161
Sumannaq, Karaeng, 148, 175, 176
Sumbawa, 109–111, 157
Sweeney, Amin, 60, 145, 167–168, 232n. 6
Syekh Yusuf. *See* Yusuf, Syekh

Taenga, Tumamenang ri, 148, 175, 176, 177, 179, 182
Talloq, 25, 28, 30–32, 42, 46–48, 73, 81–83, 86–87, 103, 105–106, 111–112, 114–115, 122–124, 130, 137, 140, 141, 142, 148, 154, 156, 158, 160–161, 163, 174–175, 209–210
Talloq Chronicle, 13, 25, 28, 42, 46, 75–79, 81–82, 84, 86, 106–107, 112, 136, 140, 146, 160
Talloq, Tumammaliang ri, 140. *See also* Sirajuddin, Sultan
Tanisamaang, 80, 121–122, 124
Tanruq Ballanga, 85, 101
Tomboloq, 155–156, 158
Toraja, 8–9, 32
translation, xi–xiii
Tuanta ri Dima, 148, 174
tumabicarabutta, 29, 46, 112
tumailalang, 29, 42, 73, 76, 112
tumakkajannang, 75–76, 179
tumanurung, 11–12, 14, 25, 29, 55, 79, 97, 98–106, 113, 115, 121–122, 125, 133–134, 139–140, 149–153, 167, 207, 224n. 15, 227n. 76

Tumapaqrisiq Kallonna, 25–26, 28, 42, 80, 88, 111–113, 131–132, 135, 180, 207
Tumassalangga Barayang, 79–80, 98, 152, 207
Tunatangkaqlopi, 80, 81, 86, 122, 207
Tunibatta, 26, 46, 65, 69, 97–98, 111–112, 207
Tunijalloq, 26, 27, 46, 73, 85–86, 112, 138, 180, 183, 207
Tunikakasang, 112, 140, 144
Tunilabu ri Suriwa, 82, 209
Tunipalangga, 26, 28, 68, 87, 111–112, 123, 138–139, 143, 207
Tunipasuluq, 26, 27–28, 30, 72, 73–74, 84, 140, 141, 208, 209
Tunipasuruq, 42, 87, 111, 140, 209

Ujung Tana, Tumamenang ri, 49, 148, 175, 180–181

Valentijn, Francois, 186
VOC, 22, 30, 32, 33, 34, 40, 124, 125, 183, 185, 188, 189–190

Wajoq, 27
Wallace, Alfred, 120
Weiner, Annette, 67
white blood, 14, 94, 98–107, 111–114, 116–117, 122–124, 126, 140, 142, 179, 180, 185–186, 194
Wiener, Margaret, 121, 135, 163
Windschuttle, Keith, 2–3
Wolters, O. W., 127, 196
women in Makassar, 70, 107–111, 114, 178–179, 186–187, 220n. 22
Woodward, Mark, 157, 183
Wyatt, David, 195–197

Young, James, 204–205
Yusuf, Syekh, 52, 54, 61, 155, 157, 158, 169

Zagorin, Perez, 201–202

ABOUT THE AUTHOR

William Cummings is an assistant professor of interdisciplinary studies at the University of South Florida. An ethnographic historian by temperament, his research interests include the nature of historical consciousness in early modern Indonesia, American perceptions and uses of the body as a historical archive, and the politics of memory. He has published articles on early modern Makassar, and is currently working on a cultural history of translation in Makassar that examines royal court chronicles and records.